EUROPEAN HISTORY:

AN OUTLINE AND SYNTHESIS

Donald H. Barry
Tallahassee Community College

KENDALL/HUNT PUBLISHING COMPANY
4050 Westmark Drive Dubuque, Iowa 52002

Copyright © 1995 by Kendall/Hunt Publishing Company

ISBN 0-7872-1326-8

All rights reserved. No part of this publication may be reproduced, stored in a retrieval system, or transmitted, in any form or by any means, electronic, mechanical, photocopying, recording, or otherwise, without the prior written permission of the copyright owner.

Printed in the United States of America
10 9 8 7 6 5 4 3 2 1

TABLE OF CONTENTS

Chapter 1. Prehistory and the Study of History	1
Chapter 2. The Ancient Near East	8
Chapter 3. Greece--Hellas	18
Chapter 4. Rome: Republic and Empire	31
Chapter 5. The Middle Ages	44
Chapter 6. The Italian Renaissance and Protestant Reformation	58
Chapter 7. Early Modern Europe and the Age of Absolutism	76
Chapter 8. The Old Regime of 18th-Century Europe	99
Chapter 9. French Revolution--Napoleon	106
Chapter 10. Karl Marx & Marxism	124
Chapter 11. 19th Century Europe: National Developments	131
Chapter 12. The New Imperialism through World War I. (1870--1920)	146
Chapter 13. Inter-War Europe: 1919--39	159
Chapter 14. World War II. and After	176
End Notes	196
References	199
Subject Matter for Essay Exams	201

PREFACE

It has been my belief and my experience for over three decades that a person acquires knowledge more quickly, more effectively, and more permanently when the material to be learned is outlined and organized in an efficient and orderly manner. Drawing on that conviction, I have written this book with two objectives in mind, one of them being to assist my students and friends in their efforts to study and understand European History, and the second one being to provide certain basic information that can support and supplement the teaching process in my specific courses at the freshman and sophomore college level.

Let me emphasize at the outset, however, that this book is not a comprehensive survey of European History. Many significant events, trends, and developments have been deliberately withheld because either they are being covered in classroom lectures in my courses, or they do not lend themselves well to the format of this volume, or they are treated much more capably by the prose rendition of a textbook. As one will clearly perceive, moreover, the stress in subject matter is on political, social, and economic history. In addition, the reader will observe that, while some passages of the text are composed in complete sentences with subjects and verbs, the vast majority of passages are presented in sentence fragments only. The purpose for such a structure is to present the material succinctly and directly but without simultaneously losing its significance or meaning.

Furthermore, it is important to note that the information in this book has been derived from literally dozens of works on the subjects of European History, Western Civilization, and even World Civilization. Also, the book is based on many years of personal reflection as well as the experiences of travel and residence in more than thirty countries in Europe, the Middle East, and North Africa. Finally, my hope is that this volume will provide insights and edification to a wide audience of people from very diverse backgrounds, interests, and educational levels.

Chapter 1   PREHISTORY AND THE STUDY OF HISTORY

I. The Study of History
   A. Definition of "History"--the recorded (based mainly on written records) and interpreted (analyzed & examined from many different perspectives and subject to numerous theories) deeds, thoughts, & words of mankind since the beginnings of civilization (which commenced only about 5-6,000 years ago with the invention of writing)
      1. Thus History is the recorded memory of humanity and includes everything--<u>all</u> forms of human activity; it is the basic foundation for all studies
      2. The great significance of History is this all-encompassing, all-inclusive, comprehensive scope--it is the <u>only</u> subject to include & cover so many other branches of knowledge and fields of study
         a. For example, in this course we will focus on the awesome impact on our world of Freud (psychology), Darwin (biology), Marx (economics & sociology), & Einstein (physics & mathematics)...
         b. These men are associated with areas of study other than History, yet a person cannot understand our contemporary world without comprehending the tremendous influence of their work & their contributions
      3. Subject matter in the study of History:
         a. Prior to a century ago, when people studied History they concentrated on politics & government, warfare, international relations, religion, and the lives of famous persons such as emperors & kings & queens & popes & generals
         b. But since the late-19th century (latter 1800's) we have included & added economics, sociology, science, culture & the arts, and the lives of ordinary & anonymous folk (and since the late 1960's, women as well as men)
         c. These additions are attributable at least partly to the impact of the four men mentioned above
      4. Absolute certainty vs. knowledgeable probability:
         a. It is important to emphasize that the study of History can never be totally objective or attain absolute truth & certainty---instead it is always highly subjective, based on each individual's opinions & values & prejudices, and capable of achieving only relative rather than absolute truth
         b. However, History that is relatively accurate, objective, & meaningful must have a strong basis on factual information, statistical data, and rational thought; otherwise, it is simply propaganda & falsehood
         c. The subjectivity & relativity of our world is partly attributable to the imperfection & fallibility of human beings--famous quotation by German philosopher Immanuel Kant in 1784: "Out of the crooked timber of humanity no straight thing was ever made."[1]
         d. Regarding the judgments of your professor, he is a passionate proponent of democracy, equality of opportunity, human decency, social consciousness, & individual accountability---actually, few people even in

     our own society are truly committed to fulfilling these
     principles
  B. Reasons for studying History:
     1. Most importantly, the betterment & improvement of ourselves,
        our society, & our world
        a. Obviously, the more we know about our world, which is a
           product of the past, the more our decisions will be
           intelligent ones & the more successful will be our
           solutions to problems
        b. Everyone is a product of his society; every society is a
           product of its past---to know the past & that of other
           people is to know oneself
        c. Thus progress is possible by avoiding past mistakes &
           emulating positive accomplishments
        d. Celebrated quote of Spanish-American philosopher George
           Santayana: "Those who cannot remember the past are con-
           demned to fulfill it."[2] and H.G. Wells: "Human history
           becomes more and more a race between education and
           catastrophe."[3]
        e. Prediction & anticipation of future events--a knowledge
           of the past can provide clues regarding what is likely
           to happen in the future
     2. Pleasure & enjoyment--nearly everyone is fascinated with at
        least some aspects of past peoples & cultures & civilizations
  C. Why should Americans study European History:
     1. American civilization is nothing more than an extension or
        transplant of the European world--our institutions & language
        & culture were brought here by our European ancestors; indeed
        most Americans are ethnically European
     2. Certainly there have been influences on America from Black
        Africans & Orientals & Middle Easterners & Native American
        Indians, but our nation is overwhelmingly European in origin-
        ation & development
     3. Furthermore, European (or Western) Civilization became the
        dominant world civilization of today, affecting the lives of
        humankind worldwide--we will study that civilization rising
        in the Middle East, maturing in Europe, & being exported to
        the rest of the world
     4. Europe uniquely produced the most significant forces in our
        world today---modern science & technology, ideals & institut-
        ions of democracy, reliance on rational thought, concepts of
        individual freedom, etc.

II. Origins of Our Universe, Life, & Civilization
  A. Our universe commenced its vast expansion (the "Big Bang") around
     15 billion years ago; our earth burst away from the sun about 4
     billion years ago; organic life in primitive one-celled forms
     appeared about 3 billion years ago:
     1. Man-like creatures (primitive ancestors of humans) emerged
        around 4.4 million years ago, and...
     2. Modern man (<u>homo sapiens</u>--"man who knows") evolved approximat-
        ely 35-50,000 years ago
  B. Evolution--idea that lower & primitive forms of life evolved, grew,
     or developed into higher & more complex forms of life over bill-
     ions of years--it is considered factual law by serious scientists

today and not mere theory, although disagreement exists over how evolutionary changes in species occurred:
1. Charles Darwin suggested in 1859 that changes came gradually & slowly & cumulatively by a process (called "natural selection") of relentless competition among individuals in a struggle for "survival of the fittest"
2. Recent scholarship supports the theory of "punctuated equalibrium" by Stephen Jay Gould of Harvard & others that physical & mental changes proceeded in rare yet sudden & dramatic leaps, known as mutations

C. Prehistory is that period of human existence before written records; History began when mankind mastered the ability to write & thus to record his thoughts & deeds:
1. The ratio of prehistoric time of man & man-like creatures on earth to historic time since 3-4,000 B.C. is like the ratio of three hours to one minute
2. Much of humanity's physical & cultural foundation of behavior (our emotions, appetites, subconscious lives) formed during the many millennia of Prehistory
3. Three chronological periods of Prehistory, divided & determined by the material & methods for making tools & weapons:
   a. Paleolithic (Old Stone) Age: beginning a million years ago & ending around 10,000 B.C. and characterized by a wandering & nomadic existence for mankind in small groups as foodgatherers & hunters
   b. Mesolithic (Middle Stone) Age: 10,000--5,000 B.C. marked by a gradual transition from Old to New Stone Age and its revolutionary changes
   c. Neolithic (New Stone) Age: 5,000--3,000 B.C. featuring the development of agriculture, domestication of animals, & thus permanent settlement of populations in large groups--these constitute a "Neolithic Revolution"
4. A significant measure of progress from 8,000 to 3,000 B.C. was the transition from "cultures" to "civilizations":
   a. A culture was characterized by primitive life in small & isolated groups or villages
   b. A civilization was characterized by greater maturity & featured three things:
      (1) Art of writing
      (2) Urban existence in cities, requiring higher organization & greater complexity
      (3) Capability of metallurgy--fusing several elements together at high temperatures for products of superior quality (copper & tin were made into bronze) --thus an indication of scientific advancement
   c. Four "cradles of civilization" developed around 3-4,000 B.C. in major river valley, from which other peoples living in adjacent regions learned of civilizing ways:
      (1) Nile Valley in Egypt
      (2) Tigris-Euphrates River Valley in Mesopotamia (Iraq)
      (3) Huang Ho or Yellow River Valley in China
      (4) Indus River of India (in modern Pakistan)
5. Ironically, Western Civilization did not begin in Europe with the European peoples, but arose among non-Europeans in the Near East or Middle East--in Egypt, Mesopotamia, & the Fer-

tile Crescent (modern Palestine, Lebanon, Syria, & Turkey) as early as 3,500 B.C.
6. Prior to 2,000 B.C. the European barbarian tribes resided & thus originated in the southern region of Russia known today as Ukraine before migrating into Europe and elsewhere

III. Race, Ethnicity, & Linguistic Groups
   A. Definition of "race"--a division of mankind possessing certain hereditary traits & physical features (such as skin color, texture of hair, shape of head & nose) which distinguish it as a distinct human type--- three major races of the world:
      1. Caucasoid or Caucasian--whites of Europe & brown-skinned peoples of the Middle East & India
      2. Mongoloid--yellow-skinned Asians & red-skinned Native American Indians
      3. Negroid--blacks of central & southern Africa
   B. Definition of "ethnic group" or "nationality"--a distinct body of people distinguished by a common language & popular culture, which are environmentally acquired through learning & not inheritance
   C. Four main families of human languages in the Western World:
      1. Hamitic--dialects of ancient Egyptian & a few modern Moslem peoples of north Africa
      2. Semitic--dialects of modern Hebrew & Arabic and ancient peoples of the Near East
      3. Aryan or Indo-European, with seven separate branches:
         a. Germanic--modern dialects of English, Dutch, Flemish, Yiddish, Danish, Swedish, Norwegian, & German
         b. Italic or Romance--ancient dialect of Latin; modern dialects of French, Italian, Spanish, Portuguese, Rumanian
         c. Celtic--Irish Gaelic, Scottish Gaelic, Welsh, Breton (of Brittany in France) dialects
         d. Hellenic--ancient & modern Greek dialects
         e. Baltic--modern dialects of Lithuanian & Latvian
         f. Slavic--modern dialects of Russian, Ukrainian, Polish, Czech, Slovak, Serbo-Croatian, Slovene, Bulgarian, & Macedonian
         g. Indo-Iranian--ancient & modern dialects of Persian (spoken in Iran) and ancient Sanskrit & modern Hindi of India
      4. Uralic, with the main branch being Finno-Ugric and the primary dialects being Hungarian (Magyar), Finnish, Estonian, & Lapp

IV. Religion
   A. The first religious beliefs, practices, & attitudes began among prehistoric peoples as much as 50,000 years ago
   B. All religions have in common two ideas--that there are higher & unseen (we say "supernatural") powers in the universe, and that mankind must deal with them
   C. Thus a fundamental definition of "religion"--religion is the effort to make sense of a mysterious world and to get into satisfactory relations with the mysterious powers that control it
   D. Science explains how things happen; religion tries to explain why things happen the way they do
   E. An explanation why religion has always exercised such tremendous power over the human mind & behavior--religion involves many things:

1. Hope--people wish for a better future beyond the pain & suffering of this world in a blissful paradise of another world
2. Fear & insecurity--humans have usually feared death as well as danger in this life; modern psychology has illuminated much for us:
   a. As children, we are protected, fed & cared for by parents
   b. As adults, we still feel threatened by the world's troubles and thus create a spiritual "protector-father"
3. Provision of purpose & meaning to life--religious practices & beliefs have served as many people's "reason for existence" in a confusing & complicated world
4. Wealth--the general populace has always been encouraged to believe in the divine powers & inherent superiority of an inspired priesthood; the consequent prestige & privileges were then used to accumulate vast riches at the expense of the gullible masses, as evidenced today by our millionaire televangelists (who claim as their Saviour a man who lived & died around 2,000 years ago in <u>poverty</u>)
5. Power & social control--small, ruling upper classes employed religion as a means of dominating & repressing the lower-class masses with encouragement to focus their energies & attention on the heavenly hereafter rather than on the exploitation & misrule of the here-and-now
   a. This tactic was immensely successful throughout most of history until the past two centuries; rarely did the masses revolt against oppression, degradation, & ignorance--thus religion truly was an "opiate of the masses"
   b. The brilliant & perceptive Napoleon Bonaparte would later comment on these matters: "In religion, I see not the mystery of the Incarnation but the mystery of the social order. Religion associates with Heaven an idea of equality which prevents the rich from being massacred by the poor."[1]
6. Obsessions with conformity--strong desires for social acceptance & "fitting in" among their peers lead people blindly to adopt the views & practices of friends & associates; on this subject, Irish playwright Oscar Wilde wrote that "most people are other people"[2]

F. Emergence of a belief in "immortality", or life after death, by the keen observation of nature (especially the cyclical procession of the seasons, among other things) on which mankind was totally dependent for survival--to be discussed further in class

J. Developments in Prehistory
  A. Origination of many things still a part of our contemporary world:
    1. Social or class structures, with some possessing more property & power & status than others
    2. Male domination of females
    3. Acquisition by men of greater strength & size (physical endowment) than women
    4. Glorification of violence & aggression
    5. A rooting of these phenomena in the vital activities of hunting and fighting for survival

B. Warfare:
   1. Warfare began as a form of organized theft; groups of men decided to steal from others what they could not or would not acquire for themselves
   2. Most men involved in warfare derived excitement & pleasure from the activity; thus it became a sport, adventure, & profession supposedly demonstrating "manliness" & superiority
   3. However, aggressive warfare has actually been a reversion to barbarism & beastliness rather than a mark of advancement or civilization
   4. In most cases throughout the human experience, conquerors are much less civilized than those being conquered--we will study many examples of this
C. Cultural creativity:
   1. When mankind has devoted his energies toward creative & imaginative pursuits, some spectacular yet rare works & advances in civilization have been achieved--when usually pursuin destructive or mindless activities, mankind has regressed or languished or behaved no differently than lower animals
   2. Homo sapiens possesses a superior brain to all other animals, but if brains are not used productively, the consequences of human life are negative
   3. This pessimistic appraisal led British philosopher-mathematician Bertrand Russell in the mid-20th century to write: "Most people would rather die than think (rationally)-and in fact, do so."[3]
   4. The next generation of Americans must reverse that fact--why?
      Richard Leakey (one of the foremost experts on Prehistoric Man) recently noted in his book Origins Reconsidered that Earth has seen five mass extinctions of living species on the planet, and he predicts the probable extinction of humanity by "the inexorable growth of human population"[4]
D. Lifestyle & behavior:
   1. Prehistoric peoples manifested a wide range of lifestyles, behaving very differently depending on circumstances & time & location
   2. For examples, there were:
      a. Warlike as well as peaceloving people
      b. Individual as well as common ownership of property
      c. Monogamy in marriage as well as polygamy
      d. Relative equality between the sexes as well as male domination of females
      e. Fairly balanced distribution of commodities as well as major disparities between wealthy & poor
      f. All sorts of religious beliefs & rituals
E. Conclusions about Mankind drawn from a study of Prehistory:
   1. Humanity is definitely a product of a long evolutionary development & has existed for tens of thousands of years as a single species
   2. Man is unique when compared to other animals in two significant ways:
      a. Capacity to use words & symbols and thus to communicate his thoughts

    b. Capability of adapting his environment to himself instead of simply adapting himself to his environment
3. Human beings have progressed over the ages, attaining higher standards of living & greater contentment in physical needs
4. Man is a highly creative & inventive animal, potentially changing nearly everything in his world
5. Humanity has developed subspecies (races) within the species of homo sapiens after residing in certain regions & areas for many millennia:
    a. Yet none of the races remained pure or completely isolated from the others; much interbreeding occurred throughout history--we can refer to humans in the present & the past as mongrels
    b. The most important variations & differences in human beings are based on physical & mental abilities of <u>individuals</u> and not of races or ethnicities

Chapter 2   ANCIENT NEAR EAST

I. Introduction
   A. Western Civilization began not in Europe but in the Near or
      Middle East among mainly non-European peoples residing in
      fertile river valleys or habitable lands of eastern regions of
      the Mediterranean Sea, with its generally dry climate, mild
      winters, & hot summers
   B. This involves a study of the peoples & civilizations of Egypt,
      Mesopotamia, and the Fertile Crescent (modern Palestine,
      Lebanon, Syria, Turkey or Asia Minor in ancient times) as well
      as the island of Crete

II. Class Divisions & Social Structures
    A. Civilization brought great advances & much improvement in
       certain areas for mankind
    B. However, it also resulted in heightened socio-economic
       inequities and brutal exploitation of the weak by the strong,
       the unskilled by the skilled, & the unfortunate by the
       privileged elite
    C. Thus there was the formation of rigid class systems &
       hierarchies almost invariably based on heredity and
       concentrating wealth & power in the hands of a few
    D. Factors & developments contributing to the formation of
       classes:
       1. Emergence of private property rather than common ownership
       2. Necessity to organize governments to dispense resources
       3. Specialization & division of labor
       4. Enslavement of conquered peoples
       5. Superior intelligence or talents of some individuals
       6. Basic human greed & selfishness
    E. General class structure in most ancient Near Eastern societies:
       1. Aristocracy--landowning nobility, priests, emperors or
          kings & their royal families--less than 5% of the
          population
       2. Freemen--businessmen & professionals & skilled workers &
          government administrators later known collectively as the
          "middle class" or bourgeoisie--roughly 5 to 10% of the
          population
          a. This group of people was small but very significant
          b. Yet its status & living conditions varied radically
             between comfort & a good income to the usual misery
             & almost endless toil of the masses
       3. Peasants--farmers & agricultural workers with few or no
          rights, little if any control over their destiny, & a
          life of ceaseless drudgery only slightly better than
          slavery--approximately 85-90% of the population
       4. Slaves--these were usually captives in war assigned the
          most arduous tasks; their numbers & percentage
          drastically fluctuated from time to time depending on the
          frequency & success of military matters

III. Egypt
     A. Lecture material will provide an understanding of the Nile
        River Valley, its irrigation system, its government, & its
        religion

B. Great achievements of ancient Egypt--its contributions to Western Civilization:
   1. Engineering feats & applied science--much technical skill & maturity was demonstrated in the construction of pyramids, religious temples, royal palaces, monuments such as the obelisk, irrigation canals, reservoirs, dikes, etc.
   2. Mathematics--use of a numbers system up to a million, ability to add & subtract & multiply & divide and to use fractions and to calculate the volume of solids & the area of circles, some understanding of the Pythagorean theorem regarding right triangles--yet no use of the zero or a positional system of numbers
   3. Invention of a solar calendar:
      a. A year contained 12 months of 30 days each with five days added at the end
      b. Its accuracy was based on centuries of precise astronomical records
      c. Later Julius Caesar adopted it for Rome and we use it today in modified form
      *d. This was their greatest contribution to civilization
   4. Development of writing, known as hieroglyphics, meaning "sacred carvings" in Greek--yet the Egyptians were not the first people to invent a form of writing
      a. Cumbersome use of picture-words & idea-words with each sign representing a single object or idea
      b. No indigenous development of an alphabet, which was introduced later from elsewhere in the Middle East
   5. Use of an inexpensive & efficient type of paper, called papyrus because it was made from a water reed of the same name growing in the Nile delta--papyrus was utilized extensively for purposes of writing & records preservation
   6. Art & craftsmanship--their jewelry, small carvings, wall paintings, and statues & busts were often superb & exquisite in quality as well as brightly colored, lively, & imaginative
      a. Much technical skill was required in their production
      b. Some experts believe that Egyptian art was equalled in the Ancient World only later by the brilliant Greeks
   7. Some advances in chemistry & medicine--Egypt employed a wide range of over 700 drugs for treating illnesses and practiced simple surgical techniques, although their medical knowledge suffered from beliefs in superstition & magic

IV. Mesopotamia
   A. Significance of geography:
      1. Geographic & climatic conditions always influence & shape significantly the institutions, values, & historical experience of every people & civilization
      2. Mesopotamia ("land between the waters" in Greek) was located in the valley of the Tigris & Euphrates Rivers; to the south were open grasslands & desert, and to the north were sloping plains & mountain ranges with a

proximity to Central Asia
   3. The lands on all sides of Mesopotamia were occupied by nomadic less civilized & more barbaric than the valley population
   4. Thus Mesopotamia lacked natural frontiers or boundaries to protect against hostile outsiders
   5. Its vulnerability & exposure resulted in a pattern of numerous invasions from without in addition to usual internal war between different states as well as the rise & fall of successive kingdoms
B. Absorption of later invaders & their cultures into the original cultural foundation of a people known as the Sumerians--a common civilization enduring for 3,000 years was developed & carried on by peoples of many different languages & cultures as a veritable melting pot
C. Contrast & comparison of Egypt & Mesopotamia:
   1. Egypt was ethnically quite pure & homogeneous--Mesopotamia was very mixed & heterogeneous
   2. Egypt possessed natural boundaries, security against invaders, an orderly society, & relative geographic isolation--Mesopotamia lacked natural frontiers, was exposed to invasions, & experienced frequent insecurity & disorder
   3. In Egypt flood waters were regular & predictable--in Mesopotamia river floods were erratic, capricious, & unpredictable
   4. Because of conditions mentioned above, Egyptians usually manifested a mood of confidence & optimism--in Mesopotamia the public mood was generally one of fatalism & pessimism & uncertainty
D. Succession of empires & states & peoples of Mesopotamia:
   1. The first inhabitants occupied the valley sometime after 5000 B.C. and passed from a Neolithic village culture after 4000 B.C. to a well-developed civilization before being conquered & enslaved by the:
   2. Sumerians (3200--2350 B.C.)
      a. One of the most gifted people in all of history-- their impressive civilization was very important in providing the foundation on which others later built & into which they were absorbed
      b. Their language was not Semitic or Aryan & unrelated to all others in the region--later invaders adopted many of their institutions & techniques, especially the elaborate canals & irrigation system
      c. They became united culturally but remained usually dis- united politically--division into many independent city- states frequently warring among themselves
   3. Akkadians (2350--2100 B.C.)
      a. A Semitic-speaking people who gradually infiltrated the valley & fused with the Sumerians
      b. They eventually conquered all of Mesopotamia & established the first true empire in the region--its collapse led to chaos & a power vacuum
   4. Amorites, or Old Babylonians (1760--1530 B.C.)
      a. These Semitic people invaded the valley around 2100 B.C. & completed their conquest by 1760 B.C., establishing their capital city at fabled Babylon, whence their name

                b. Their king Hammurabi (1792--1750) issued the most famous
                   codification of laws in the Ancient World
          5. Kassites--these highly destructive European barbarians from
             Central Asia to the north ushered in an era of anarchy &
             decentralized government around 1550 B.C.
          6. Assyrians (900--612 B.C.)
                a. These Semitic warrior people conquered the first empire
                   including most of the Middle East: Mesopotamia, Syria,
                   Palestine, & Egypt
                b. Their empire & capital city of Nineveh later experienced
                   destruction at the hands of the:
          7. Chaldeans (612--538 B.C.) and Medes
                a. The Chaldeans were Semitic speakers known as the New
                   Babylonians for their brief but brilliant revival of
                   the old city
                b. The Medes were Aryans from the east related to the Pers-
                   ians who are mentioned below
          8. Persians (538--330 B.C.)
                a. These Aryan-speaking ancestors of modern Iranians invaded
                   from their lands to the east
                b. Their empire ruled from the capital of Persepolis would
                   constitute the largest in the Western World thus far,
                   extending from Libya in north Africa to the Indus River
                   in modern Pakistan and including all of the Near East
    E. Achievements & contributions to civilization by the Mesopotamians:
          1. These contributions will be listed in the chronological order
             of kingdoms & peoples occupying the valley region
          2. Writing--the Sumerians were the absolute first people to de-
             velop this art, known as <u>cuneiform</u> ("cuneus" in Latin means
             wedge); this was picture-writing without an alphabet by im-
             pressing wedged signs on wet clay tablets with a square-
             shaped stylus
          3. Use of the wheel & the saddle for riding horses--the Sumer-
             ians invented these devices that revolutionized work and
             transportation
          4. Theory of government:
                a. The Sumerians & Old Babylonians viewed their mortal rul-
                   ers not as gods or autocrats but as servants of higher
                   powers (the gods) to whom the rulers were held account-
                   able for even the lowliest subjects
                b. This view (in spite of many violations) was more enlight-
                   ened than that of other peoples such as the Egyptians
          5. Literature--the Sumerians & later Old Babylonians were the
             first to write epic poetry, in the form of stories & legends
             about the hero <u>Gilgamesh</u>
                a. An epic is a long narrative poem in a lofty or embellish-
                   ed style recounting the deeds of a legendary or semi-
                   historical hero
                b. Many peoples & nations would compose epics, such as the
                   <u>Iliad</u> & <u>Odyssey</u>, <u>Aeneid</u>, <u>El Cid</u>, <u>Song of Roland</u>, <u>Beowulf</u>
                c. Gilgamesh was typical in embarking on hazardous journeys,
                   achieving great feats of courage, saving damsels in dis-
                   tress, cavorting with gods, etc.
          6. Religion--unique contribution of <u>astrology</u>, which is a belief
             that the movement of stars & their positions in the heavens
             affect the destiny of events & one's life--use of the 12

signs of the zodiac for predictions
   a. The Sumerians introduced this belief & the Old Babylonians greatly enhanced its practices with detailed studies of the stars--some people still subscribe to it now
   b. Reputable scientists today give no credibility to its sham theories, which certainly does not prevent bubble-brains like Nancy Reagan from basing major White House decisions on its hocus-pocus suggestions
7. Mathematics--again the Sumerians & Old Babylonians made impressive advances, which were extended later by other Mesopotamians:
   a. The number 60 was the fundamental basis for their number system, thus the sexagesimal system--consequently, our hours have 60 minutes with 60 seconds, & a circle has 360 degrees
   b. In geometry they could also calculate the volume of some solids, area of a circle, & area of a right triangle
   c. In algebra the Old Babylonians were probably the best in the Ancient World capable of figuring compound interest, solving quadratic equations, squaring & cubing numbers, and formulating tables for square & cube roots
   d. A true positional system of numbers was used by the Sumerians; Mesopotamians routinely used the zero for calculations by 500 B.C.
8. Law--the Sumerians & Old Babylonians were first to codify systems of law; "codification" of laws meant the combination of many different systems of law into one uniform body that is universally applied throughout a nation or empire, which can be a significant milestone in fairness & consistency--most famous (but not the first) was <u>Hammurabi's Code</u>--examples:
   a. Recognition of the principle: "an eye for an eye and a tooth for a tooth"[8], meaning punishment according to the degree of harm done to another on exactly the same basis
   b. Foundation on a strongly stratified class structure--thus injuries to men of the upper class were fined more heavily than to freemen or peasants or slaves
   c. Yet protection by the law of even slaves who possessed some rights & status & guarantee of three days of rest monthly--also emancipation possible through service or purchase--fines to be paid if slaves injured or killed by superior
   d. Severe penalty of death for crimes such as treason & bribery & adultery
   e. Treatment of women--not regarded as equal to men, but recognition of rights to divorce, occasional inheritance, demand from husband for proper care of children
   f. Regulation of all problems such as theft, injury, property rights, business practices, inheritance, etc.
   g. Frequent appearance of being brutal & barbarous, yet probably one of the most humane in the world at the time
9. Contributions of the Assyrians:
   a. Military tactics--first organization of armies into separate units of infantry, cavalry, engineers, supply, & intelligence (spying)--this efficiency made their armies invincible for several centuries
   b. Engineering--construction of roads, the first aqueduct

              ever (elevated pipes for carrying water to cities), and
              a massive library
           c. Sculpture--their wall carvings of animals & humans in the
              form of bas-reliefs still judged as excellent in quality
           d. Government administration--division of empire into dis-
              tinct provinces for tax & efficiency purposes
       10. Astronomy--the Chaldeans (New Babylonians) were the most
           learned astronomers of the Ancient World with detailed re-
           cords of eclipses, precise charts of the heavens, and minute
           calculations of the length of a year
       11. Achievements of the Persians:
           a. Engineering--construction of the finest roads in the
              world prior to the Romans, one alone stretching 1600
              uninterrupted miles from near the Persian Gulf to near
              the Mediterranean Sea in Asia Minor
           b. Establishment of a postal service utilizing horseback
              riders & relay posts anticipating our pony express of
              the American West--a renowned Greek traveller wrote of
              its excellence: "Neither snow nor rain nor heat nor
              gloom of night stays these couriers from the swift com-
              pletion of their appointed rounds."[9]
           c. Introduction of the camel to Egypt & the chicken to the
              West from India--probable invention of the windmill
           d. Government--efficient division into 20 provinces (each
              one called a <u>satrapy</u>) with an appointed governor (<u>sat-
              rap</u>)--annual secret inspections of provinces by royal
              agents--quite remarkable toleration of religion & cul-
              tural diversity
           e. Religion--Zoroastrianism, named after the prophet Zoro-
              aster (his appellation in Greek, Zarathustra in Persian)
              who lived & taught in the 6th century B.C. (625--551);
              containment of his beliefs in 17 hymns--the <u>Gathas</u>:
              (1) Monotheism--existence of a supreme god (Ahura-
                  Mazda) of virtue, goodness, light, & truth
              (2) Dualism--opposition from an evil spirit (Ahriman)
                  representing evil, sin, darkness, & falsehood
              (3) Constant war & struggle between these two forces
                  for control of the world, with humans free to
                  choose on which side to fight & live by example
              (4) Last judgment, with an ensuing afterlife of heaven
                  or hell--view of Zoroaster as a savior or messiah
              (5) Belief in a resurrection for all in a final apoca-
                  lypse or fiery destruction of the devil & the
                  world with the triumph of Ahura-Mazda & supporters

. The Hebrews & Judaism
   A. Introduction
      1. An understanding of the ancient Hebrews (sometimes called
         Israelites or Jews) and Judaism (their religion) is essen-
         tial to a comprehension of our modern world
         a. Their tragic experiences laid the foundation for prob-
            lems & conflicts in the contemporary Middle East
         b. Their religious evolution provided the basis for modern
            Judaism, Christianity, & Islam--the world's most power-
            ful faiths today
         c. Their conceptions of morality and of social & political

    justice have profoundly influenced Western Civilization
  2. The Jewish past might be the most fascinating saga in all of human history, providing great significance & meaning to us:
   a. Extreme glory & tragedy marked their existence as an ethnic group
   b. No people has ever consistently demonstrated such adaptability, indomitable energy, resourcefulness, brilliance, passion for learning, and will to survive
   c. No people has perpetually suffered such horrors of persecution, discrimination, & eventual mass extermination (the "Holocaust" during World War II.)
B. Early history--the first Hebrews (Semitic in language) originated in the Arabian Desert with a reputation as wanderers, raiders, captives, & primitive people who eventually migrated into Mesopotamia around 2000 B.C. and borrowed heavily from other cultures
C. Constant dissension--severe disunity always characterized the various Hebrew tribes--sometime before 1800 B.C. one group migrated westward & began its occupation of Palestine
D. Egypt--a bit before 1600 B.C. certain tribes of Israelites moved into Egypt to escape the consequences of famine--according to Biblical accounts (no Egyptian records mention these events) they were gradually enslaved by the Egyptian government
E. Impact of Moses--one of their most influential leaders ever:
  1. Indomitable personality leading (between 1300 & 1150 B.C.) Jews out of Egypt & into Sinai Peninsula while welding various tribes of followers into a loose confederation that reoccupied Palestine thereafter
  2. Foundation of religious Judaism & Jewish Law in his inspiration of what later became the first five books of the Old Testament (Pentateuch), containing the Ten Commandments and a specific body of wisdom & law known as the Torah:
   a. The Torah embodied many stern & strict & rigid & detailed practices, rituals, & moralistic laws such as insistence on circumcision, the observance of certain fasts & holy days, and dietary rules requiring kosher preparation & prohibiting consumption of pork
   b. Adherence to these rules would identify the Hebrews as a very unique & peculiar people
  3. Commencement of an evolutionary process toward monotheism by persuading the tribes to accept the worship of one god (named "Yahweh" in Hebrew, later "Jehovah" in Latin) to the exclusion of all other deities, thereby replacing an earlier & primitive polytheism
  4. Possession by Yahweh of the physical body & emotional qualities of a man, being at times capricious & irascible & wrathful & arbitrary as well as beneficent
   a. This is "anthropomorphism"--the attribution of human qualities & characteristics to nonhuman things & objects
   b. Most religions would feature this concept
  5. Introduction of the idea of the "Covenant"--a special agreement or compact in which Yahweh promised protection & favor to Jews in return for faithful worship & unquestioning obedience to His laws & commandments--this included belief in the:
   a. Promised Land--God granted the territory of Palestine exclusively to the Hebrews as long as they earned divine grace in the Covenant

    b. Chosen People--a superiority & special status in comparison to other people resulted by virtue of Yahweh's favoritism, yet it demanded greater human effort & moral dedication--thus a kind of ancient nationalism
    c. Consequences--these ideas were inspirational to Jews but also caused them frequently to manifest arrogance, intolerance, militancy, & narrow-mindedness that created numerous enemies & much resentment
  6. Political objective of Moses--there was more than a religious motive in his mind for the Torah & Ten Commandments & ideas of God; his political goal was to unite the diverse groups & tribes for survival & strength & common effort
  7. The legacy of Moses--for the next 3,000 years Yahweh & His Law would be the main (and sometimes the only) source of unity & common identity for Jews scattered all over the world
F. Efforts to conquer Palestine & to found an independent nation:
  1. Neighbors--the Hebrews shared this region with others such as the Canaanites & Philistines (from whose Latinized name came "Palestine")--their threat compelled greater political unity among the Jewish tribes
  2. Replacement of a loose confederation of twelve independent tribes with a monarchy around 1025 B.C. under King Saul-- greater discipline & organization brought military & political success for a brief while
  3. Achievement of their zenith of power & prestige under kings David (1000-960) and Solomon (960-922):
    a. A magnificent capital at Jerusalem & the Temple were constructed under the absolute monarchy
    b. Yet powerful government & military glory & material splendor were accompanied by heavy taxes, conscription, exploitation of the masses, and eventual weakness & decline
    c. The Hebrew nation was always vulnerable against more powerful neighboring empires due to its exposed geographic location on the land routes between Egypt & Mesopotamia
  4. Split & division of the kingdom in 922 B.C. after Solomon's death into a northern state of Israel & a southern state of Judah separate existence for two centuries as small & feeble kingdoms until the:
    a. Conquest of Israel (722 B.C.) by the Assyrians and the scattering of its inhabitants throughout their empire
    b. Conquest of Judah (586 B.C.) by the Chaldeans who plundered & burned Jerusalem & enslaved its citizens during the Babylonian Captivity until 539 B.C.
  5. The Persian conquest of the Middle East brought liberation to the Jews & the right to return to Palestine for a reconstruction of Jerusalem & the Temple--yet future domination by the Persian Empire (539--332), later Greek Hellenistic regimes (332--63 B.C.), and the Roman Empire
  6. The Roman Period:
    a. Mounting frustration over thwarted hopes of political independence, outside threats to religious exclusiveness, and corrupting foreign influences led to fanatical hostility toward the Romans culminating in a renowned rebellion

b. The Jewish Revolt (66--70 A.D.) was a suicidal uprising against the Romans ending in death or enslavement for more than one million Jews--simultaneous destruction of Jerusalem & the Temple & thus all tangible symbols of national identity
  c. The Hebrews interpreted this catastrophe as God's punishment for their failure to achieve their mission as the Chosen People & for their unworthiness of Yahweh's favoritism, thereby breaking the Covenant--further punishment was to be the loss of the Promised Land for most Jews, resulting in the:
  d. Diaspora (Great Dispersion)--their departure from Palestine and the resumption of their wandering existence or residence elsewhere--it was believed that a return was impossible until they regained God's special grace
  e. However, Jews living elsewhere in small groups or as individuals became (due to their unusual lifestyle & habits as well as their extraordinary will to survive) blameworthy as scapegoats for social problems and as easy targets for discrimination, persecution, & worse--former Jewish intolerance toward others in Palestine now turned into desires for tolerance in the outside world
  f. An independent Jewish nation never existed again until after World War II. and the Holocaust with the return of many Jews to Palestine (where they found many Arabs) and creation of the modern state of Israel in 1948
  g. Masada--this ancient mountaintop fortress towering above the Dead Sea is where 1000 Jews made their final stand against a besieging Roman army for two years (71--73) before committing suicide when the final assault imperiled them with enslavement--it is today a symbol of defiance & dedication to Israelis with the motto: "live free or die"
G. Hebrew religious evolution:
  1. Their religion developed & changed over many centuries from the crudest superstitions to the loftiest spiritual & ethical conceptions
  2. This evolutionary process occurred because of a diversity of influences from many peoples & civilizations, thus a legacy of their migrations & exiles as well as their geographic situation on the crossroads of the Middle East
  3. <u>Four</u> different stages of evolution:
    a. Period before Moses (earliest beginnings to 1250 B.C.): belief in magic & animism [polytheistic worship of spirits in nature] & sacrifices & anthropomorphic tribal gods--no national worship of Yahweh yet
    b. Period of Moses (1250--800 B.C.): stage of national <u>monolatry</u> [exclusive worship of one god without denying the existence of other gods] yet continuation of many superstitious beliefs & practices from the previous stage--ethical standards & spiritual ideas were still unimportant (scholars believe that the Ten Commandments as preserved in <u>Exodus</u> date only from the 7th century B.C.)
    c. Period of the Prophetic Revolution (800--600 B.C.): refinement of Judaism into pure monotheism under the influence & teachings of a series of prophets [meaning

"speak for" in Greek], who were preachers believing in their direct contact with the deity
- (1) Most important were Isaiah, Jeremiah, Hosea, Amos, Micah, & Elijah
- (2) Regard for Yahweh as the universal & only true god of all humanity
- (3) Important stress on social & economic & political justice as well as goodness & humane behavior
- (4) Their main focus was on the material & not the spiritual world

d. Period of Persian Influence (539--300 B.C.): emergence of modern Judaism with the addition of:
- (1) Dualism--first belief in Satan as a spiritual author of evil and the rival of God
- (2) Messianism--belief in the future coming of a deliverer or savior ("messiah") who will preside over a last judgment & resurrect the dead
- (3) Apocalyptical tradition--view that the material world will end in cosmic cataclysm and fiery & terrible destruction ("apocalypse"), followed by the messianic kingdom of heaven for the righteous
- (4) Otherworldly focus--emphasis on salvation in a heavenly paradise or damnation in hell
- (5) Idea of a revealed religion--conviction that the authors of biblical books were directly inspired by God to proclaim divine truth

Chapter 3   GREECE--HELLAS

I. Introduction
   A. Some scholars believe the ancient Greeks were the most brilliant, creative, & remarkable people who ever lived, because:
      1. They originated so many ideas & institutions that have powerfully shaped our modern world, such as democracy, personal freedom, religious toleration, rational thought, modern science, cultural standards, athletic games, and commercial & business practices
      2. Thus they truly began most of the meaningful values of Western Civilization
      3. Obviously, we in the modern world have gone far beyond their accomplishments but only because we built on a solid foundation that the Greeks laid
      4. This fact makes them very unique & fascinating to us because they were the first people in history to think & act the way we still do today
   B. Why were they so brilliant, creative, & remarkable? The explanation is found in the following combination of factors:
      1. Personal qualities--typical Greek view of life as an adventure to be experienced passionately--tendency to be restless & immoderate, impulsive, volatile, turbulent, & quarrelsome
      2. Deep curiosity about the world & love of travel--frequent wanderings abroad, intermingling with foreigners, & borrowing of ideas & methods from others
      3. Open-mindedness & flexibility--a consequence partly of their recognition of themselves as a mongrel people with pride in their racial & ethnic impurity
      4. Principle of challenge-and-response: much adversity (such as a lack of natural resources) stimulating the necessity of great energetic effort & imaginativeness
      5. Less religiosity with more focus on humanity--the gods & the hereafter of less importance to most Greeks than the here-&-now and this world of mankind & human endeavor--only this attitude could have produced such a brilliant civilization

II. Chronological Periods
   A. Minoan or Cretan Civilization: 2600--1100 B.C.
      1. Neolithic & non-Greek invaders from North Africa & Asia Minor settling on island of Crete after 6000 B.C. and eventually developing an impressive civilization after 3000 B.C.
      2. Great wealth deriving from overseas trade & colonial empire in eastern Mediterranean--famous for exquisite craftsmanship, artistic beauty, & luxurious lifestyle of its upper class
      3. Conquest of Crete around 1460 by first group of Greeks, who learned much from their more advanced neighbors
      4. Violent destruction of this civilization about 1405 B.C. by awesome volcanic eruption and accompanying earthquakes & tidal waves & fires emanating from nearby island of Santorini --very slow recovery thereafter
   B. Mycenaean Age: 2000--1100 B.C.
      1. This first wave of primitive & barbaric Mycenaean Greeks invading the peninsula & its islands from the north around 2000 B.C.--destruction of native culture & subjugation of Stone Age population

2. These people named for the most impressive fortress-palace & town of Mycenae--rule by powerful kings & social organization into clans, or large extended families
3. Heavy cultural borrowing from Minoans--bronze technology--zenith of power & development of civilization (1600--1200) cut short & overwhelmed by 2nd wave of Greeks, the Dorians
4. Most famous event & grandiose endeavor--the siege & destruction of the city of Troy in northwestern Asia Minor around 1260 or 1240 B.C. later immortalized in the epic poem of the Iliad by Homer (the Odyssey described a Greek hero's wanderings & adventures after Troy was sacked)

C. Dark Ages: 1200--800 B.C.
1. This era of chaos & violence & backwardness ushered in by the invasion of Dorian Greeks between 1200 & 1100--very gradual reconstruction after initial shock & disorder
2. Flight of some Mycenaeans to western coast of Asia Minor where they became known as Ionian Greeks--contacts there with more civilized peoples stimulating a faster recovery that later spread to the Greek mainland through commercial enterprises:
   a. Alphabetic writing learned from Phoenicians--adaptation to Greek spoken language about 825 B.C.
   b. Homeric epic poems initially written down in 8th century---oral transmission only prior to that time
   c. Adoption of iron-making technology in 9th century
   d. Introduction of coined metal money in the 8th century--a practice learned from the Lydians
3. Persistence for a long time in a hunting & herdsman stage of economy with farming as a secondary occupation--tendency of life to be crude, warlike, & insecure
4. Emergence of the basic political unit as a tribal region or small kingdom ruled by a chieftain or king--gradual development of a market & homes & a fortress into the "city", or polis, as the center of communal life
5. Formation of fundamental governmental institutions:
   a. Kings limited in authority by a powerful nobility class
   b. Councils of aristocratic elders to advise the monarchs
   c. Popular assemblies of male citizens for consultation & for the election of certain leaders (invariably nobles)

D. Archaic Age (Age of Nobles, Colonization, & Tyrants): 800--500 B.C.
1. Economic expansion & diversification:
   a. Existence of farming as the primary occupational pursuit of most Greeks from this period on, in spite of many problems with poor soil, small plots of land, & poverty
   b. Yet necessity of agricultural shifts away from production of cereal grains to more profitable cultivation of olives & grapes
   c. Development of overseas trade for food such as wheat & barley, raw materials like wood, & cash profits while exporting surpluses of wine, olive oil, & manufactured products (listed below)--mastery of the seas by 750 B.C.
   d. Emergence of urban manufacturing of pottery, woolen cloth & textiles, wood & leather products, metalworks, and perfume--thus the:
   e. Simultaneous creation of new occupational professions & socio-economic groups known as the bourgeoisie or middle class and including skilled workers (artisans, crafts-

    men, tradesmen) & merchant businessmen & professionals
2. Appearance of major problems:
 a. Significant increases in population, yet lack of adequate natural resources to sustain them
 b. Impoverishment of many small-scale independent farmers & tenant farmers and enslavement following their inability to pay off debts--rising numbers of landless & poor people in rural areas
 c. Enlargement of land holdings by wealthier aristocratic families at the expense of poorer farmers either selling or forfeiting their possessions--thus a trend of the rich getting richer & the poor becoming poorer
 d. Total domination of government & politics by the aristocracy--the right to vote confined to citizens with a certain amount of landed property, and the right to hold office limited to members of a few families of noblemen
 e. Existence of a kind of Marxian class struggle between the aristocracy on one side and business & farming & laborer interests on the other side
3. Results of & responses to these major problems:
 a. Emigration of surplus population & foundation of overseas colonies all over the Mediterranean world--these <u>poleis</u> became politically independent yet maintained cultural & commercial ties with the mother city-state in Greece
 b. Period of greatest emigration: 750--550 B.C.
 c. Pressures from class conflict eventuating in reform measures beneficial to many lower-class commoners & addressing their grievances yet initiated by the...
 d. Political rise of <u>tyrants</u> (650--500 B.C.)--dictators seizing power illegally with popular lower-class support in opposition to aristocrats, even though the tyrants were ambitious politicians from the aristocratic class
4. <u>Three</u> developments or trends undermining aristocratic predominance & encouraging a more democratic society:
 a. Rule of tyrants--these dictators came to power with armed coercion from the popular masses, but they could obviously be deposed in the same fashion--thus ultimate authority truly rested with the people if they insisted
 b. Commercial Revolution--the export trade & its products enriched & emboldened & later empowered many of the popular masses
 c. Changes in military tactics & methods of fighting during this era (800--600 B.C.):
  (1) De-emphasis on cavalry (horses affordable only by noblemen) & more stress on infantry (foot soldiers equipped with more moderately-priced shields, helmets, spears, small swords, & breastplates)
  (2) These heavily armed infantrymen (<u>hoplites</u>) attacking in massed formations (the <u>phalanx</u>)--coordinated & perfectly disciplined lines of troops charging & maneuvering to commands of their leaders
  (3) Such changes introducing a sense of the equality of man to man & of solidarity among the citizens of one state--dependence of every man in line on the man next to him for his safety & survival

E. Hellenic Age: 500--330 B.C.
1. Attainment of the greatest glory & achievement for Greece during this era & the following one--in the Greek language, "Greece" is <u>Hellas</u> and "Greeks" are <u>Hellenes</u>
2. Greek civilization centering on the Greek peninsula, the surrounding islands, & the western coast of Asia Minor--no political unification into one nation & division instead into hundreds of usually small & independent & often remote states
3. Culmination of 300-year governmental evolution by most city-states from:
    a. Monarchy--"rule by one person" in Greek, usually a hereditary king or queen, to:
    b. Aristocracy--"rule of the best", a small & privileged class of landowning nobility who claim genetic superiority over all others in society, or: Oligarchy--"rule by the few or handful", meaning nobility & some wealthy businessmen without pedigree bloodlines, to:
    c. Tyranny--absolute rule of a usurping dictator or despot, yet regard for most Greek tyrants as benevolent, reform-oriented, & populist in their policies
    d. Democracy--"rule of the people" in Greek, implying a majority of the male citizens
4. The two leading & rival powers in Greece:
    a. Athens--the foremost democracy & most culturally creative city-state of all the <u>poleis</u>
    b. Sparta--the most repressive, authoritarian, & militaristic aristocracy in Greece
5. Attainment of the zenith of power & wealth & cultural creativity during the 5th century B.C. (499--400) as well as the beginnings of Greek demise in savage & devastating wars
6. Reasons for the downfall of Hellenic Greece:
    a. Suicidal wars reflecting a fatal militarism & glorification of fighting
    b. Vicious class conflicts within all states between the haves & the have-nots
    c. Failure of Greeks to achieve unification into one nation & one economy & one society
    d. Excessive individualism, leading to an absence of community identification & self-sacrifice as well as greed & selfishness & attitudes of the-public-be-damned (these qualities are dangerously apparent in America today)

F. Hellenistic Age: 330--30 B.C.
1. This stage witnessing the expansion & internationalization of Greek civilization after the conquest of Greece by Macedonia & its king Philip II. in 338 B.C.
2. Distant ethnic relationship between the primitive & backward Macedonians and the more civilized Greeks
3. Later conquest of the entire Middle East by the Macedonian king Alexander the Great (336--323 B.C.) in the largest empire yet known in Western Civilization
4. Collapse of political unity of Alexander's empire after his death, but achievement of cultural & commercial unity plus the fusion of Greek & Oriental societies for three centuries thereafter

21

III. Greek Religion
   A. Greek religious beliefs would play a central role in the great cultural achievements and would strongly influence daily life
   B. There were <u>two</u> separate yet often complementary & overlapping forms of Greek religion:
      1. Worship of the Olympian Gods--named thus because of the belief that the gods resided on top of 9000-foot Mount Olympus in northeastern Greece, its snow-covered peak usually being shrouded with clouds
      2. Fertility and Mystery Cults--nature religions quite popular throughout the eastern Mediterranean World
   C. Worship of the Olympian Gods:
      1. The primary literary source for our knowledge of the gods is Homer's epic poems of the <u>Iliad</u> & <u>Odyssey</u>, followed secondly by Hesiod's <u>Theogony</u> (9th or 8th century), with later additions by various Greek & Roman poets & dramatists & writers
      2. These many different sources of reference brought some conflicting & contradictory ideas & views--the following are the mainstream & prevailing features & characteristics
      3. Features & characteristics:

(margin note: Not Specific gods)

         a. Polytheism--belief in many gods representing the forces or phenomena of nature as well as human qualities & activities--examples:
            (1) Zeus was God of the Sky, chief of all the others, & the most powerful of divinities--Hera was his wife & sister & Goddess of Marriage--their brothers were Poseidon, God of the Seas, & Hades, God of the Underworld & ruler of the dead
            (2) Apollo was God of the Sun & Light & Truth and called "the most characteristic & beloved of the Greek gods"[1]--Aphrodite was Goddess of Love & Beauty--Athena was Goddess of Wisdom--Ares was God of War
            (3) Later the Romans would adopt the Olympian Gods as their own while assigning each god a new name in Latin rather than Greek, thus Zeus became Jupiter & Poseidon became Neptune & Hades became Pluto
         b. Anthropomorphism--attribution of human characteristics & qualities to non-human things--the Greeks regarded their immortal deities as possessing perfect human physical appearances & with typical human emotions & aptitudes
         c. Absence of morality--Greeks were as moral & ethical as other peoples of the Ancient World, but they did <u>not</u> believe such conduct was required of them by their gods:
            (1) Christianity & Judaism & Islam usually appealed to negative feelings of fear, guilt, & dread to inspire proper behavior--a jealous & wrathful God would punish human indiscretions with eternal misery in hell
            (2) To the Greeks morality was a positive matter of reason & pragmatism--everybody will benefit and the world will be better if we treat each other with compassion, decency, & humanity--it is a simple matter of common sense
         d. Rejection of belief in an afterlife of heavenly paradise--the dead all went to the dark & shadowy & miserable underworld of Hades

                        (1) Much later some Greeks & Romans developed the idea
                            of Elysium or the Elysian Fields
                        (2) It was a very pleasant region in Hades reserved for
                            a few military heroes & poets
                e. Existence of no authoritative sacred book, creed, com-
                    mandments, doctrine, powerful priesthood or prophets or
                    saints, or extensive ritual & ceremony--stress instead
                    on much freedom of thought & imagination for each
                    individual
            4. Importance of sacred shrines such as Delphi & Olympia--sources
                of inspiration for culture & athletics (to be lectured on in
                class)
    D. Fertility and Mystery Cults
        1. These religions fulfilled personal & emotional & mystical &
            otherworldly desires lacking in the Worship of Olympian Gods-
            --the roots of these faiths traced back to the ancient wor-
            ship of regenerative forces in nature
        2. General beliefs & practices:
            a. Resurrection & salvation--faith in a god or specially-
                inspired mortal who died & then arose to become a
                savior for his initiated believers
            b. Existence of a soul--a distinct "son of starry heaven"[2]
                dwelling in a corrupted & sinful body
            c. Promise of immortality in a blissful & heavenly paradise
            d. Ceremonies of ecstacy & wild rites of initiation, some-
                times including frenzied & emotional & orgiastic acts
            e. Stress on a high level of ethical conduct in seeking
                "beauty, truth, & goodness"[3]--thus the necessity of an
                austere & pure lifestyle
        3. Examples: Worship of Dionysus, the Mysteries of Eleusis invol-
            ving the Goddess Demeter & her daughter Persephone, and
            Orphism (to be lectured on in class)

V. Comparison of & Contrast Between Athens and Sparta
    A. The two most powerful city-states during the Hellenic Age were
        Athens and Sparta, yet they were radically different in nearly
        every way
    B. Differences--Athens vs. Sparta:
        1. Democratic vs. aristocratic & authoritarian
        2. Free & open & thinking society vs. closed & narrow-minded &
            thoughtless society
        3. Individualistic vs. group or collective-oriented
        4. Commercial & capitalistic economically vs. backward & agrarian
        5. Culturally creative & brilliant vs. sterile & barren
        6. Liberal in its attitude toward change vs. conservative
        7. Social & class mobility vs. rigid & hereditary class structure

VI. Democracy & Political Institutions in 5th-Century Athens
    A. The Greek experiment in democracy (brief, turbulent, & overwhelmed
        by difficulties) was a radical & revolutionary development in his-
        tory without precedent:
        1. It was a society operating in an atmosphere of free discussion
            on the assumption that human beings are worthy of governing
            themselves
        2. Even today very few people in our world reside in a democratic
            society respecting individual rights & civil liberties

B. Greek city-states, like contemporary nations, divided government into **three** branches:
   1. Executive--to administer & carry out laws
   2. Legislative--to formulate & discuss & pass laws
   3. Judicial--to apply & interpret laws
C. Athens became the best & most famous example of Greek democracy, & we will examine its evolution and study how it functioned
D. Earliest governmental institutions *before* democracy:
   1. End of monarchy about 750 B.C. and replacement of a power-sharing between hereditary kings & landowning aristocrats with a pure aristocracy:
      a. <u>Archons</u>--3 to 9 executive officials from the aristocratic class elected for a one-year term, after which they automatically became members of the:
      b. <u>Areopagus</u>, or Council of Elders--composition of former veteran officials with meetings on the small, rocky Hill of Ares near the Acropolis--most powerful body in Athens prior to 5th-century advent of democracy with broad authority to supervise officials, make policy-decisions, judge legal matters, and veto laws passed by the:
      c. <u>Ekklesia</u>, or Popular Assembly--legislative body including most male citizens yet organized by class & social status to guarantee control by the aristocratic few with wealth & family connections
   2. Reforms & modifications by Solon (archon & lawgiver: 594-572 B.C.) after class conflict between nobility & small farmers:
      a. Cancellation of mortgages for small farmers & abolition of the practice of enslaving debtors
      b. Division of citizen body into four classes based on income derived from land
      c. Permission of Ekklesia to elect archons (formerly chosen by Areopagus) from the two wealthiest classes and to supervise the conduct of all elected officials
      d. Creation of the <u>Boule</u>, or Council of 400 (later 500)--a steering committee preparing & selecting all subjects brought before the Assembly--100 members chosen by the Assembly from the four tribes represented there
      e. Addition of <u>Heliaea</u>, or Court of Appeal--6,000 jurors chosen by lot & at random from volunteer citizens and forming separate courts of between 101 & 1001 members empowered to hear all cases except murder & treason
      f. Significance of Solon's reforms--grant to Athenians of equality before the law--in court, plaintiffs & defendants arguing & pleading their cases themselves without resort to lawyers
      g. Conclusion--retention of most power by the aristocracy, yet introduction of democratic elements to protect the lower classes from some abuses & repression
   3. Tyranny of Pisistratus & his son Hippias (546--510 B.C.) after factional strife & class warfare--no constitutional changes but protection of popular interests & stimulation of trade & manufacturing interests
   4. Reforms of Cleisthenes (570--500 B.C.): archon & virtual dictator presenting constitutional changes in 508-507 after a brief civil war against the aristocratic faction:

        a. Reorganization of districts & geographical areas for voting purposes in the Assembly to cut across aristocratic & clan & tribal lines--thus a reduction of old class identification
        b. Inclusion for the first time of almost <u>all</u> male citizens in the Ekklesia--achievement of equality in voting & at the ballot box
        c. Reconstitution of the Boule into the Council of 500--continuation of its steering committee functions yet addition of duties to administer the city as a bureaucracy or civil service & to review the actions of officials
            (1) Selection of committees of 50 citizens annually by lot from ten city districts--prohibition on anyone serving more than twice between the age of 30 & 60
            (2) Each committee of 50 governing in continual session for one-tenth of the year (roughly 36 days) with a new chairman chosen daily by lot
        d. Creation of the <u>Strategoi</u> (the singular <u>strategos</u> means "general"), or Board of 10 Governors:
            (1) Original duties to command armies & conduct war
            (2) Gradual assumption over the next 40 years of chief executive power in civil as well as military matters, thus eventually supplanting the archons
            (3) Function of the Board like a modern cabinet of ministers with its leader having responsibilities similar to a prime minister (<u>strategos autokrator</u>)
            (4) Annual election of Strategoi by Ekklesia with eligibility for reelection, thus ensuring the possibility of continuity in policies & politicians--the great Pericles served almost incessantly for thirty years (467--429) with only brief interruptions
        e. Practice of <u>ostracism</u>--ten-year honorable exile for ambitious leaders suspected of tyrannical aspirations or considered dangerous to the state:
            (1) Requirement of a majority vote in the Ekklesia of at least 6,000 members present at a meeting
            (2) Procedure of voting secretly by writing the name of the accused on an "ostrakon"--fragment of pottery
            (3) Infrequent abuse of its power--in 90 years of its usage, only ten persons were exiled
    5. Assessment of Cleisthenes' reforms--his democratic reforms were limited & neutralized & potentially negated by the retention of aristocratic institutions & powers:
        a. Continuation of the Areopagus as guardian of the laws & constitution with the authority to veto measures passed by the Assembly and to judge treason cases
        b. Maintenance of the traditional & theoretical powers of the executive archons as well as their election by the two richest classes
        c. Requirement that Boule membership come from the top three classes, thus excluding many citizens of the 4th class
        d. Consequent persistence of 40 years of uncertainty & a final power struggle over which institutions (democratic or aristocratic) held ultimate authority
E. Final transformation into democracy in 462-461 B.C. under the leadership of Ephialtes (immediately assassinated by aristocrats)

and Pericles (495--429 B.C.):
1. Approval of laws stripping the archons & Areopagus of all traditional powers except insignificant religious & ceremonial functions--transfer of their important duties to the Strategoi, Boule, & Heliaea
2. Charges of treason now being heard by the Boule
3. Determination of issues over constitutionality & conflicting laws by the Heliaea
4. Abolition of all socio-economic limitations on serving in political office (except for archon, which now wielded no real power)
5. Inauguration of a system of state payment for government service by Pericles and extension of this to jurymen & Boule members & some other officials, thus making possible the participation of even poor citizens

F. The institutions & system of democracy in 5th & 4th-century Athens:
1. Ekklesia--Assembly of the People:
   a. Supreme legislative body & the most powerful institution of government with wide jurisdiction over everything including votes on taxes & the spending of all money
   b. All officials & leaders chosen by lot or elected by it
   c. Participation accessible to all male citizens aged 21 or more--possibility of free & open debate, initiation of legislative proposals, and movement of amendments
   d. Meetings at least four times a month, ordinarily located in an open-air & semi-circular area on the eastern slopes of Pnyx Hill, west of the Hill of Ares and the Acropolis (all of which can be visited today)--votes taken by a show of hands
   e. Debates almost invariably stormy, raucous, & tempestuous with only the most trained orators subjecting themselves to heckling, personal insults, shouts of protest, whistling, & handclapping
2. Boule--Council of 500:
   a. A permanently sitting body with some legislative, executive, & judicial powers:
   b. Preparation of the legislative agenda for the Ekklesia as a steering committee
   c. Issuance of decrees to facilitate the execution of decisions while the Ekklesia was not in session--negotiations with representatives of foreign nations
   d. Collaboration with bureaucrats in the work of administration
   e. Right to preside over critical judicial cases of treason
3. Strategoi--Board of 10 Governors: the chief executive cabinet including the prime minister
4. Heliaea--Court of Appeals: the main judicial branch from which came juries for court cases
5. Archons--executive officials, & the Areopagus--Council of Elders: once powerful but now powerless institutions performing unimportant religious & ceremonial functions
6. Ostracism--the charge of & vote on an honorable ten-year exile for leaders considered dangerous to the state--introduction of this practice by Cleisthenes in 507 B.C. & later revival in 487 B.C.

G. Differences between ancient Greek democracy and modern American or European democracy:
   1. Direct vs. indirect--Greek citizens personally voted on issues & laws & participated in government, but we must vote for representatives who then vote for us (supposedly)
   2. Small vs. large size of the political unit--most Greek poleis were smaller than a county in one of our states, and Athens at its height had roughly 40,000 citizens, thus permitting direct & frequent involvement; our modern nations include millions of citizens & vast territorial expanses
   3. Theoretical foundation--exclusive vs. open:
      a. Athenian democracy was exclusive--slightly less than 15% of all residents were "citizens" (those born of Athenian parents) out of a total population of over 300,000
         (1) Excluded from politics were all women, slaves (more than one-third of all people), foreign residents (mostly businessmen known as metics--30,000), and unskilled workingmen
         (2) In practice, only a small percentage of citizens ever attended Ekklesia meetings--farmers from outlying districts particularly found it almost impossible to travel that far
      b. Modern democracy is theoretically open to all regardless of status, sex, race, ethnicity, or religion--yet this has not always been true realistically:
         (1) Before condemning Greek narrowness, we must remember that the U.S. Constitution of 1787 effectively eliminated from voting rights all women, blacks (most of them slaves yet nearly 20% of the population then), Indians, and white males not owning landed property or paying a certain sum of taxes
         (2) Thus the early American electorate was 30% at most
         (3) Women were granted the vote in 1920 & blacks in 1964, yet civil equality is often denied even today
   4. Evolutionary vs. revolutionary process of development:
      a. Both ancient & modern democracy experienced evolutionary change (over a long period of time with a minimum of violence & bloodshed and with a stress on debate & persuasion), and revolutionary change (sudden destruction with force & violence of the old system and its replacement with a written constitution & democracy)
      b. Yet the Greeks seemed to have more evolutionary & less revolutionary change, while modern nations have seemed to emphasize the reverse

VI. Achievements & Contributions of Hellenic Greece
   A. Democracy--the Greeks were first to experiment with the "open society" with its stress on individual rights, liberty of conscience, and ideas of freedom & citizenship--the Greek citizen was freer in his private life by law & custom than even modern Americans
      1. Three types of "freedom" recognized & defined by the Greeks:
         a. Personal freedom--the individual right to do whatever one wishes without interfering with others
         b. Civic freedom--the right of community members to participate in government for the purpose of guaranteeing per-

sonal freedom as well as of protecting the collective social interests of the entire group
   c. Sovereignal freedom, or "freedom as power"--the right of an inspired & superior individual to rule over & dominate & exploit others--to us today, this constitutes two things not regarded as freedom:
      (1) Imperialism--the conquest, domination, exploitation, or rule of one people by another people or their ruler, and...
      (2) Autocracy or tyranny or dictatorship or authoritarianism--rule of one person imposing his will on all others, thus destroying the other two freedoms
      (3) Example of Plato, who described in his Republic the ideal state as an aristocracy of a few educated philosophers heading a hierarchy of inferiors who "willingly submit to virtuous laws" while "socially dead" slaves at the bottom did not count[4]
  2. Tragic failure of Greek democracy after less than a century & a half of turmoil from international, civil, & class warfare
  3. Revival of modern democracy in the late-18th century only after the passage of more than two thousand years
B. Political science--the Greeks were the first people to study and analyze the basic principles, comprehensive theories, & different forms of politics & government:
  1. The two fathers of political philosophy were Plato (428--347), whose views are mentioned above, and Aristotle (384--322)
  2. Both were writing in a period immediately after excesses & recklessness in Athens had resulted in military disasters & democratic governmental demise; consequently, they repudiated true popular democracy as unstable & disorderly mob-rule and as a prelude to anarchy & tyranny
  3. Impact of Aristotle--for 2,000 years after his time, he was celebrated as "the master of those who know"[5] (Dante) because of the encyclopedic range of his work & the compelling common sense of his arguments, thus a colossal influence on all subsequent thinkers:
     a. To him, the ideal state was one possessing a "mixed" constitution with elements of all three different types of government: monarchy, aristocracy, & democracy--these views strongly influenced the writers of the American Constitution
     b. Acceptable to him was monarchy (a hereditary king or queen ruling according to traditional laws); yet one-person authority could degenerate into tyranny (an ambitious politician seizing power illegally & changing laws drastically)
     c. Permissible was aristocracy (rule of the best & most capable men), which could give way to intolerable oligarchy (rule of the few yet incapable & unscrupulous men)
     d. Acceptable was moderate democracy (or "polity", in which all citizens participated in the governmental process & elections but always deferred to their "superiors" for leadership); yet this could degenerate & fall victim to radical democracy (or "anarchy"--lawlessness or chaos, as if having no ruler at all--when people supported uneducated & unprincipled demagogues)

             e. He also excluded & banished women from governing pro-
                cesses because they were (he believed, like all Greek
                men) biologically inferior to men, flawed humans, &
                "mutilated males"[6]--politics was for superior people,
                meaning a few men of education & experience
   C. Stress on reason, logic, & rational thinking--the Greeks again
      originated this method of thought indispensable to solving prob-
      lems & understanding the world
      1. The most educated & thoughtful Greeks dominating their society
         developed a critical & inquiring spirit that denied magical
         or supernatural causation in the belief that nature was in-
         telligible to humans
      2. They were the first people in history to seek answers to ques-
         tions without appealing to tradition or divine revelation
   D. Primary focus on mankind & humanism rather than on religion & the
      gods--thus religion was important to the Greeks, but not as impor-
      tant as human affairs--the Greeks again introduced this concept to
      the world
      1. To them, the proper study of mankind was man & not the gods--
         they acted as if humans possessed a high degree of free will
         to control their own destiny & the world
      2. They were less otherworldly & less interested in the afterlife
         than other civilizations, and their religion usually lacked a
         deep spirituality
      3. Religion in Greece was not a branch of government or an insti-
         tution controlled by powerful nobles
      4. Only these attitudes could have made them so perceptive &
         brilliant & creative
   E. Creation of our "classical" standards of culture--thus the ideals
      of nothing in excess, moderation in all things, pursuit of the
      golden mean of balance & harmony & proportion, the goal of precise
      form & line & restraint, and the achievement of simplicity & clar-
      ity & symmetry
   F. Literary origination of tragic drama, comedy, & history--their
      works are still read, performed, and enjoyed today as relevant &
      profound & inspirational to the modern era
   G. Philosophy:
      1. Greek thinkers were the first in history to concern themselves
         with every aspect of life and the world around them
      2. They explored such questions as the meaning of life, ethical &
         moral problems, the true nature of the universe, the means of
         achieving the most perfect form of life for individuals &
         society, and the idea of justice
   H. Science:
      1. The Greeks began science as we understand it today with their
         crucial & all-important reliance on rational thought as well
         as their pursuit of natural rather than supernatural explana-
         tions of the world
      2. Many of their conclusions would not be challenged for over two
         thousand years
      3. Yet Greek science was very limited & not truly modern by being
         overwhelmingly speculative & theoretical while usually lack-
         ing the experimental & empirical side, thus failing to seek
         factual evidence in support of hypotheses--there was little
         technological progress due to scorn for the practical uses of
         knowledge

    I. The Arts:
        1. There were spectacular contributions to architecture, sculpture (perfect representations of the human body), and painting of pottery & statuary & buildings
        2. Most experts agree with scholar Edith Hamilton that Greek art was the creation of: "Artists than whom the world has never seen greater, men endowed with the spirit's best gift..."[7]
    J. International athletic games--their Panhellenic contests almost annually at one of the sacred shrines reflected an obsession with competition & achievement as well as an admiration of physical prowess, endurance, finesse, & gracefulness
    K. Banking & commercial practices:
        1. The Greeks introduced the first banks owned & operated by businessmen rather than by governments or religious organizations--their commercial loans at interest promoted more economic growth & expansion than other banks with very narrow & limited objectives
        2. In the 4th century a real credit system developed with the issuance of checks, money orders, letters of credit, & bonds for business loans--banks received deposits and served as agents in the investment of other people's money

VII. Negative characteristics & weaknesses of Hellenic Greece
    A. Low position of women--total social domination by men, menial existence, much life in seclusion, few opportunities for education, & very restricted legal rights for Greek females
    B. Acceptance of slavery--a significant minority of the population in Greek democracies (one-third in Athens) living in servitude
    C. Militarism & glorification of war--the consequences being centuries of horrifying atrocities & ultimate destruction of their civilization
    D. Excessive individualism--too much personal freedom resulting in selfishness, greed, & concerns mainly for oneself even when proven harmful & disastrous for the entire community & society
    E. Immoderation & extremism--the aspiration & ideal of balance & moderation rarely being fulfilled due to most Greeks manifesting exactly the opposite traits: passionate, intense, high-spirited, reckless, daring, opinionated, quarrelsome, etc.
    F. Exclusive & narrow view of citizenship & the political world--their vision limited to the self-governing & very small city-state with no possibility for personal involvement in larger political states
    G. No development of higher mathematics--absence of a positional number system as well as use of the zero, thus inhibiting the final evolution of modern science as we understand it today

Chapter 4   ROME: REPUBLIC & EMPIRE

I. Outline of the Chronological Periods & Stages of Roman History
   A. Earliest beginnings of the Roman people & state: 2000--509 B.C.
      1. Migration of the Latins into central Italy--division into many small states, one of them being Rome
      2. Cohabitation in the Italian Peninsula with other peoples: Etruscans, Samnites, Greeks, & Celts or Gauls
      3. Conquest by & profound positive influence of the Etruscans during the 7th & 6th centuries
      4. Assertion of independence in 509 B.C. and establishment of:
   B. The Republic: 509--27 B.C.
      1. Early Republic (509--200 B.C.):
         a. Imposition of the class structure--patricians & plebians
         b. Development of the political institutions & system
         c. Resolution of socio-economic conflicts in compromise
         d. Emergence of their famous character traits & values
         e. Beginnings of territorial expansion to embrace the Mediterranean World
      2. Late Republic (200--27 B.C.):
         a. Diversification of the economy & class system
         b. Rise of enormous social & economic & political & military problems resulting from rapid territorial expansion of the state
         c. Occurrence of devastating civil wars & illegal seizure of power by ambitious generals leading to a destruction of the Republic & its replacement with:
   C. The Empire: 27 B.C.--476 A.D.
      1. Early Empire (27 B.C.--180 A.D.):
         a. Existence as a bureaucratic & authoritarian despotism ruled by emperors (called <u>Caesars</u>) wielding virtual absolute & unlimited powers
         b. Attainment during this <u>Pax Romana</u> (Roman Peace: 30 B.C.--180 A.D.) of the zenith of the Ancient World--an unprecedented era of peace, prosperity, & stability during which most of Rome's achievements reached fulfillment
      2. Late Empire (180--476 A.D.):
         a. Decline & eventual fall over a period of 300 years emanating from a complex & interconnecting series of economic, social, political, military, & miscellaneous causes
         b. Final destruction in the West during the 4th & 5th centuries by invasions of German barbarians
         c. Yet survival & frequent success of Rome for nearly one thousand years, truly one of the most incredible & enduring achievements in human history

II. Famous Roman Values & Traits
   A. Early appearance of certain characteristics contributing significantly to the long-term stability & cohesiveness of their society
   B. Identification of these values with Roman greatness:
      1. Respect for authority & obedience to law
      2. Loyalty to the state--a form of strong patriotism committing <u>all</u> classes to serve & sacrifice for the nation
      3. Willingness to compromise--importance of flexibility & adaptability & pursuit of practical solutions to problems
      4. Devotion to family--a general solidarity & strength of the

            male-dominated family-unit extending eventually to society as an organic whole and assigning more influence & authority to females than any civilization we have studied so far
        5. Hard work, self-discipline, & sacrifice for the common good--encouragement of a sense of togetherness & community spirit that was very different from the reckless Greek individualism

III. Territorial Expansion of the Republic
    A. Roman achievement of renown for its emphasis on military virtues & its eventual rule of a vast empire covering the entire Mediterranean World
    B. Reasons for the early development of a warlike spirit & desires for expansion:
        1. Existence of constant warfare in central Italy--Rome was a small city-state surrounded by numerous & belligerent enemies whose threats required self-defense for survival
        2. A rapidly swelling Roman population and depletion of soil & forests--thus a hunger & necessity for additional lands
        3. Desires for greater wealth through plunder of other peoples
        4. Major Roman successes by the mid-4th century arousing fears & hostility from neighbors as well as inciting ambitions & aggressiveness in Romans
    C. Factors explaining Roman victories & success:
        1. Political & social stability--lack of internal dissension & thus total unity of society in prosecuting wars & making sacrifices--this phenomenon being a product of earlier compromises between patricians & plebians
        2. The nature of its "citizen-army", meaning that all men were liable for service & drafted into the armies--dual status of Romans as civilians most of the time but often called to duty as soldiers when required, resulting in the development of a sense of fairness & equality
        3. Superior organization--Roman fame for their precise chain-of-command & hierarchies of officers & soldiers all knowing their duties & functions--recognition of this systematic structure as a critical factor in winning on the battlefield
        4. Skillful & lenient treatment of conquered peoples--conversion of former enemies into allies & friends--Roman extension of much local control & eventual grant of full or partial citizenship to subdued Italian neighbors
    D. Conquest of Italy:
        1. Involvement in many local wars during the mid-4th century bringing triumphs & frightening former allies of the Latin League of tribes & states--conflicts between Rome & the Latin League ending in defeat & absorption of the latter by 338 B.C.
        2. Attainment of victory over & inclusion of the Etruscans to the north and the Samnites to the southeast by 295 B.C.
        3. Conquest of Greek city-states in southern Italy by 270 B.C., giving Rome control over all of the Italian Peninsula south of the Po River Valley in the north & making her a major power in the Mediterranean World
        4. End of this first phase of expansion in 265 B.C.--beginnings of contacts in Sicily with the empire of Carthage
    E. Punic Wars with Carthage (to be lectured on in class)

F. Victory in the 2nd Punic War (218--202 B.C.) drawing Rome irrevocably to involvement in & invasion of the eastern Mediterranean regions where states in Greece & Macedonia & Asia Minor had formed alliances with Carthage--acquisition of lands & populations there

IV. Governmental Institutions & System of the Republic
   A. Definition of a "republic"--a government in which supreme power resides in a body of citizens entitled to vote & is exercised by elected officials responsible to them & governing according to law
      1. Thus its main feature is representative government through elections--this term deriving from the Latin res publica, meaning "public thing" or commonwealth
      2. The constitution of the Roman Republic always remained essentially conservative & arstocratic despite patrician grants of reform concessions & political participation to plebians and despite an early & gradual evolution toward theoretical (not real or meaningful) democracy
      3. Its executive & legislative branches were balanced to prevent radical action, and political power was theoretically exercised by & spread thin throughout numerous offices & agencies
      4. Consequently, Rome was actually an oligarchy dominated from the Senate by about 26 wealthy & landed families and never became a true democracy--the substance of its government was quite different from the form or theoretical appearance
      5. Division (as in the Greek states) into three branches of government--executive, legislative, & judicial:
   B. Executive:
      1. Consuls--the two chief executives elected by the Centuriate Assembly for a term of one year, each exercising supreme political power ("imperium") alone in alternate months--almost always from the patrician class, although plebians eligible by 336 B.C.
         a. Consuls advised by & almost totally dependent on Senate
         b. Each consul having the right of veto over the other's actions, so that both had to support measures before implementation possible
      2. Dictator--a temporary position as commander-in-chief of the armies & state during a wartime crisis, with complete authority over persons & property
         a. Election by the Centuriate Assembly for six months or one year
         b. Legal necessity to obtain power constitutionally & to surrender it upon expiration of the term
         c. Celebrated example of Cincinnatus, who returned to his land & plow in 456 B.C. immediately after saving Rome from its enemies, thus refusing to abuse his authority
      3. Censors--two elected by the Centuriate Assembly from ex-consuls for 18-month terms with powers to:
         a. Take the census for determining which members of society were financially qualified for army service
         b. Investigate the moral qualifications of men nominated for the Senate (Council of Elders) and to:
         c. Bar those considered corrupt or profligate from the Senate, thus our words "censor" & "censorship"
      4. Tribunes--originally two & later 10 officials (created in 494 B.C.) elected annually by the Tribal or Plebian Assembly

after its introduction in 471 B.C. to protect plebians from unfair & harsh applications of the law
- a. Authority to <u>veto</u> ("I forbid", in Latin) acts of another tribune, rulings of magistrates, & decisions of consuls
- b. Frequent failure to protect plebian interests because of the Roman "principle of no salary" or pay for public service, the results being:
- c. Disqualification from holding office of poor or lower-class plebians and election of only wealthy candidates usually cooperating & identifying with the patricians

5. Conclusions about the executive branch:
- a. The existence of so many elected officials capable of counteracting or overruling each other resulting in few if any accomplishments while in office
- b. This political paralysis, deadlock, & stalemate only enhancing the awesome powers of the experienced & permanently-sitting Senate

C. Legislative:
1. Centuriate Assembly--<u>Comitia Centuriata</u>
- a. Composition of all males (plebians & patricians) capable of military service, which included most men during the early Republic--named for the smallest unit in the army, a "century" of 100 men--voting procedure by group or century rather than by individual soldier
- b. Powers theoretically great yet actually small--election of consuls and approval or rejection of laws submitted by consuls or the Senate
- c. No authority to initiate legislation or to discuss matters proposed by the Senate--predominant influence in the voting units of richer & older men

2. Plebian or Tribal Assembly--<u>Concilium Plebis</u>
- a. Establishment in 471 B.C. originally to elect tribunes only--later recognition in 339 B.C. as a law-making body equal to the Centuriate Assembly--yet introduction of legislative proposals by tribunes or the Senate
- b. Minor advance in 287 B.C. with an end to Senatorial veto over Assembly decisions, yet persistence of its role as a usually weak & divided body ratifying Senate wishes
- c. Limitations on authority--impossibility to initiate legislation and voting collectively as "tribes" or residential districts rather than by individual citizen (as did the Greeks), thus circumventing potential democracy
- d. Efforts during the late Republic by Marius & Gaius Gracchus to strengthen its powers & introduce democratic changes provoking bloody & fatal constitutional crises

D. Judicial:
1. Necessity for a politician to pass through an apprenticeship in other positions before becoming eligible for the office of consul--leading directly to the consulate was the job of:
2. Praetor--judges numbering between one & eight and serving one-year terms after election by the Centuriate Assembly, the word deriving from the Latin <u>prae-itor</u>: "the one who goes in front"
3. Requirement of men seeking election as praetor or consul to wear a special robe whitened with chalk known as the <u>toga candida</u>, whence our word "candidate"

E. The Senate, or Council of Elders--<u>Senatus</u>:
1. The most powerful & influential organ in government with vast legislative, executive, & judicial (all three areas) authority--known by its famous initials: S.P.Q.R. or <u>Senatus Populusque Romanorum</u>, meaning "The People & the Senate of the Romans"
2. Composition--around 300 former consuls & praetors appointed for life from patricians or plebians of extensive wealth & property & land
3. Rule of Rome in practice by the Senate:
   a. The cumbersome & balanced nature of the other state machinery guaranteeing the necessity that one institution take the initiative in order to make government function
   b. Weakness & division of popular assemblies & short-term magistrates--possession only by the Senate of enough knowledge & experience to conduct affairs on a permanent basis, almost by default
4. Powers & authority:
   a. Conduct of foreign affairs & administration of conquered provinces--very significant in a nation so often at war
   b. Control of finances & supervision of the permanent bureaucracy running the state
   c. Strong advisory capacity over all elected officials who lack the experience of Senators, and control over elections--initiation of most legislative proposals to the Centuriate & Plebian Assemblies
   d. Judgment of crimes for treason, assassination, & conspiracy--appointment from its membership of most judges in major civil trials
5. Perpetuation of effective direction of the Senate by a small & wealthy governing class due to the tradition of non-payment of salary for service in political office--example: in the century before the year 133 B.C., 159 out of 200 consuls came from only 26 patrician families
6. Similarity of the Senate in Rome to the aristocratic Areopagus in Athens, yet very different eventual fates:
   a. Democracy in Athens ultimately stripping the Areopagus of all its important traditional powers
   b. Oligarchy in Rome continuing to dominate the Republic and resisting any surrender of its enormous powers until violence & revolution destroyed the entire political system in the first century B.C.
F. Assessment & great impact of Polybius (204--122 B.C.), a Greek historian of early Rome:
1. Admiration & praise of the Republican constitution inaccurately as "the best of all existing governments",[1] a system perfectly balanced among its three branches and providing maximum protection of personal freedom, the best model of good government with its "system of checks & balances" & principle of "separation of powers"
2. These ideas on the best possible government later influencing strongly the 18th-century French political thinker Montesquieu (1689--1755) in his monumental work <u>The Spirit of the Laws</u>, which profoundly impressed...
3. The Founding Fathers of the American Constitution (1787), who incorporated the separation of powers and checks & balances

             into our system, as well as the mixture of autocratic, aristocratic, & democratic elements
        4. Mistakes & misunderstandings of his analysis & interpretation:
            a. Its checks & balances resulting in political paralysis & deadlock for most institutions, inability to solve problems, & failure to achieve constructive change--these same difficulties constantly plague our government also
            b. Bare survival of the Republic as actually a clumsy confusion of institutions & offices that functioned by muddling through a mass of structural defects
            c. The constitution in reality only appearing to be balanced because most powers concentrated in the Senate while plebian institutions & offices were very ineffectual--existence of very few if any "democratic" aspects--the lower-class masses having no organized party or trained leaders
            d. Existence of Republican Rome for centuries as the modern U.S.A. exists today--"upper class government masked by democratic forces"[2]

V. Emergence of Major Problems During the Late Republic
    A. Rise of enormous social & economic & political & military problems after 200 B.C., the fundamental & central cause being the rapid territorial expansion & conquest of lands surrounding the Mediterranean Sea
    B. Specific problems: (to be explained in greater detail in class)
        1. Misgovernment of conquered provinces & revolts against Roman rule due to corruption & over-taxation
        2. Decimation of the class of small-scale farmers
        3. Importation of huge numbers of slaves for cheap labor
        4. Creation of a large class of alienated proletariat
        5. Failure to solve the problem of high rates of unemployment
        6. Dangerous trend for the rich to get richer and the poor to get poorer & more numerous
        7. Changes in the method of army recruitment inaugurated in the late-2nd century B.C. by Marius, the catastrophic consequence being civil wars, military intervention in civil politics, & dictatorships by ambitious generals
        8. Inadequacy of the Republican governmental machinery (established originally to administer a tiny city-state) to rule an extensive empire
        9. Corruption of civic virtues & personal values

VI. Transformation to Empire
    A. Pursuit by Augustus (31 B.C.--14 A.D.) & other early emperors of certain policies & practices necessary to transform Rome from a city-state to a world-state (empire) and the practical absolutism of the emperors' authority to a constitutional absolutism
    B. The measures in this transformation binding the empire together: (details to be provided in the classroom lecture)
        1. Nullification of the authority of the Senate
        2. Development of an efficient, centralized administrative system
        3. Allowance of much local self-government for provincial cities
        4. Extension gradually of full citizenship to the vast majority of residents throughout the empire

5. Army recruitment by voluntary enlistment from all male inhabitants of the empire
6. Emperor-worship, a ceremonial form of imperial patriotism
7. Roman law, equally applied to all citizens & the best system of law in the world up to that time

II. Achievements & Contributions to Civilization of Rome
   A. Capacity for large-scale organization, such as its governmental bureaucracy & army & legal system & communications--rule by Rome at its height of a heterogeneous empire containing 100 million people of widely mixed ethnicity with much tolerance & with little racial or cultural prejudice (more so than ourselves)
      1. Ideal of "unity amid diversity"[3] in maintaining the empire
      2. Inability of the Western World after the fall of Rome to regain these organizational talents until the 18th century A.D. & well over 1000 years later
   B. Government & administration--combination of a high degree of centralization in Rome under the emperors with the allowance for elected officials & councils over local city government--thus "authority from above and initiative from below"[4]:
      1. Existence of a large bureaucracy of trained & professional civil servants promoted generally on merit & open to most citizens--this institution providing stability & order & strength during bad times as well as good
      2. Maintenance by the Roman Empire of one of the most efficient & effective governments in all of history while enduring for half of a millennium
   C. Communications:
      1. A superb system of roads on land & shipping on sea making travel conditions throughout the Mediterranean World the best yet known & not surpassed until the introduction of railroads & steamships in the 19th century
      2. Traversal by Julius Caesar on one occasion of 800 miles in eight days; travel of 332 miles in 36 hours by a messenger in the 1st century A.D.
   D. Engineering & applied science--the Romans were the greatest builders in the world prior to the 19th century A.D.--some edifices still in use today:
      1. Invention & wide use of concrete in construction
      2. Establishment of a vast network of roads 50,000 miles in extent (American Interstate System is currently around 45,000 miles long) with each averaging 40 feet in width & 3-5 feet in thickness
      3. Construction of bridges, aqueducts, dams, reservoirs, harbors, sewers, tunnels, mines, multi-storied apartments, temples, palaces, bathhouses, open-air theaters, & oval stadiums (the Colosseum held 50,000 spectators; the Circus Maximus seated over 150,000 people)
   E. Architecture--first extensive exploitation of the rounded arch & vault and the invention of the dome for roofs of their monumental buildings
   F. Law--development of a system of fair, rational, humane, flexible, & universal justice throughout the empire--our modern systems of law are based either directly or indirectly on that of the Romans--***this was their greatest contribution to us:

         1. Frequent reinterpretation to stay in harmony with changing
            needs for different eras
         2. Belief in the principle of equity, meaning that all men were
            equal before the law which theoretically protected individ-
            uals ever from the state
         3. Application of certain fundamental principles based on the
            uniformities of human nature, thus inspiring the use of the
            expression: "laws of nature"
      G. High standards of living, public sanitation, personal hygiene, and
         literacy--no society in history prior to the 19th century A.D.
         achieved what the Romans did in these areas:
         1. Possession by many private upper-class houses of running water
            & sewage systems & central heating & glass windows & well-
            prepared foods & wines
         2. Public bathhouses (direct ancestor of Turkish baths & Scandin-
            avian saunas) open to men & women & sometimes freely avail-
            able to all classes--over 1000 existing in the city of Rome
            alone with some having restaurants, shops, libraries, mus-
            eums, gymnasiums, & continuously flushing marble latrines
         3. Medicine--existence in most major cities of hospitals where
            surgeons performed numerous operations (removal of gallstones
            & tonsils & goiters, for example) using over 200 different
            surgical instruments
            a. Application occasionally of anesthetics
            b. Adoption of the practice of taking a patient's pulse
               while making a diagnosis
            c. Provision by dentists of gold teeth & bridgework
         4. Attainment by Rome of heights in individual & public levels of
            cleanliness unequalled until the mid-19th century with the
            introduction of soap & cheap cotton clothing
         5. Estimation of those capable of reading & writing at roughly
            25-40% of the entire population during the Pax Romana, this
            being a greater proportion of literate people than at any
            time in history before the late-18th century A.D.
            a. Even many small towns in possession of public libraries
            b. Conclusion by recent studies of the U.S. Department of
               Education that 20% of Americans are functionally illit-
               erate while another 35% possessed barely minimal skills
               of functional literacy
      H. Dissemination of Graeco-Roman culture & civilization throughout the
         Mediterranean World and eventual transmission of them to the mod-
         ern Western Civilization:
         1. Direct derivation from Latin of the Romance languages of Ital-
            ian, French, Spanish, Portuguese, & Rumanian (and from French
            comes at least one-fourth of our English words)
         2. Roman lack of the individual brilliance & cultural creativity
            of the Greeks, the former being more practical than the
            thoughtful latter--thus imitation & borrowing of Greek cul-
            tural standards, literary styles, philosophical concerns, &
            religious beliefs in the Olympian Gods and Fertility & Mys-
            tery Cults

VIII. Causes of the Decline & Fall of the Roman Empire
   A. One of the most fascinating phenomena in all of history--the sub-
      ject of how an empire achieving such spectacular heights could

collapse & eventually disintegrate in Western Europe over a period of 300 years:
1. Existence beneath the surface even during the Pax Romana of problems & difficulties which were not addressed for centuries & which worsened with time
2. Most famous conflicting interpretations of Rome's fall:
    a. St. Augustine (354--430) expressing in his work <u>The City of God</u> that Rome was dying because of its continuing embrace of pagan religions rather than Christianity--this was inaccurate because paganism was increasingly declining as Christianity was being forcibly imposed on people
    b. Edward Gibbon (1737--94) advancing the controversial theory that one contributing factor among many others was the rise of Christianity, which encouraged people to abandon all efforts to save the material world and instead fatalistically to join monasteries & pray for salvation in the next or spiritual world--this was an accurate assessment but a minor factor in Rome's decline
3. Discovery of true explanations in a complex & interconnecting series of economic, social, political, military, & other causes that are elaborated below:

B. Economic--decline of agricultural productivity:
1. Deforestation--resulting in soil erosion in many regions
2. Overcropping of marginal lands--resulting in soil exhaustion & depletion of fertility with the consequence of permanent destruction of soil capabilities
3. Abandonment of scientific farming on large estates using slave labor to produce one or two specialized crops in great volume efficiently & effectively for distant markets
    a. Tendency toward tenant farming & sharecropping by freemen as large & wealthy landowners rented out small plots only being farmed for personal or local consumption
    b. The problem being that these tenant & sharecropping farmers lacked capital & expertise to produce large volumes
    c. Consequence of significant loss of efficiency & effectiveness as well as a sharp decline in agricultural production--this shift in methods occurring around 200 A.D.
4. Governmental mismanagement & poor allocation of natural resources in general--formulation of no plans or policies to deal with these problems

C. Economic--other causes:
1. Unfavorable balance of trade, as the Empire imported more than it exported over a long period of time--thus a lack of self-sufficiency, as cash payments to foreign states drained the treasury in order to cover this commercial imbalance
2. Heavy taxation--resulting in dwindling consumer purchasing power, economic stagnation, & paralysis of individual enterprise for the upper as well as lower classes
3. End of territorial expansion & conquest in the 2nd century A.D.--thus no new lands & peoples & resources being added to the empire for exploitation & development
    a. Any capitalistic economy requiring steady growth for strength & prosperity--thus the termination of imperial conquests ending the stimulus of external economic growth

  b. Simultaneous halt to internal economic expansion for all other reasons being mentioned here--no introduction of any inventions or new methods of cheaper mass production to lower prices or to encourage consumption
 4. Basic inequitable distribution of wealth between rich & poor:
  a. An increasingly large percentage of money & land concentrated in the hands of a relatively small upper class, thus diminishing the buying power of the lower-class masses while shrinking the size of the economy
  b. Dangerous tendency for the rich to get richer and the poor to get poorer & more numerous--interestingly, this was also a fundamental cause of the Great Depression during the 1930's in America and is much in evidence now
 5. Role of governmental policies:
  a. Extreme measures of under-regulation & too little control of the economy during the Pax Romana before 200 A.D. leading to chaos in some economic sectors followed by over-regulation & too much control after 300 A.D. causing strangulation of economic activity
  b. No achievement of that vital & delicate balance between governmental interference & planning on the one hand vs. free enterprise for business & labor on the other hand
 6. Slavery--its continuous existence limiting economic growth & expansion while posing a constant problem:
  a. Competition between free labor & slave labor perpetually depressing the wages of freemen--resulting in lower living standards as well as a limitation of the purchasing power for free laborers
  b. Diversion of important investment capital from business & commercial enterprises to the acquisition of slaves
  c. Degradation & discouragement of manual labor--existence of a humiliating & demeaning stigma associated with those people performing hard work with their hands--wish among freemen not to be identified with slaves, thus frequent avoidance of manual labor
  d. Differences between slavery in the Ancient World and slavery in the Modern World (to be explained in class):
   (1) Race--meaningless to the Ancient, not to the Modern
   (2) Theory of innate superiority or inferiority--not so important to the Ancient, very meaningful to the Modern
   (3) Status & type of labor--more diversity to the Ancient, less to the Modern
   (4) Possibility of gaining freedom--easier in the Ancient, harder in the Modern

D. Political & military causes:
 1. Failure of the imperial government to evolve a law of orderly succession to the throne--no hereditary principle--policy of the emperors to adopt an heir & successor never working properly--thus an encouragement to intrigue, conspiracy, & political power plays
 2. Inability of the civilian branch of government to control the military (as during the dying days of the Republic)--thus independent armies & ambitious generals fighting among themselves for power

        3. Consequences--civil wars & power struggles during the Century
           of Anarchy & Chaos (180--284):
           a. In the 50 years after 235 there were (24) soldier-
              emperors, only <u>two</u> of whom died natural deaths
           b. Constant destructive interventions by the armies into
              politics, with the tendency of the generals to be rigid,
              unimaginative, poorly educated, & uncompromising leaders
           c. Response to these problems in disastrous laws & policies
              aspiring to end the disorder, disruptions, lawlessness,
              & uprootedness (mentioned below under the <u>social</u> causes)
              --promotion of those laws by the autocratic emperors
              Diocletian (284--305) and Constantine I. (313--337)
    E. Social causes:
        1. Loss of class or social mobility when occupations made heredi-
           tary--the consequences being the restriction of freedom, the
           inhibition of individual initiative, & the impossibility of
           social or economic improvement
        2. Permanent freeze of wages & prices in 301 A.D.--termination or
           at least severe limitation of opportunities for advancement--
           allowance for no incentives to work or contribute to society
        3. Results--psychological depression & popular views of fatalist-
           ic resignation in the face of seemingly overwhelming troubles
        4. Heavy loss of population in the millions due to civil wars &
           widespread epidemics of plague as well as crop failures &
           famine--resulting in manpower shortage for work & military
           service
        5. Slavery--<u>social</u> effects:
           a. Brutalization & dehumanization of the entire populace by
              cheapening the value of life & encouraging a resort to
              violence as a solution to problems
           b. Perpetuation of a callous, brutal, & coarse society in-
              sensitive to suffering and conditioned or inured to vio-
              lence as an everyday way of life (the rural South here
              in America lives under such a legacy still today)
    F. Invasion by German (Teutonic) barbarian tribes:
        1. Armed & hostile migrations into the empire beginning in the
           late-4th century & continuing until deposition of the final
           emperor in 476 A.D.
        2. Possibility of these conquests of the western regions of the
           empire (parts of the empire in the east survived for another
           one thousand years) only because of Roman decline in so many
           ways for such a long period of time
        3. Accuracy of the description of the Germans finishing off a
           greatly decayed & expiring Roman Empire

IX. Rise of Christianity
    A. Jesus Christ (8 to 4 B.C.--29 A.D.):
        1. The name "Jesus" deriving from the Hebrew name "Joshua", while
           the Greek word <u>Christos</u> ("anointed one") referring to the
           belief in the Messiah, or "Deliverer"
        2. Much debate & controversy among scholars & historians about
           the life & teachings of Christ due to contradictions & incon-
           sistencies in the Synoptic Gospels as well as dubiousness of
           their objectivity--yet this matters not at all to believers
        3. His message--universal brotherhood & love of humanity devoid
           of elaborate ritual or doctrine

       a. According to the Gospels, Christ seemingly not a revolutionary leader wishing to establish a new world religion, but a simple & illiterate Jewish prophet teaching non-violence & non-attachment to the material world (both of which are usually ignored by most American "Christians")
       b. Claim by his followers of Christ's resurrection & divinity after execution by the Romans for sedition--the first "Christians" were Jewish friends of Christ living only in Palestine

B. Role of St. Paul:
  1. The true founder of Christianity was Saul of Tarsus (St. Paul: died in 64 A.D.) who:
    a. Made the new religion universal in appeal by eliminating elaborate Jewish laws & rituals and by refining its basic doctrines
    b. Conducted crucial missionary activities in the eastern Mediterranean regions
    c. Died possibly as a martyr in Rome during persecutions
  2. Early expansion of Christianity--by 50 A.D. existence of a congregation in Rome, & by 150 A.D. every province & major city having a Christian community
  3. Persecutions--six waves over three centuries inconsistently applied by various emperors--general exaggeration of severity later by Christian commentators
    a. Practice by Rome of a higher degree of religious toleration & freedom than at any time in history before the late-18th century
    b. Cause of persecutions--<u>not</u> religious but political, due to Christian refusal to discharge their duties as citizens by venerating the emperors through a ceremony of sacrifice & tribute
    c. Thus a popular consideration of Christians as unpatriotic & subversive & disloyal traitors to the Empire

C. Reasons for the triumph of Christianity in the Roman Empire by the 4th century A.D.:
  1. Appeal of its doctrines--fulfillment of spiritual longings & satisfaction of deep human desires for immortality--yet previous existence of such ideas in many other religions
  2. Unification of the Mediterranean World under the Empire and Rome's official policy of religious toleration--facilitation of the spreading faith by easy travel & a fairly open society
  3. Disintegration of Roman civilization & culture after the 2nd century--collapse of the real & material world inducing the suffering masses to escape & take refuge in a mystical & spiritual world--thus perfect & advantageous historic timing
  4. Status as a well-organized & dedicated minority group:
    a. History usually made & great events determined by well-organized, aggressive, intolerant, & dedicated minorities--existence of much strength in smallness--winning & losing ordinarily controlled by differences in the degrees of organization & efficiency
    b. Estimation of the percentage of Christians in comparison to the believers in other religions at the time of their 4th-century triumph placed at merely around 10% by most historians today

  c. Deceptive appearance by Christians of greater numbers & influence than in reality because of their superior organization, location in urban centers, & moral intensity
 5. Absorption (known as the process of "syncretism") of all its doctrines & beliefs & practices from other religions such as Judaism, Zoroastrianism, Mystery & Fertility Cults as well as from Greek philosophy
  a. Resulting in nothing of originality in Christianity, yet:
  b. Broadening its attractiveness & strengthening its claim as a universal religion
 6. Endorsement & support of a powerful emperor, Constantine I. the Great (313--337) who issued a decree granting a final end to persecution and official toleration of Christianity with the pursuit of a favorable status permitting the movement to prosper & to destroy other faiths
  a. Why Constantine favored Christianity--recognition of it as one of the few vital forces in the decadent empire and the hope that it could reunify & revitalize society
  b. Later in life Constantine becoming a sincere convert
  c. Result--success of the religious movement but failure to save the material empire
  d. Later proclamation by Emperor Theodosius I. (379--395) of Christianity as the one official religion of the empire and the beginning of forcible suppression of the others
  e. Deprivation of civil rights for heretics, with religious orthodoxy becoming the price of citizenship for perhaps the first time in the history of Western Civilization
  f. Thus occurring the destruction of religious freedom for nearly a millennium & a half--endorsement of the death penalty by Pope Leo I. the Great (440--461) for "erroneous beliefs"

D. Aftermath:
 1. Adoption of the Roman pattern of governmental organization by the official Roman Catholic Church
 2. Theological controversies & heresies over doctrine & ritual plaguing the Church in the 4th & 5th centuries
 3. Victory over paganism in the 5th century & survival in a very weakened condition after the fall of the Roman Empire in 476
 4. Gradual drifting apart of the Catholic Church in Rome and the Greek Orthodox Church in Constantinople (administrative capital of the eastern half of the Empire after 330 and named for its founder & builder--Constantine I.) after the fall of Rome in the west

Chapter 5   THE MIDDLE AGES

I. Chronological Division of the Medieval Era or Middle Ages:
   A. Low Middle Ages: 500--1000
   B. High Middle Ages: 1000--1300
   C. Late Middle Ages and/or Renaissance: 1300--1550
   D. Thus the Medieval Era was literally in the "middle" chronologically between the Ancient World of Greece & Rome and the Modern World of the 16th century & after

II. Low Middle Ages: 500--1000
   A. Division of Western Civilization after the collapse of the Roman Empire in 476 into <u>three</u> geographical parts:
      1. The Barbarian West--northern & western European kingdoms dominated by numerous German tribes (Franks, Angles & Saxons, Vandals, Burgundians, Lombards, Visigoths, Ostrogoths, etc.) and subjected to frequent invasions by Vikings from Scandinavia & by Magyars (Hungarians) from Central Asia
      2. The Byzantine Empire--a survival until 1453 of remnants of the Roman Empire in the East centering on the impressive city of Constantinople and usually including the territories of Asia Minor, Greece, & the Balkan Peninsula--this Empire was generally much more advanced than northwestern Europe
      3. The Moslem World--an enormous empire founded & inspired by the new religion of Islam and its prophet-leader Mohammed (570--632) and embracing the territories of the Middle East, North Africa, Spain, & parts of Central Asia--commercial & cultural unity under the Arabic language--a very advanced civilization in comparison to Europe
   B. Description of the Low Middle Ages as the "Dark Ages" because of:
      1. An almost complete breakdown of civilization--a society in an acute stage of disintegration
      2. An inability to organize on a large scale, & weak government
      3. A primitive economy & lawless, chaotic, undisciplined society
      4. A near total disappearance of literacy & artistic culture
      5. A loss of the understanding of advanced technology & applied science--all of these were things <u>lost</u> from the glory days of the Roman Empire
   C. Striking contrast between the Roman Empire of the Pax Romana and Europe of the Low Middle Ages:
      1. Rome was urban (importance of city life), cosmopolitan (a universal outlook on the world), commercial (economy of trade & business), politically centralized (governmental authority emanating from rulers in Rome), and possessing class mobility (capacity to move up the social scale)
      2. The Middle Ages was rural (cities had almost vanished), provincial & narrow, agrarian or agricultural (farming as the major occupation), decentralized (government influence only on the local or regional level), and class-conscious (hereditary social stratification into two classes)

III. The Byzantine Empire
   A. Background--also known as the Eastern Roman Empire surviving & often succeeding for nearly one thousand years after the fall of Rome until 1453

1. Focus on its magnificent capital city of Constantinople (significantly built up in the 4th century A.D. by Constantine I. the Great)--originally founded by the Greeks in 660 B.C. as Byzantium & renamed Istanbul in the 20th century
    a. Important strategic location on the "Straits" (Bosphorus Peninsula, Sea of Marmora, & Dardanelles) connecting the Mediterranean with the Black Sea
    b. Very favorable geographic position on the trade routes running in all directions--at this point Europe meets Asia, West meets East, the Occident meets the Orient
    c. This strongly defensible location & awesome fortifications providing the city with impregnability & impressive longevity till the 15th century
2. Diverse characteristics of the empire:
    a. More Hellenistic Greek than Roman--Greek in language & culture & religious ideas; Greek & Oriental in its social & political institutions
    b. Retention of many important Roman institutions such as law, governmental administration, & army organization
    c. Highly heterogeneous population reflecting the traditional mixture of peoples in the northeastern Mediterranean Sea region
3. Experience by the Byzantine Empire of a fascinating, exciting, colorful, & remarkable history while exertion of great influence on the future of the world
    a. Yet bare survival in a severely weakened condition during the half century after the fall of Rome in the west untill the reign of a vigorous & capable emperor
    b. Establishment of a firm foundation for long-term preservation of the empire by Justinian the Great (527--565), whose ambition was to restore its former greatness

B. Rule & accomplishments of Justinian (527--565)
1. Consolidation of personal power after suppression of the Nika Rebellion in 532--critical role of his wife & constant companion Theodora as a woman of intelligence, resourcefulness, iron nerve, & courage
2. Conquest of parts of the old Roman Empire in the west including areas of northern Africa, Italy, & southern Spain---actually, this was not a good idea because of its:
    a. Waste of much money & resources & manpower in regaining these territories, yet lack of capabilities to maintain them in the future
    b. Thus permanent loss of these lands to the Empire after the death of Justinian
3. Most notable achievement--the revision & codification of Roman law after centuries without major reinterpretation--the Code is our main source of knowledge for Roman law today
4. Massive program of public works to stimulate the economy & build an infrastructure & create architectural glory--roads, bridges, theaters, palaces, the magnificent cathedral of Sancta Sophia ("Holy Wisdom"), & the sports arena known as the Hippodrome seating 80,000 spectators
5. Caesaropapism--unique relationship between church & state in which the emperors as secular rulers completely dominated & controlled the religious institution--appointment by the emperor of church leader (the patriarch of Greek Orthodoxy)

      6. Reform of governmental administration & a strengthening of imperial control over the central government--salaries increased, civil service made efficient, corruption checked, sale of offices prohibited, & taxation made equitable
      7. Adoption of an unscrupulous & devious diplomacy (still known today as "byzantine") as well as a defense policy of "divide & rule"--the use of any means to keep enemies separated & fighting among themselves
      8. Conclusions on the reign of Justinian & Theodora:
         a. Successful application of many of his reforms & policies in the future for stability & strength
         b. Exhaustion of the treasury from too much war & building--a weakened empire after his death and three centuries of peril (565--867) from enemy attacks & weakness
         c. Yet possession by the Empire of remarkable powers of recuperation & astonishing vitality
  C. Strengths of the Empire and reasons for its long survival:
      1. The absolute powers of emperors--a source of great strength when wielded by an able & strong man controlling every department of state--the title of the emperor: <u>Autokrator</u>, thus our word "autocracy" & autocrat--the rule of one person with absolute & unlimited power
      2. An efficient civil service or central administrative system functioning always, even during crises & revolutions
      3. Religious unity (Greek Orthodoxy) and cultural unity (Greek)
      4. A balanced economy as a source of wealth, vitality, & power:
         a. Well-planned agriculture & efficient industry & prosperous trade all combining to provide most necessities
         b. Circulation of a strong system of money--meanwhile, a near total disappearance of currency during the Low Middle Ages in Western Europe
         c. Dominant role of the central government in planning & managing & controlling production and the economy in general--strict yet effective regulation of wages & prices & working hours
         d. Fabulous wealth & luxury of Constantinople giving it the reputation as "<u>the</u> City" of Europe and the "New Rome"
      5. A well-organized & proficient army & navy for defense--also possession of a secret weapon known as "Greek fire", which was an incendiary liquid compound squirted from tubes & igniting upon contact with other objects
      6. Skillful diplomacy & defense policies
      7. Impregnability of the city--defensive invincibility of heavy fortifications & geographic location (against everything except cannon & artillery, introduced in the late-14th century)
  D. Weaknesses of the empire & the reasons for its eventual collapse:
      1. No fixed rule of orderly succession to the throne
         a. Thus the encouragement of intrigue, violence, revolution, military involvement in politics, & civil war--all threatening the security of the state as in Rome earlier
         b. Occurrence in 1000 years of Byzantine history of 65 revolutions and 60 abdications or murders of emperors
      2. Religious disputes within Greek Orthodoxy, the most famous being the Iconoclastic Controversy (725--843):
         a. Concern by some emperors & scholars over discovery that the gullible & superstitious masses actually worshipping

"icons"--painted wooden images of saints--consideration of these activities as dangerous examples of idolatry & contrary to the spiritual teachings of the Bible
- b. Government campaign of forcible removal from churches & the destruction of icons--violent popular reactions gaining support from many monks of the monasteries--results of riots & massacres & civil disturbances
- c. Final outcome--capitulation by the emperors & return of the icons with the attitude that attaining theological purity was not worth destroying all of society
- d. Origins of a modern term in this dispute--an "iconoclast" being someone who attacks cherished traditional beliefs & practices as falsehood & sham--thus iconoclasm is equated with "image-breaking"
- e. A development unrelated to the above--the disintegration of Christianity into the Greek Orthodox Church headed by the patriarch in Constantinople and the Roman Catholic Church headed by the pope (il papa) in Rome--a division or split (the "Schism") becoming official in 1054
    - (1) Doctrinal disagreement over the exact nature of the Trinity: God, Christ, & Holy Spirit--also a problem with celibacy not always being practiced in Orthodoxy--& painted wooden images of Orthodoxy vs. carved statuary of Catholicism
    - (2) Primary difference causing separation--issue of Caesaropapism, with the popes in Rome wishing to maintain independence from secular rulers
3. Factional strife between rival sports teams & political groups--notorious rivalry between the Greens & Blues--two of several athletic clubs whose members & supporters were so fanatical (the word "fan" aptly derives from "fanatic") that contests & games resulted in riots, bloodshed, & even deposition of several emperors rooting for the "wrong" team
4. Omnipresence of outside enemies--perpetual encirclement by many hostile tribes, states, & empires--ultimate conquest by the powerful Ottoman Turks whose growing Near Eastern empire wore down the Byzantines & stormed Constantinople in 1453

E. Significance & influence of the Byzantine Empire in history:
1. Preservation & eventual transmission to Western Europe of the classical works in literature & philosophy of ancient Greece:
    - a. Irony in Byzantine retention of ancient Greek culture, yet lack of appreciation & neglect & even condescension toward these works of genius because of the religious paganism of ancient Greece
    - b. Meanwhile, production of almost nothing culturally valuable for 1000 years by the Christian Byzantines
    - c. Acquisition by Western Europe during the High Middle Ages of a knowledge of ancient Greek culture from the advanced Moslem World, which borrowed Greek knowledge from the Byzantines & which recognized its brilliance
2. Profound influence in culture & institutions on the Slavic nations of Eastern Europe and especially on Russia--adoption of the Byzantine church, form of government, law, literature & art styles, and cyrillic alphabet

3. Role as a buffer state (barrier or wall of protection) in defending a weak Western Europe for long centuries against Middle Eastern invaders such as the Arab & Turkish Moslems

IV. Islam & the Moslem World
   A. Introduction--Islam today perhaps the most powerful religion in the world, with over 900 million believers (nearly one-fifth of humanity) spread over the entire globe
      1. Arabia--place of origination & center of the religion--a large peninsula between the Red Sea & the Persian Gulf with the Indian Ocean to the south and Syria to the northwest and the Tigris-Euphrates River Valley (modern Iraq) to the northeast
      2. Conditions in Arabia before Mohammed:
         a. Mainly deserts of rock & sand with nomadic tribes of Bedouins living in tents near oases with their herds
         b. No settled or agricultural life possible in most regions
         c. Existence of some richer lands along the east & west coasts of the peninsula
      3. Arab people, government, & religion:
         a. Use of a language in the Semitic family common throughout the Middle East
         b. Total absence of any central government--division into social & political units of tribes or clans--constant conflicts & bloodfeuds raging over oases & pasture lands
         c. Religion before Mohammed--a crude & superstitious & polytheistic paganism worshipping tribal nature gods & idols
            (1) Source of religious unity--common veneration of certain sanctuaries, especially a sacred black rock (actually, a meteor fragment) housed in a square temple known as the Kaaba in Mecca
            (2) Pilgrimages to Mecca & the Kaaba during sacred months when fighting was prohibited
   B. Mohammed: 570--632 (also spelled Muhammad & Mahomet)
      1. Humble birth in Mecca--orphaned at an early age--life of poverty till age 24--entrance into the service of a wealthy widow named Khadija & work as a camel driver leading caravans to the more civilized regions to the north
      2. Immense success--marriage to his employer in 595 & enjoyment of the comfortable life of a wealthy merchant in Mecca for the next 15 years until his revelation experience--belief that heavenly voices persuaded him to be the "Prophet" of a new religion
      3. Description--kindly man, charismatic personality, strong will & ruthless determination, sound practical sense, good ability in judging men
      4. Belief in a prophetic mission in 610 at age 40--passage of one month in solitary meditation on a mountain--sufferance from nervous seizures of a hysterical nature during which fits & convulsions & high fever were experienced--later development of the ability to conjure up hypnotic trances at will
      5. Determination to establish a new religion:
         a. Islam, meaning "submission" in Arabic to the will of God---its followers known as Moslems or Muslims, meaning "those surrendering themselves"
         b. Initial conversion of family members & friends--rise of a small following after the formation of a secret society

  c. Provocation after the public introduction of Islam of opposition & persecution from pagan Meccans fearing that insistence on the worship of one god would destroy popular faith in idols & end the profitable trade with perennial pilgrims
  d. Severe persecution precipitating the <u>Hegira</u>, or "migration" to Medina in 622--conversion of the city & spread of the faith--commemoration by the <u>Hegira</u> of the beginning of the Moslem calendar on July 16, 622
  e. Significant assumption by Mohammed of the position of both religious & political leader, thus a <u>theocracy</u>--a form of government in which the religious leader is also the secular political ruler, with "divine guidance"
  f. The Sacred Book known as the <u>Koran</u>, meaning "recitation" in Arabic--compilation after Mohammed's death into 114 chapters arranged in order of length from the longest to the shortest--belief that it contains the word of God as dictated to Mohammed by the angel Gabriel reading from the golden books in heaven (Koran in Arabic is <u>Qur'an</u>)
 6. Triumphant return to Mecca in 630 and acceptance of the city & the Kaaba as the center of the new faith--conversion of all Arab tribes to Islam by his death in 632
 7. Belief among Moslems that at the moment of Mohammed's death in Mecca, angels whisked his body away to Jerusalem where he ascended to heaven from a large rock on Temple Mount--the rock later enclosed by a mosque known as the Dome of the Rock
C. Doctrine & practices of Islam:
 1. Monotheism--belief in only one god, Allah
  a. Belief in Mohammed as the greatest prophet, yet recognition of other prophets such as Adam, Noah, Abraham, Moses, & Christ
  b. Adherence to the view that some truth was revealed to all of the prophets, but the final revelation made only to Mohammed
 2. Many obvious influences from Judaism & Christianity: a Last Judgment, an afterlife in hell or heaven--the latter described enticingly as a "paradise of sensuous pleasures"[1] with lovely women, delicious food, shade, & an abundance of water (exactly the things lacking in Arabia)
 3. Emphasis on a holy life--prayer five times daily toward Mecca, charity to the poor, humility & patience, forgiveness of enemies, fasting from dawn to dusk during the holy month of Ramadan
 4. A pilgrimage (<u>hadj</u>) to Mecca at least once in a lifetime
 5. An ascetic lifestyle--prohibition of gambling, drinking intoxicating beverages, idol worship, charging interest rates, eating pork, & public expression of affection between the sexes (kissing & caressing to be a strictly private matter)
 6. Authorization of slavery yet discouragement of cruel treatment--none of the major religions realized the contradiction & inconsistency in urging the brotherhood of humanity while simultaneously permitting the ultimate degradation of mankind
 7. Allowance of polygamy--men taking a maximum of four wives, with Mohammed setting the example after the death of Khadija--consequence of actual improvement of women's position in

society and a safeguarding of their rights in comparison to the past
8. Proclamation of a holy war or crusade (<u>jihad</u>) against non-believers with a militant desire to spread the faith throughout the world--guarantee to those dying in battle of an afterlife in heaven
9. Great appeal in its simplicity of no priesthood or sacraments or elaborate ritual for most Moslems--universalism in its message of "equality of all believers" regardless of race or class or ethnicity

D. Expansion of Islam & the Moslem Empire
1. Inclusion in the Moslem World at the death of Mohammed in 632 of only Arabia--yet possession within a century afterward of a larger empire than ancient Rome (though not as effectively governed) stretching from Spain & northern Africa to northwestern India & western China
2. Two main periods of expansion & conquest:
    a. Incorporation of Egypt, Syria, Mesopotamia, & Persia by the year 655
    b. Spread to northern Africa, Spain, Sicily, & much of Central Asia by 732
3. Beginning of this movement as a uniquely Arab phenomenon but rapid conversion into an international & cosmopolitan one as new peoples & territories embraced the new religion & joined its growing armies
4. Description of the Moslem Empire--a diverse & multinational entity united by a common religion & the Arab language--its cosmopolitanism & cultural unity very reminiscent of the Roman Empire and the Hellenistic World of the ancient Greeks
    a. Rule over the empire of secular & spiritual autocrats known as the <u>caliph</u>, or "deputy" of the Prophet--two major dynasties of Moslem history: Umayyad (661--750) and Abbassid (750--1258)
    b. Transfer of the political capital city from Mecca to the more central location of Baghdad in the Tigris-Euphrates Valley--attainment of its high point of prestige & power during the caliphates of Haroun-al-Rashid (786--809) and Mamun (813--833)
    c. Disintegration of the empire into political disunity after 945 as various regions & territories became independent, yet preservation of its cultural & commercial unity for many centuries thereafter
5. Practice of a high degree of religious toleration in the empire with the requirement only that non-Moslems pay a special tax--thus Jews & Christian minorities in the Moslem World much freer to practice their faith & worship without persecution or discrimination than their counterparts in Europe
    a. This remaining true until the 19th century in Europe and until the late-19th century rise of Zionism (the movement for establishment of a Jewish homeland & nation in Palestine) in the Middle East & in Europe
    b. Moslem conquerors often being welcomed as deliverers by subjected peoples of other empires & territories
6. The Moslem World much more advanced economically & culturally than Europe during the Low Middle Ages (500--1000); the Euro-

pean revival after 1000 was actually stimulated by increasing contacts with the Middle East

7. Emergence of the two major sects within Islam--origination in a 7th-century power struggle for the position of caliph between rival claimants:
   a. Sunnites or Sunnis--including the vast majority of Moslems and the mainstream beliefs & practices
   b. Shi'ites--including a small minority (about one-tenth of all believers, living mainly in Iran or ancient Persia) and featuring a powerful professional clergy who studied the Koran & offered advice to the faithful
8. Later invasion of the Middle East by various tribes of Turks (initially Seljuks & later Ottoman Turks) from Central Asia--eventual conquest by the Ottoman Empire of the Byzantine Empire and rule over the entire Middle East & southeastern Europe at their capital of Constantinople from the 15th century until 1918

E. Moslem Cultural Achievements:
1. Spread of the Arabic language--a flexible & powerful instrument still in use today as a significant international medium
2. Science & medicine--attainment of knowledge far beyond the ancient Greeks with experiments in chemistry & physics as well as the use of compounds--then compilation of this learning into textbooks
3. Mathematics--introduction of "Arabic" numbers (actually invented in India) and use of the zero in calculations to Europe--greater progress than others in analytic geometry & trigonometry & algebra
4. Philosophy--no original works, yet translations of & commentaries on the ancient Greek philosophers--Europe actually learning of Greek philosophy from the Moslems who appreciated its genius & not from the Byzantines who did not
5. Literature--brilliant love poetry as well as popular fiction & short stories (such as <u>The Arabian Nights</u>) that influenced Europe heavily (& that made Disney hundreds of millions)
6. Music--invention of instruments such as the lute, guitar, & tambourine as well as improvement of the flute & drum--first use of the "fanfare"--a showy musical flourish often inaugurating an event or introducing an important person
7. Architecture--original development of the pointed arch, ribbed vaults, & stone tracery later used extensively in the Gothic cathedrals & buildings of Europe
8. Art--beautiful secular paintings of nature, animals, & people as well as book illustrations--famous geometric patterns & intricate designs known as "arabesque"

V. Medieval Europe
A. The "Age of Faith":
1. Possession & exertion of enormous power & influence over people's lives by the Roman Catholic Church & religion generally--domination of all phases of life by religion
2. Yet popular adherence only in ritual & certain beliefs rather than in the conduct of ethical & moral behavior, which remained abysmally low in this age of unbridled violence, disorder, & ignorance

3. Perception of religion by the common man (illiterate & poor) in terms of superstition, blind faith, & magic--popularity of beliefs in the divine powers of saints & relics
B. Major political theme throughout the Middle Ages:
   1. A constant power struggle between the kings or emperors (representing national government & centralization) and the nobility or landed aristocracy (regional & local government and decentralization)...
   2. Usually resulting in victory for the latter but with the passage of time gradually favoring the slow accumulation of power by the former in the distant future
   3. Local government (often a knight in a nearby castle) normally having the strongest impact on the average person's life
C. The Feudal System--a description of all social, economic, & political institutions pervading all aspects of life and giving the Middle Ages its unique & peculiar character
   1. Chronology:
      a. Origins in the 8th & 9th centuries; movement toward definite shape around 900--1050; highest development from 1050 to 1250; then several centuries of slow decay; most feudal institutions dead or greatly modified by the early 1500's in Western Europe, but gaining strength in Eastern Europe
      b. Yet persistence of some vestiges of the System in the West until the French Revolution (1789--1815) and in Eastern Europe until the 1st World War (1914-18)
   2. Emergence of the Feudal System in a backward & primitive society existing in an extreme condition of near collapse & disintegration
   3. Main features of the Feudal System:
      a. No ownership of private property--instead, people holding a hereditary right to use land from a social superior in return for personal services
      b. Rigid hereditary division of society into two classes:
         (1) Commoners--mostly rural peasant serfs (about 90% of all in society) farming the land in conditions of near slavery for the upper class, and possessing few rights & many obligations of work & special services & taxes
         (2) Nobility--the fighting & ruling aristocracy supposed to provide political supervision & military protection for the lower class serfs--less than 5% of all in society
      c. Economic retardation--exchange of goods & services by barter with little or no money in circulation--land as almost the only source of wealth--mostly agriculture & little industry & commerce--cities almost non-existent--economic localism with every community requiring self-sufficiency (autarky) for survival
      d. Decentralization of government--passage of authority from kings to the local nobility with jurisdiction over the populace and with power over justice, taxation, police (small local armies), & issuance of primitive coins
      e. An elaborate system of relationships & services between & within the two classes:

                (1) Everyone theoretically possessing rights as well as
                    obligations & commitments to others
                (2) Village life among the serfs especially stressing
                    "socialistic" qualities of communal sharing, close
                    cooperation, group ownership of tools & livestock,
                    and mutual assistance for survival
         4. Division of the Feudal System into two types of relationships:
             a. Feudalism--the military & political arrangements only
                among the aristocracy (kings, barons, counts, dukes, &
                knights in the social pyramid or hierarchy) involving
                the exchange of a landed estate (fief) for fighting ser-
                vices in the armies of a superior
             b. Manorialism or seignorialism--the economic & social
                arrangements between nobility & serfs involving the
                exchange of protection from above for food & services
                from below

VI. High Middle Ages in Europe: 1000--1300
    A. Occurrence of a dramatic economic & social recovery from backward-
       ness & semi-barbarism with prosperity to the point of a business
       boom and with great technological advances
    B. This "Economic & Social Revolution" bringing specific improvements
       in a series of connected developments:
         1. Rise of external security--decline of threatening invasions
            from Moslems, Vikings, Magyars, & all others
         2. Rise of internal security--greater safety & less violent dis-
            order due to the influence of the Church & stronger central
            governments
         3. Population growth--a doubling in four centuries (950--1350)
            that ended a critical manpower shortage
         4. A migratory expansion into (or colonization of) previously
            undeveloped or underdeveloped lands all over Europe
         5. Major improvements in farming methods, the results being sig-
            nificant increases in agricultural production
         6. Revival of international trade--local surpluses eventually
            finding far-away markets & stimulating further production
         7. Return of capitalism & a money economy replacing barter:
             a. Emphasis in capitalism on personal accumulation of mater-
                ial wealth & money, more individual rather than group
                effort, and importance of private property
             b. Appearance of an urban "middle class" (between the nobil-
                ity & rural serfs, freemen like the former yet commoners
                like the latter) or bourgeoisie (burghers, burgesses) as
                the group of people practicing & benefitting from capit-
                alism (the term "bourg" or "burg" meaning walled city)
             c. The bourgeoisie consisting of the business & professional
                occupations such as merchants, bankers, small shopkeep-
                ers, skilled workers known as craftsmen & tradesmen &
                artisans, lawyers, doctors, professors, & government
                bureaucrats
             d. Simultaneous existence for several centuries of capital-
                ism side-by-side with feudalism, with capitalism eroding
                & eventually destroying the backward feudal system based
                on hereditary land tenure & communal labor
         8. Growth of towns & cities--major increase of the urban populat-
            ion during these three centuries from less than 2% to about

10% of the entire society & remaining at that level for nearly five more centuries
9. Greater social mobility & betterment for most commoners--disappearance of slavery, rise of the middle class, income increases for peasant serfs

VII. The Crusades
　A. Introduction--a series of military expeditions launched by the Catholic Church and organized & fought usually by noblemen during the High Middle Ages against the Moslem World of the Middle East & Spain & southern Italy, against heretics in certain regions of Europe, and against heathen pagans in Eastern Europe
　　1. The Crusades providing evidence of social, economic, & political revival & strength--emergence from the Dark Ages bringing aggressive drives for territorial expansion & conquest
　　2. Preaching of the 1st Crusade by Pope Urban II. in 1095 at Clermont, France & directed against the Moslem Middle East
　　3. Pretext for the 1st Crusade--recent conquest of the Middle East by the Seljuk Turks in the 11th century and accusations of their harassment of Christian pilgrims visiting holy shrines in Palestine
　B. Reasons for the Crusades
　　1. Motives of the popes for preaching the Crusades:
　　　a. To liberate the "Holy Land" (region of Palestine associated with the ancient Hebrews & the life of Christ) from Moslem domination & to protect Christian pilgrims there
　　　b. To expand the realm of Christendom & the Catholic Church territorially
　　　c. To channel the destructive fighting spirit of the European nobility into work useful to Christianity
　　　d. To strengthen claims of the Papacy to universal supremacy in their power struggle with European kings & emperors
　　2. Factors explaining participation by Crusaders:
　　　a. Religious promises by the popes of personal salvation for those fighting & dying in battle against the infidel ("unfaithful") Moslems as an act of atonement for sins
　　　b. Desires by the nobility for adventure, glory, plunder, land, & power in the Middle East--also guarantees by Church leaders of freedom from debt & exemption from taxes for all
　　　c. An end of serfdom & oppression for the few commoners
　　　d. Profits, commerce, & trading posts in the Levant (Middle East) for Italian businessmen & merchants financing the expeditions--these were the most tangible benefits
　C. The Crusades--a total of eight directed toward the Holy Land:
　　1. 1st Crusade (1096--99): success in "liberating" Palestine & Syria by mainly French noblemen and establishment of temporary feudal kingdoms falling subsequently to the Moslems by 1144--two parts of this movement:
　　　a. The conquest by 12,000 knights & infantrymen
　　　b. The Peasants' Crusade preceding the other & consisting of 20,000 serfs recruited by popular preachers like Peter the Hermit & Walter the Penniless--this untrained rabble mostly perishing in a Turkish ambush in Asia Minor
　　2. 3rd Crusade (1189--92): the most famous one because of participation by the three greatest rulers of Europe

            a. Richard I. the Lionhearted (King of England), Philip II.
               Augustus (King of France), & Frederick I. Barbarossa
               (Emperor of Germany)
            b. Consequence of complete failure, with Frederick drowning
               in a river, Philip cleverly abandoning the expedition to
               return home & steal lands from Richard, and Richard wag-
               ing battle ineffectively before leaving Palestine
         3. 4th Crusade (1202--04): the most notorious & scandalous one
            a. Diversion of this expedition from its goal of Palestine
               to an attack on Constantinople by greedy & ambitious
               leaders & merchants of the Italian city-state of Venice
            b. Result--Constantinople sacked by the Crusaders & ruled by
               the Venetians till 1261, with the Crusade never reaching
               the Holy Land
         4. 8th Crusade (1270): the last expedition to the Middle East be-
            ing led by French King Louis IX. (known as "Saint Louis"),
            who died in Egypt
         5. Several other Crusades fought *in* Europe, such as the protract-
            ed & celebrated struggle in Spain (the *Reconquista*, or "Re-
            conquest") between Moslems & Christians
   D. Results & importance of the Crusades:
         1. Final failure to conquer the Holy Land & to establish perman-
            ent Christian kingdoms in the Middle East
         2. Stimulation & accompaniment of a great revival of internation-
            al trade with the Middle East and introduction to Europe of
            many new luxury products--spices, fruits, sugar, perfumes,
            unique fabrics & clothing
         3. Contribution to a dramatic rise in standards of living & to a
            greater secularization of society ("secular" meaning worldly
            & less religious--with improvements in society, people were
            now enjoying the here-&-now rather than concentrating on the
            heavenly hereafter)
         4. A broadening of intellectual horizons and the adoption of new
            ideas with less provincial attitudes--benefits resulting from
            shaking up a settled society
         5. Tendency of the nobility as a class to die or fail to return
            to Europe, thus contributing to political & social gains in
            Europe for their potential opponents: monarchs, serfs, church

III. The Beginnings of National Representative Assemblies
   A. Introduction--the emergence of "national representative assemblies"
      around 1300 to become for the future of Europe & the World one of
      the hugely important medieval developments:
         1. These council or assembly meetings summoned by kings to assist
            in governing the nation and included delegates or represent-
            atives from various classes & localities throughout the realm
         2. Assemblies beginning as relatively weak & powerless, infrequ-
            ently-called, and seldom-used institution
            a. Yet some of them exploited circumstances & gradually
               accumulated power over many centuries
            b. They eventually became the primary legislative & execu-
               tive authority whose political leaders today are the
               real rulers of European democracies
            c. Thus their origins & evolution are very significant
         3. Application of this practice of calling assemblies all over
            Europe--a common tendency in most nations, sometimes in

            provinces or regions within nations, and often on the local
            level in medieval cities
        4. Most renowned & important of all--Parliament in England and
            the Estates-General in France
    B. Roots, origins, & early development:
        1. The German barbarian tribes--rule by chiefs with the assist-
            ance of the great warriors--a chief merely being the highest
            among equals--all major tribal decisions necessitating dis-
            cussions & consultations among all warriors plus the chief
        2. By the Middle Ages, the chiefs becoming known as kings and the
            warriors known as the highest aristocrats or noblemen--their
            gatherings now being called meetings of the "Great Council",
            where the nobility offered advice & held discussions under
            supervision by the king
        3. Conversion of Great Councils into "national representative
            assemblies" by the simple yet revolutionary addition to the
            meetings of commoners, almost invariably from the small mid-
            dle class (bourgeois, burghers, burgesses) of the cities
            a. Initial meeting of Parliament (from the French parler &
                parlementer, meaning "to speak" & "to parley") called by
                King Edward I. (1272--1307) in 1295
            b. First meeting of the Estates-General in France called by
                Philip IV. (1285--1314) in 1302
        4. Reasons for the addition of bourgeois commoners:
            a. Need for more money by monarchs due to increasing ex-
                penses & much growth of royal government--realization by
                the kings that tax collection would be easier if consent
                given by representatives and that the bourgeoisie was
                rising in wealth & influence
            b. Bid for greater popularity among their subjects by kings
            c. Efforts by monarchs to make their governments more nat-
                ional in scope, with representative institutions being a
                means to bring royal rule into closer contact with the
                people
            d. Increase in the prospects for a closer political alliance
                between kings & bourgeoisie against their traditional
                political rivals, the nobility
        5. When summoned--infrequently & irregularly & only at times of
            crisis or when unusual taxes needed--the monarchs arbitrarily
            called & dissolved all meetings
        6. Functions & powers & authority--very little & very few in the
            initial stages:
            a. Consent or approval of the king's proposals after debate
                & votes
            b. Advice & counsel if requested by the monarch, which could
                be ignored--no possibility of dictation to the king
            c. No initiation of legislation or control of government
            d. Thus a very one-sided relationship between the monarchs &
                the assemblies, with the former almost totally controll-
                ing the agenda
        7. Organization & composition--acquisition not at once but with
            repeated meetings over decades--division into separate bodies
            based on class for voting & for deliberation:
            a. Continental Assemblies (typical example of the Estates-
                General)--division into three houses based on "classes,

orders, or estates" of the: (1) Clergy, (2) Nobility, & (3) Commoners
  b. English Parliament--unique & meaningful division into only <u>two</u> houses: House of Lords (including great noblemen & church dignitaries) and the House of Commons (including town burgesses & lower-level aristocrats, or knights from the shires, sitting together)
    (1) This special composition of the House of Commons encouraging cooperation between the two classes
    (2) Gradual development of common interests by some of the nobility & the bourgeoisie against the monarchy in future confrontations
C. Different medieval fates of Parliament & the Estates-General:
  1. Evolution of Parliament over three centuries into a regular, necessary, & permanent part of the national government as a legislative body
    a. Eventual recognition of the power to vote taxes in combination with the right to present "petitions for the redress of grievances" to the king
    b. Stamps of the royal seal of approval making these petitions the first pieces of legislation in English constitutional history
  2. Failure of the Estates-General to limit royal authority with only occasional meetings, weak & ineffective leadership, and inability of the three houses & classes to cooperate against the monarchy

Chapter 6   THE ITALIAN RENAISSANCE

I. Introduction
   A. The Late Middle Ages-Renaissance (1300--1550): great significance of this era as a transition from the medieval to the modern world
      1. Institutions & attitudes of the Middle Ages such as feudalism being gradually phased out & dying while more modern phenomena increasingly gaining strength & replacing them
      2. These monumental changes occurring initially & most dramatically in the cities of Italy, where in so many ways the modern world was inaugurated
   B. The term <u>Renaissance</u> literally meaning "rebirth" in French (<u>Rinascita</u> in Italian)--it originally referred to a revival of interest in the classical learning & culture of ancient Greece & Rome
   C. Belief by Renaissance scholars in a sudden rebirth of civilization & great creativity in Italy around 1300 inaugurating a new & different & superior age that contrasted sharply with the earlier Middle Ages, which was all portrayed as the "Dark Ages":
      1. This judgment was partly untrue--the High Middle Ages (1000--1300) witnessed some cultural greatness in many areas
      2. However, this judgment was partly true from the standpoint that the Renaissance in Italy far surpassed Medieval culture
   D. Assessment of the Renaissance as one of the (perhaps <u>the</u>) most spectacular periods of creativity in all of history completely overshadowing the accomplishments of the previous millennium
      1. Few eras displaying greater intellectual & artistic vitality and striking genius--the only possible equal being the Golden Age of Athens in ancient Greece
      2. The inspirational & unifying factor of the age and a one-word description of the Italian Renaissance--<u>secularization</u> of society & culture more & more ("secular" meaning worldly or materialistic as distinguished from religious or spiritual)
      3. Thus a revival of <u>humanism</u> that began with the Greeks--the study of mankind & his many activities rather than a focus on God & religious matter
         a. This concentration of human attainment being a more optimistic view in contrast to the more pessimistic view of the human condition by medieval religion
         b. Renaissance regard for humans as beings of great dignity & worth capable of improvement & brilliance when applying rational thought & when granted free expression

II. Achievements of the Renaissance
   A. Great development of the creative arts such as painting, sculpture, and architecture:
      1. Painting--replacement of medieval techniques & emphasis on abstract & inexact depiction with modern stress on "naturalistic" realism & exact representationalism--in other words, depiction of objects & persons as they truly appeared
         a. Medieval art was also religious in purpose & in subject--Renaissance art portrayed worldly subjects as well as religious ones
         b. Introduction of the principle of perspective by presenting a three-dimensional effect on a two-dimensional surface--use also of light & shadow (<u>chiaroscuro</u>)
         c. New portrayal of dramatic action & strong human emotions

         d. Development of new pigments for vivid colors as well as
            the common use of canvas for a superior surface
      2. Sculpture--inspirational borrowing from classical models to
         produce impressive statuary of realism, poise, & grace
      3. Architecture--imitation of Roman & Greek buildings with their
         domes, round arches, fluted columns, & balanced proportions
   B. Literature:
      1. Discovery of many formerly lost Greek & Latin manuscripts of
         classical antiquity and establishment of libraries to pre-
         serve them
      2. Expectation that all scholars learn at least Latin & perhaps
         Greek with some even studying Hebrew & Arabic--many writing
         plays & poetry in the elegant & polished style of original
         Latin
      3. Foundation of schools to provide secular education in the
         humanities, although available only to the very few
      4. Rise of national literatures in the vernacular languages of
         the common people--the finest works of this era written in
         Italian, French, Spanish, German, & English--probably the
         greatest person ever to put pen to paper was Shakespeare
   C. Philosophy:
      1. Rejection of medieval scholasticism of the universities that
         utilized Greek philosophy only insofar as it supported or
         demonstrated "truths" in religious teachings & the Bible
         a. Attempt by scholasticism to reconcile Greek logic or rea-
            son with Christian Biblical revelation--in essence, it
            endeavored to make many irrational aspects of religion
            seem perfectly rational
         b. Thus subordination of Greek philosophy to Christian
            faith as the primary purpose of scholasticism
      2. Study by Renaissance humanists of Greek & Roman thinkers in
         their pure form as ends in themselves for what they offered
         to the universal human experience--glorification by the best
         Renaissance minds of the value, dignity, potentiality of all
         persons regardless of ethnicity, religion, class, or status
   D. Music:
      1. Vigorous developments only during the Late Renaissance of the
         late-1400's & early-1500's
      2. Further maturation & development of the earlier medieval form
         of polyphony--a style in which two or more independent yet
         related voice parts sound against one another:
         a. Musical compositions characterized by increasing complex-
            ity, integration of the entire work, and expansion of
            the voice range
         b. Production of an immense number of secular chansons
            (French polyphonic songs in a setting of poetry & gen-
            erally simple enough to be performed by amateurs) and
            madrigals (Italian songs of greater sophistication sung
            by professionals on themes of lofty literary poetry) for
            princely courts & bourgeois mansions
      3. Rise of secular music performed exclusively by small orchest-
         ras (though less common or popular with composers than relig-
         ious music & voice forms) for royal & aristocratic courts
         a. Gradual development of instrumental dance forms such as
            the pavane and sarabande

   b. Instrumental changes--the viol (ancestor of the violin) becoming the favorite bowed instrument, and the harpsichord (which plucked strings with a quill) gradually supplementing the older clavichord (which struck the strings)--the former instrument had more accent & power
 E. Science:
  1. Addition during the Renaissance era of very little new scientific knowledge to the world
  2. Yet the foundation being laid for the structure of modern science and the future 17th century Age of the Scientific Revolution that established science as we understand it today
   a. Renaissance scholars often attacking abstract & unproven philosophy of the Middle Ages while fostering the growth of a more secular & rationalistic spirit
   b. Introduction of the idea of approaching nature through the medium of observation & experimentation--also the increasing integration of theory & practice--these views & practices first being advanced by artists & craftsmen
   c. Growth in popularity of the mechanistic interpretation of the universe--view originally taught by the ancient Greek mathematician & physicist Archimedes that the universe operates on the basis of mechanical forces like a great machine, predictably & measurably
  3. Greatest accomplishment of the period in the area of astronomy by a Polish clergyman named Nicholas Copernicus (1473--1543) who formulated & demonstrated mathematically the heliocentric theory that the earth & planets revolved around the sun
   a. Thus disproving the geocentric theory of an earth-centered universe as interpreted from the Bible
   b. This breakthrough in knowledge leading to a future explosion of astronomical information
 F. Inventions & technological advances:
  1. Mechanical clocks--invented shortly before 1300
  2. Printing press with movable type--replacement (1200--1400) of expensive parchment (from animal skins) with cheaper paper (made from rags & wood pulp)
  3. Eyeglasses--perfected in the 14th century
  4. Magnetic compass (around 1300)--also improvements in shipbuilding, mapmaking, & navigational devices
  5. Artillery & firearms--developed around 1330
  6. Telescope--invented soon after this era in 1609 by Galileo
 G. The Age of Exploration:
  1. Occurrence during this epoch of adventure & excitement & curiosity of the voyages of discovery and thus the beginnings of New World colonization as well as expansion of European civilization throughout the world
  2. No participation in these enterprises by the Italian states, although individual Italians did sail under the employment of England, France, Holland, Spain, & Portugal
 H. Modern politics:
  1. Open pursuit of "power politics" as analyzed by Machiavelli in <u>The Prince</u> (more on this subject later)--role of Machiavelli as the father of modern political science
  2. Development of a corps of diplomats to serve national interests abroad &, of course, to spy on potential enemies

3. Reliance on mercenary soldiers foreshadowing their general future use with the abandonment of feudal levies (noblemen obligated to fight in the armies of a social superior in return for land use--yet often disloyal & unreliable)
4. Application to international affairs of the "balance of power" concept--states learning to co-exist & to avoid war occasionally by forming alliances & coalitions to match powerful & aggressive adversaries
5. All of the above being innovations exclusively by the Italians

II. Reasons for the Decline of Italy & the Destruction of the Renaissance
   A. Invasions of Italy by France & Spain beginning in 1494 and continuing thereafter in devastating warfare--thus rapid destruction of Italian brilliance & creativity & wealth & power by 1550
   B. Loss of political liberty & independence--invasions & defeats bringing foreign conquest or domination as well as exploitation to many Italian states
   C. Suppression of intellectual freedom--this mainly being a consequence of repressive actions by the Catholic Church during the Counter-Reformation Era of the 2nd half of the 16th century--heavy censorship of all art & thought
   D. Decline of economic prosperity--this resulting from shifts in the trade routes to the west & the Atlantic Ocean & thus outside of the Mediterranean Sea, thereby sapping the energy of Italy

IV. The Northern Renaissance
   A. Commencement of the Renaissance in Italy as early as the late-1200's--spread over the Alps Mountains to Northern Europe much later, around 1450
   B. Significant differences between the Italian & Northern Renaissance:
      1. In Italy the Renaissance affecting everything in society (politics, economics, social institutions, etc.) and penetrating to the grass roots--in the North the Renaissance consisting of only a cultural movement in literature & the arts
      2. Stress of the Renaissance in Italy on secularism & individualism in an urban environment--emphasis in the North on a traditional & strong religious orientation and on educational & church reform in a society little changed from previous centuries, thus not particularly focused on city existence

V. Reasons Why the Renaissance Attaining Its Earliest, Highest, & Fullest Development in Italy and Not Elsewhere in Europe
   A. Obviously, the existence of most favorable conditions in Italy as already the most progressive & modern area of Europe economically, socially, & politically throughout this era
   B. Economic prosperity--the Italian city-states from 1000 to 1500 were collectively the dominant economic power of Europe:
      1. Explanation for this prosperity in the strategic geographical proximity to the Middle East--Italian city-states profiting enormously from their monopoly over this trade--Italy as the commercial center of Europe
      2. Importation of silks, spices, sugar, cotton products, & other luxuries from the Levant and frequent reshipment to northern Europe for fabulous profits
      3. Earlier end of feudalism in Italy than elsewhere & earlier advent simultaneously of capitalism
      4. Prevalence of economic depression for most of Europe during

the general period of 1300--1450, yet Italy usually suffering less from its ravages & reviving sooner
C. Higher development of capitalism than elsewhere--much wealth generated by aggressive bourgeoisie eager to patronize culture & surround themselves with ostentation
D. Vigorous urban society--cities in Italy were larger, richer, & more important than elsewhere, thus more of a focus of all activity--city life always offering an encouragement to greater thought & creativity & freedom & economic opportunity
E. More class or social mobility--careers thrown open to talent in these urban environments with fewer limits on what men might accomplish--creation by the new secular spirit of more incentives for fame & fortune
F. Stronger feelings of individualism--men awakening in the Italian cities to a new consciousness of themselves as individuals rather than as members of medieval groups or a community or a class
G. A higher degree of freedom & self-expression--artists & scholars & writers practicing their trades in a freer atmosphere and exerting more control over their work--even despotic patrons & rulers often encouraging experimentation
H. Greater awareness of the Roman tradition & heritage--constant physical reminders in monuments & edifices of the glory & grandeur of Rome--use of Roman law & Latin expressions in Italy

VI. Evolution of the Italian States
A. Birth & maturation of the Italian Renaissance in an atmosphere of chaos, turmoil, frequent warfare, & political disunity--13th & 14th-century Italy very similar to ancient Greece in being divided into several hundred city-states:
  1. Cities fought each other for complete conquest or for control of trade routes--rural areas rebelled against urban domination--class warfare between rich & poor raged within cities--rival political factions battled for control of government
  2. Efforts by various overlords earlier to extend their supremacy over Italy failed:
     a. Frankish kings in the 8th & 9th centuries ruled northern & central Italy briefly & weakly
     b. A long struggle for domination in Italy during the High Middle Ages between German emperors and Church pope (1075--1254) resulted in destruction of the emperors and exile of the popes to France a bit later in 1305
     c. Thus the Italian city-states were left completely independent of the sovereignty of any single ruler
  3. Social & political trend--constant lawlessness & disorder & class conflict & revolution always threatening the peace & stability necessary for economic prosperity--the result:
     a. Demands by the upper classes (especially the bourgeoisie) for restrictions on freedoms & civil liberties and increases in the power of police & armies & authoritarian government to curb the social unrest & violence
     b. The primary purpose--to protect upper class property, privileges, status, & power
     c. Trend toward despotic rulers and the use of mercenary generals & soldiers (<u>condottieri</u> in Italian) to maintain internal order & to defend against invaders

B. Two general political tendencies during the 14th & first half of the 15th centuries:
   1. Governmental evolution from "democratic" republics ("democratic" in the sense of holding elections or having votes of approval in which a male majority might participate) to oligarchic republics (controlled entirely by a wealthy or privileged minority) to despotism (signori meaning dictators or despots by force of arms)
   2. Expansion & consolidation of larger city-states at the expense of smaller & weaker ones--by 1450 only five great states & around four lesser ones remained
C. Impact of Niccolo Machiavelli (1469--1527) & his book The Prince:

   1. The founder of modern political science with his description best form of government but only what worked best
   2. Analysis of "power politics" & the principle that the end justifies the means, even when it involved illegality & immorality--separation of statecraft & politics from ethics
   3. Occasional admiration of despots as ruthless & cruel & treacherous yet very able & intelligent leaders maintaining their positions by winning popular gratitude and by providing order & stability--they owed their careers to performance & talent and not to blood or tradition
   4. Utilization of rational thought & scientific analysis of the modern world to support his conclusions

VII. Description of the Major States of Renaissance Italy
   A. Duchy of Milan (Milano):
      1. Location in the central & northern region of Lombardy--wealthiest city in Italy during the High Middle Ages leading the defense earlier against the invasions by German emperors
      2. A balanced economy providing great wealth due to its strategic geographic situation--a focus of international trade flowing north & south through Alpine passes--bountiful agriculture in the fertile Po River Valley--textile & metallurgical manufacturing
      3. Typical political transition from democratic republic to oligarchy to despotism--rule by the Visconti family from 1277 to 1447 when the male line died out--replacement by the condottiere Francesco Sforza (1450--66), who married a Visconti
      4. Impressive cultural achievements under his son Ludovico "Il Moro" Sforza (1479--1500) until driven from power by the French--many works of genius performed in Milan during this period by Leonardo da Vinci (1452--1519)
   B. Republic of Florence (Firenze):
      1. Situation geographically in the region of Tuscany midway between Rome & Milan
      2. Much wealth deriving from woolen & silk-weaving industries and from banking--the most famous banking families & operations in Italy were Florentine during the Renaissance
      3. Political retention of a republic throughout the era with wild swings between an oligarchical & a democratic one--usual domination by the rich merchants, bankers, & manufacturers yet occasional exercise of power by the common laborers, craftsmen, & small shopkeepers
         a. Political life characterized by factional strife, party

    feuds, turbulent elections, & infrequent revolutions
    with a seizure of the government by the lower classes
  b. This active popular involvement in civic affairs result-
    ing in profound pride & patriotism & participation in
    political as well as cultural events--known as "civic
    humanism" and unique to Florence & the Florentines
  c. Community interest & involvement partially explaining the
    brilliant cultural achievements of Florence--relevance
    of the theory of "crisis and creativity"
 4. Famous reputation as the "Athens of the West" during the Renaissance era because most of the great artists & scholars &
  writers were Florentines
 5. Ultimate surrender by Florentines to the despotic rule of Cos-
  imo de'Medici (1434--64) who headed a very rich banking &
  woolen-manufacturing family
  a. Retention of the republic in name & institutions by the
    de'Medicis while controlling most offices & rigging
    elections for political dominance--similar to the meth-
    ods in Rome by Augustus during the early Empire
  b. The prestige of the de'Medicis attaining its zenith under
    Lorenzo de'Medici (1469--92) who was renowned as a ver-
    satile genius & the ideal of the "Renaissance man" be-
    cause he excelled in so many different phases as a poet,
    writer, diplomat, statesman, & patron of arts & learning
  c. Florence after Lorenzo experiencing invasions & wars &
    rapid political as well as economic decline
C. Republic of Venice (*Venezia*):
 1. Existence as the richest city in Western Europe following the
  revival of trade with the Middle East after 1000--dominance
  over the lion's share of that commercial activity with its
  vast naval & merchant fleet of ships
 2. Unique political evolution into a very stable & unchanging
  system of government without revolutions or civil strife--
  probable explanation in the security from constant warfare
  due to its geographic separation from the mainland & its construction on hundreds of tiny islands within the Adriatic
  Sea lagoon approximately one mile from shore
 3. The perfect example of an oligarchy--monopoly over government
  councils by the wealthiest merchant, shipping, & banking fam-
  ilies--rule by about 2% of the entire population
 4. Triumphant emergence over its main rival Genoa in their 14th-
  century struggle for dominance of the Mediterranean commerce
  & its fabulous profits
 5. Acquisition throughout 15th-century conquest of territory on
  the Italian mainland and an overseas empire including Cyprus,
  Crete, southern Greece, & the Dalmatian Coast
D. Republic of Genoa (*Genova*):
 1. Also very wealthy from overseas commerce--the principal rival
  of Venice located on opposite or northwestern coast of Italy-
  --famed for its adventurers & mariners such as Cristoforo
  Colombo (we call him Columbus)
 2. Notoriety for its turbulent politics & drastic fluctuations
  between a democratic & oligarchic republic, often with victory for the former--celebrated 14th-century democrat Simon
  Boccanegra, about whom Giuseppe Verdi later composed an opera

E. The Papal States in Rome (Roma):
  1. Disastrous papal neglect of its spiritual duties during the 14th & 15th centuries in order to pursue worldly wealth & power--concentration in the 15th century on reconquering independent despots & cities within the Papal States
  2. A series of scandalous popes:
     a. Alexander VI. (1492--1503) & his son Cesare Borgia---notorious pervert & drunkard assassinating his political enemies & reducing the Papacy to its lowest moral level
     b. Julius II. (1503--13): the "Warrior Pope" spending much time & money fighting battles & wielding secular power
     c. Leo X. (1513--21): a weak leader lacking knowledge about religious matters who nonetheless appreciated & patronized high culture
F. Kingdom of Naples, or the Two Sicilies (Napoli & Sicilia):
  1. The largest Italian state in its territorial area, yet the poorest & least prominent of the major states--no significant cultural achievements under French & later Spanish rulers
  2. No recovery from the vigor & prosperity & cultural leadership of the High Middle Ages under Norman & then German regimes
G. Duchy of Savoy, or Piedmont (Savoie, Piemonte)--location in the extreme northwestern region of Italy--totally insignificant during the Renaissance yet destined for a great political future as the state forging all of Italy into a unified modern nation in the mid-19th century

THE PROTESTANT REFORMATION

I. Early Christianity
  A. Assumption by Christianity of many hundreds of forms since the life & teachings of Christ:
    1. The central reason for this diversity (in the judgment of Biblical scholars) is that the Bible is replete with contradictions, inconsistencies, fallacies, & myths as well as some factual historical information
    2. Thus people have picked & chosen to emphasize whatever variety of practices & beliefs they wished while strongly disagreeing with others
  B. Christ was initially portrayed in the Synoptic Gospels & the Book of John (the 1st four books of the New Testament), yet his earliest followers differed sharply in opinion over his teachings:
    1. There were at least 20 varieties of Christianity by the 2nd century A.D.--more than 80 types existed by the 4th century
    2. Then St. Paul & St. Augustine distorted & twisted Christ's message with their own views & interpretations
    3. Later medieval Roman Catholicism presented even more contrasting & contradictory opinions & practices
    4. With the 16th century Reformation came many hundreds of varieties which continue to proliferate today
    5. These conflicting interpretations led Christians to slaughter each other by the millions in the name of Christ, who taught love & brotherhood--historian F.S.C. Northrop concluded: "Any serious attempt to remove present causes of war must concentrate on the roots of the Christian religion and of Western idealism."[1]

  C. Essential to any understanding of modern Christianity are the ideas
   & profound impact of St. Paul & St. Augustine

II. The Extraordinary Mission of St. Paul (Saul of Tarsus: 10--64)
  A. One critical reason why Christianity triumphed over all other religions in the Roman Empire was the attraction of this remarkable
   missionary renowned for his dedication, fervor, & capabilities
  B. Paul was very different from Christ--he was an urban & Hellenized
   (culturally Greek) & fairly educated Jew as well as a fierce &
   somber man driven by a deep sense of guilt
  C. The most significant event in his life & the key to his mission:
   1. Paul began as a pathological hater of Jesus' disciples--then
    en route to Damascus on a mission of persecution he had a
    blinding vision of the resurrected Christ who called to him
    from heaven
   2. This mystical experience turned him into a zealous proponent
    of Christ, although Paul knew Jesus only by hearsay & rarely
    referred to his human life
   3. He believed in a Christ who died & was resurrected & through
    whom one achieved immortality--origination of these ideas in
    the Mystery Cults already thousands of years old
   4. Paul was typical of a zealot or fanatic swinging from one ex-
    treme to another while devoting himself entirely to a new
    cause that manifested similarities to the old one
  D. Impact & legacy of Paul:
   1. Transformation of Christianity from a minor Jewish sect into a
    separate & independent universal religion:
    a. Paul led a faction deciding to preach the new gospel to
     Gentiles (non-Jews) & to exempt them from Jewish dietary
     regulations, circumcision, elaborate ritual & ceremony
    b. He introduced the "doctrine of justification by faith"[2]
     (achieving salvation through belief in the resurrected
     Christ) and the "doctrine of the Redemption"[3] (theory
     that Christ purposefully sacrificed himself to save &
     redeem mankind, thus atoning for all sins of humanity)
    c. Paul stressed the importance of faith (a result of his
     Christian revelation & knowledge of Mystery Cults) <u>and</u>
     good works such as charity (a legacy of Judaism)
    d. Ironically Paul preached a gospel about Jesus <u>not</u> taught
     by the Christ portrayed in the Synoptic Gospels:
     (1) Jesus had proclaimed a kingdom of God (heaven) to
      be earned by simple repentance & righteousness
     (2) Paul taught that salvation was possible only
      through belief in a resurrected Christ
   2. Introduction of the "Idea of Original Sin":
    a. Paul developed a peculiar view of the Genesis story re-
     garding the Garden of Eden, from which Adam & Eve were
     expelled for disobedience to God in eating the fruit
     from the "tree of the knowledge of good and evil"[4]
    b. The prophets of Israel had earlier made little or nothing
     of this myth
    c. Christ never mentioned it at all
    d. Yet the plain meaning of this Biblical story was twisted
     into a different interpretation:
     (1) The Curse of Original Sin--the belief that the en-
      tire human race was sinful & depraved & corrupted

                    by the evil deed of Adam & Eve in the Fall from
                    Grace and banishment from the Garden of Eden
                (2) This pessimistic view of human nature would have
                    disastrous consequences by encouraging acceptance
                    of correctable social wrongs, callousness toward
                    human suffering & atrocities, and toleration of
                    slavery & serfdom
        3. Reaffirmation of the lowly & inferior status of women to men:
            a. The Bible originally assigned to women a role of subject-
                ion to men: "...and he shall rule over you."[5]
            b. Women were created by God as an afterthought and caused
                man's Fall by succumbing to the serpent's temptation
            c. Paul required women to wear a hat in church as a symbol
                of their subjection to men
            d. Sex was something to be guarded against--Paul believed
                that bachelorhood was preferable to marriage--"those
                (men) who have wives should live as though they had
                none"[6]--marriage was only advisable as an alternative to
                sinful fornication
            e. Paul was the first of a long line of saints & reformers &
                spiritualists whose religiosity involved a morbid fear
                or hatred of sex
        4. Approval & sanction of authoritarian & absolute government:
            a. Paul provided a highly influential argument for bondage
                to absolute monarchs & dictators: "The powers that be
                are ordained of God. Whosoever therefore resisteth the
                power, resisteth the ordinance of God; and they that
                resist shall receive to themselves damnation."[7]
            b. Condemnation of political equality & freedom--even in
                spiritual life Paul taught that salvation was achieved
                by God's special grace and "not your own doing..."[8]
    E. Paul experienced martyrdom in Rome around the year 64 A.D. accord-
        ing to legend--yet his tireless efforts toward conversion, his
        ideas, & his inspirational leadership made him the true founder
        of Christianity

II. The Influence & Ideas of St. Augustine (354--430)
    A. Augustine was the greatest thinker of early Christianity with a
        powerful impact on religious history, providing the foundation
        for the Roman Catholic Church in the Middle Ages and becoming the
        chief inspiration of the Protestant reformers later
        1. Excellent education in philosophy & classical literature--a
            brilliant career of versatility as preacher, organizer, bish-
            op in north Africa, writer, & philosopher of religion during
            the dying decades of the Roman Empire
        2. Radical oscillation of his life (similar to Paul) between ex-
            tremes of debauchery & worldly pleasure on the one hand to
            severe asceticism on the other hand
    B. Impact & legacy of Augustine:
        1. The divine interpretation or conception of history
            a. In his monumental work <u>The City of God</u> Augustine traced
                the history of humanity since the Creation, representing
                all events as the purposeful unfolding of God's plan for
                the world--thus God's hand was behind all happenings
            b. This book was undertaken after the sack of Rome in 410 to
                demonstrate that the Empire's calamities were not caused

                    by Rome's desertion of the old pagan gods, but was a
                    predictable outcome for all worldly things
                c. According to Augustine, the material city & empire of
                    Rome would inevitably crumble while the spiritual city
                    of God (heaven) led to eternal peace, happiness, &
                    salvation
        2. Belief in predestination--idea that an all-powerful & all-
            knowing Deity determines (or pre-destines) everything that
            occurs, thus theoretically denying mankind any freedom of
            will to control his life
                a. According to this theory, God destines each person at
                    birth for salvation or damnation, with only a tiny
                    number of elite (the "elect") being granted God's spec-
                    ial grace through Christ's sacrifice--this means that
                    humans were powerless to affect their salvation
                b. These views easily emanated from Augustine's acceptance
                    of Paul's distorted interpretation of Original Sin
        3. Profound pessimism in his opinions toward sexuality & politics
            & human nature--Augustine was sometimes even harsher than
            Paul in these matters
                a. Augustine believed that the forbidden "knowledge of good
                    & evil" consumed by Adam & Eve was literally carnal
                    (sexual) and that the taint of sin was transmitted
                    through "the semen from which we were to be propagated"[9]
                    --one sign of Original Sin to him was sexual arousal
                b. Thus emerged the "ideal of passionless procreation"[10]---
                    sex was permissible for breeding purposes, but sexual
                    desire & pleasure was regarded as sinful
                c. The consequences ever since for people taking these views
                    seriously have been frustration, trauma, disillusion,
                    neuroses, and....divorce
                d. Augustine judged humanity incapable of self-government &
                    advocated the use of coercive secular power against doc-
                    trinal dissent

IV. Causes & Background of the Reformation
    A. Introduction
        1. Similarity of the Reformation to other major historical uphea-
            vals in having long-term causes traced back many centuries
            prior to its beginning in 1517
        2. An analysis of these causes illustrating perfectly the role of
            change in history & the necessity for powerful institutions
            to adapt to constant new developments
        3. Attainment by the Catholic Church of its zenith in power &
            prestige during the High Middle Ages (1000--1300) with the
            development of an international hierarchy of officials, a
            system of courts, powers over taxation, and the authority to
            interfere in the secular politics of nations & states
        4. Yet the seeds of destruction for the Medieval Church also be-
            ing planted during that era
        5. A listing & explanation below of (8) causes of the Reformation
    B. A growing sense of alienation & estrangement in religion after the
        year 1000 between professional upper clergymen & the common man:
        1. In other words, the religion of professional upper clergymen
            becoming more incomprehensible to the average uneducated man
        2. Domination of religion before 1000 by superstition & ignor-

ance & emotion with a belief in the importance of saints & relics & miracles
   a. This fact being the simple reflection of a barbaric age & backward society
   b. Existence also during this era of few social distinctions between the common people and the lower & upper clergy
3. However, occurrence in the High Middle Ages between 1000 and 1350 of extensive changes:
   a. The masses of common people as well as the lower clergy (parish priests) remaining the same as always in religious ideas & practices, but the...
   b. Professional upper clergy (bishops, archbishops, cardinals, popes, abbots of monasteries, scholars of universities) becoming educated and fascinated by Greek reason & complex doctrinal ideas of theology that could not be understood by simple & uneducated commoners
   c. Furthermore, the priesthood now coming to mirror the social class divisions of feudal society with the lower clergy recruited only from commoners and the upper clergy filled by the privileged nobility
4. Professional priesthoods throughout history seeking to enhance their power, influence, & wealth by making themselves indispensable to the religious needs of people--thereby increasing popular reliance & dependence on them:
5. Accomplishment of this goal by the Church in several ways:
   a. Development of the sacramental system--seven sacraments constituting formal acts necessary for salvation that were performed officially by priests--final definition of the sacraments at the 4th Lateran Council in 1215:
      (1) Among them were baptism, confirmation (marking an adolescent's conscious acceptance of the faith), marriage, extreme unction (the last rites of a dying person), penance (an act of atonement for sin following confession), & communion, or:
      (2) The Holy Eucharist (later the Lord's Supper to Protestants) as the partaking of wine & bread in a ceremony commemorating Christ's sacrifice on the cross--the Catholic dogma of "transubstantiation" expressing the belief that the priest miraculously converts the substance of wine & bread into the blood & body of Christ upon consumption
   b. Stress on the necessity of performing "good works" in life to merit salvation--powerful influence of the brilliant scholar Thomas Aquinas (1225--74) in rationalizing that God granted mankind "free will" to work out in this life his fate of salvation or damnation in the afterlife
   c. Adherence to the doctrine of divine authority in the hands of priests, without whose assistance mortals cannot achieve heaven
6. Results--increasingly by 1300 the common people rejecting the elaborate ritual & complex doctrine as too formal & mechanical & impersonal & corruptly administered & lacking in emotionalism & spirituality--the response being our 2nd cause:

C. Rise of mysticism
   1. A popular movement during the 14th & 15th centuries in northern Europe (especially in Germany where the Reformation began) stressing individual prayer & a direct personal relationship with God and involving a return to irrational beliefs & emotional expressions
   2. Acceptance by the Catholic Church of the mystic preachers & their activities & the effect of heightened piety, yet mysticism having the consequence of eroding popular dependence on the clergy & Church institutions
D. Absence of a reform movement within the Church after the 13th century--thus a failure to address the problems of corruption & abuse:
   1. Poor educational standards & frequent illiteracy of the lower clergy having little or no knowledge of Church ideology & practices
   2. Luxurious & worldly lifestyle by many clergymen plus the avoidance of vows regarding asceticism (self-denial of worldly pleasures) & celibacy or chastity (abstention from sexual intercourse)
   3. Fraudulent sale of relics; simony--sale of church offices to the highest bidder without regard for qualification; nepotism--appointment to church office of friends & relatives & favorites; pluralism--occupancy of several church positions by one person for financial gain only
   4. Profitable sale of dispensations (exemption from a church law or vow) and indulgences (a pardon eliminating punishment for worldly sins)
   5. Appearance to many people that the Church was more a profit-making business interested in secular power than a soul-saving institution interested in the spiritual needs of common people
E. Scandals & weaknesses of the Papacy:
   1. Babylonian Captivity (1305--78): exile from Rome by the popes at Avignon under the domination of the French monarchy
   2. Great Schism (1378--1417): existence of two & sometimes three claimants to be the real pope excommunicating each other
   3. Conciliar Movement (1409--49): failure of efforts to limit papal powers & to reform the Church with assemblies of equal or superior authority to the popes
   4. Notorious Renaissance popes (Alexander VI. & Julius II. & Leo X.) neglecting their spiritual duties to pursue worldly power & wealth
F. Influence of radical reformers--whenever moderate changes are not forthcoming, demands for extreme measures will arise:
   1. Marsiglio of Padua (1273--1343): publication of a pamphlet condemning the Church for meddling in worldly politics & ignoring its spiritual functions
   2. John Wycliff (1330--84): English scholar & Oxford theologian more influential than all others in anticipating the reforms of the Reformation--advocacy of important recommendations:
      a. Support of the Conciliar view that Church councils representing the entire body of Christians should be superior in authority to the popes
      b. Superiority of secular rulers to church leaders in matters of state (secular politics)

    c. Minimization of the importance of the sacraments--prohibition of sinful priests from administering sacraments
    d. Denial of the theory of transubstantiation in the communion ceremony
    e. Recognition of the Bible as the ultimate source of religious authority, rather than Church traditions or Papal pronouncements
    f. Insistence on a literal interpretation of the Holy Scriptures--this view being a reaction against the commentaries of medieval scholastics
    g. Conviction that all Christians (not just the clergy) must be able to read the Bible--and not in the traditional Latin, but in the vernacular languages of the common people--thus the need for translations
    h. Results--denunciation by the Church of Wycliff who went into hiding--his followers hunted down & executed--yet his ideas spreading all over northern Europe
  3. Jan Huss (1369--1415): Czech nationalist & university scholar espousing the views of Wycliff and eventually arrested illegally & burned at the stake as a heretic--failure of these three radicals mainly because of a lack of secular support
G. Political causes of the Reformation:
  1. Growth of national consciousness in northern & western Europe, thus intensifying feelings of popular patriotism & nationalism with a perception of the pope as a foreigner & intruder in other countries--emergence of more support for national ruler than the international Papacy under Italian control
  2. Rise in northern & western Europe of powerful monarchs & stronger nations with more efficient bureaucracies & armies than during the Low & High Middle Ages--possession by these secular states of more coercive power than the Papacy
H. Economic causes of the Reformation:
  1. Increasing resentment of Papal taxation, land ownership, & wealth--much money leaving northern Europe for Italy
  2. Development of a significant conflict between the ambitions of the new merchant class (bourgeoisie) and the ascetic ideal of the Church
  3. Opposition by Medieval Catholicism in many ways to the more dynamic aspects of capitalism & its capitalist businessmen:
    a. Imposition of Church regulations & laws prohibiting unlimited profits, which were regarded as immoral--thus statutes enforcing the "just price" for merchants & the "reasonable wage" for laborers--no concern for the principles of free competition or supply & demand
    b. Morality also at issue in the Church condemnation of usury--charging interest on loans where no actual risk was involved
    c. Businessmen often ignoring this interference into their private affairs & these hindrances to rapid expansion & wealth--yet persistence of much resentment toward the Church by the bourgeoisie
    d. Contrasting attitudes toward poverty--Church view of it as a positive virtue of humility & godliness; bourgeoisie view of it as a negative sign of laziness & a social evil or vice to be eradicated

             e. The greatest appeal of Protestantism existing among the
                socio-economic class of the bourgeoisie
    I. The Renaissance--this new era of change & upheaval with its spirit
       of secularism & individualism & humanism constituting a direct
       shock & challenge to the medieval Catholic Church, which had
       appeared more than a thousand years before
         1. Existence of the Catholic Church during the Late Middle Ages
            as an anachronism looking backward & not forward and remain-
            ing inflexible & impervious toward any change and intolerant
            toward criticism
         2. Even today, modern challenges leave Catholicism fumbling awk-
            wardly with such issues as feminism, socio-economic revolut-
            ionary movements in the 3rd World, overpopulation, abortion,
            celibacy of the priesthood, antisemitism, etc.

V. The Reformation Religions
   A. Catholicism
         1. Nature of the Roman Catholic Church--a highly centralized, au-
            thoritarian, hierarchical organization with a rigid chain of
            command commencing at the top with the Pope who passed down
            orders, policies, & appointments through archbishops, bish-
            ops, & parish priests to the non-professional faithful
         2. Emphasis on a privileged, exclusive, professional priesthood
            as intermediaries the common laymen & God's Church
         3. Absorption over the many centuries of some doctrines & prac-
            tices that were conflicting, contradictory, & confusing:
              a. Ideas advanced by St. Augustine of "predestination" that
                 God decides the future fate in the afterlife of everyone
                 at birth, and that God wills all actions & world events
              b. Belief later in the "free will" of persons to work out
                 their salvation or damnation with "good works" in this
                 life as well as faithful observance of the sacraments
   B. Protestantism
         1. Application of this term for <u>all</u> non-Catholic & non-Greek or
            Russian Orthodox Christian religions arising after 1517 when
            the Reformation commenced
         2. Derivation of the term from a formal "protest" drawn up by the
            Lutheran princes of Germany at the Diet (meeting of the nat-
            ional representative assembly, or Reichstag) of Speyer in
            1529 over Catholic leaders' refusal to recognize an earlier
            promise to consider the issue of allowing each of the hun-
            dreds of German rulers to determine the religion of his state
         3. Constant claim by all Protestant reformers to be not rebels or
            revolutionary innovators but devout Christians returning to
            an older, purer, & simpler faith of early Christianity
         4. The major Protestant Reformation religions & their main feat-
            ures, mentioned below:
   C. Lutheranism
         1. The first of the Reformation Churches to break away from Rome
            in 1521--a creation of the life & teachings of Martin Luther
            (1483--1546) who set a precedent followed by all Protestants
            in rejecting certain Catholic beliefs & practices:
              a. Abolition of all sacraments except two (baptism & commun-
                 ion)--retention of the latter only because of their
                 specific mention in the Bible, the ultimate authority to
                 Protestants

  b. Belief in only "faith" as the way to salvation rather than the performance of good works--thus the elimination of pilgrimages, fasting, veneration of saints & relics, a privileged & exclusive priesthood, clerical celibacy, & the existence of monasteries
  c. Inclusion in church services of more music, singing, and popular participation
  d. Permission of Lutheran clergymen to pursue ordinary lives and to marry & have families (the "priesthood of all believers")
  e. Translation of the Bible by Luther personally from Latin into the vernacular German language, as the final source of religious authority
 2. Decision by Luther to make his religious institution an "established" church, meaning under the domination of the secular government--this status of dependency permitting politicians to interfere in church affairs while the government undertook to pay clerical salaries & to finance literature & maintenance of buildings, etc.
 3. Yet retention by Lutheranism of much Catholic doctrine & ritual to remain one of the most conservative of all Protestant religions in its closeness to Catholicism

D. Anglicanism, or the Church of England (Episcopalianism in America after 1786)
 1. Commencement of the Reformation in England with the obsession of Henry VIII. to obtain a marriage annulment (repeatedly rejected by the pope) from his first wife (Catherine of Aragon) in order to perpetuate the power of his Tudor Dynasty with a strong male heir (Catherine produced only a sickly daughter)
 2. Proclamation of the Act of Supremacy in 1534 establishing the king as the supreme head of the new Church of England, with the Archbishop of Canterbury as his subordinate appointee
 3. Wish of Henry to change very little otherwise and to maintain most of the old Catholic doctrine & ritual & hierarchical organization--yet a contrary desire by most English people for further reforms & changes:
  a. Swing of the Anglican Church in a more Protestant direction during the reign of Edward VI. (1547--53)
  b. Then a return toward Catholicism under "Bloody" Mary I. (1553--58), whose persecution of heretics inspired us to name an alcoholic drink with vodka after her
 4. Assumption of a definitive form for the Anglican Church during the reign of Queen Elizabeth I. (1558--1603) with her enactment of the 39 Articles in 1563, known as the Elizabethan Compromise or Settlement:
  a. Allowance for the doctrine & theology to remain deliberately vague & general with the goal of attracting most English people, including many with Catholic views (High Church Anglicans) and many with Protestant outlooks (Low Church Anglicans)
  b. Elimination of Latin usage, oral confession, clerical celibacy, monasticism, & allegiance to the pope--maintenance of a professional priesthood, elaborate ceremony, & a hierarchical organization

  c. Preservation of Anglicanism as essentially a very conservative church deviating the least among all Protestant faiths from Catholicism
  d. Similarity to Lutheranism also in its acceptance of state domination & its subservience to secular authority--this condition often called <u>Erastianism</u>
 E. Calvinism
 1. The most important Protestant faith because of its universal & international appeal, its spread throughout Europe & the New World, and its pervasive influence on the values & lifestyle of the bourgeoisie
 2. Origination with the French theologian John Calvin (Jean Cauvin, in French), who became religious & political ruler (a theocracy) of Geneva, Switzerland and attracted followers from all over Europe
 3. Derivation of Calvinist uniqueness from its heavy stress on predestination, with its low opinion of human nature & its pessimistic view of mankind as depraved, evil, & corrupted by the Original Sin of Adam
 4. The most outstanding feature of Calvinism--a rigid, strict, austere, puritanical, & narrow code of moral behavior prohibiting most worldly pleasures as Satanic temptations:
  a. Forbidden pleasures such as music, dancing, gambling, cursing, fine clothes, excessive drinking, theater productions, sensuous enjoyment of sex, & general idleness
  b. Emphasis instead on the "Puritan ethic" of hard work, thrift, sobriety, & perseverance
  c. Exaltation of the pursuit of wealth and the acquisition of material possessions--regard for prosperity & riches as a sign of God's blessing--thus powerfully appealing to the bourgeoisie and an incentive to capitalism
 5. Existence by Calvinists in most countries as often persecuted minorities--thus the championing in self-defense of certain "democratic tendencies" of importance to the future:
  a. Opposition to governmental control of religious affairs
  b. Separation of church and state
  c. Avoidance of hierarchical organization, by which authority is imposed from above
  d. Permission of congregational members to choose their leaders--thus a form of local religious democracy
  e. Individual freedom of worship
  f. Yet denial of these practices to others when Calvinists dominating as the majority--consequently, they were truly not lovers of democracy as we understand it in the modern era
 6. Recognition of Calvinists by different names in different countries:
  a. In England--Puritans or Separatists (later Independents or Congregationalists)
  b. In Scotland--Presbyterians
  c. In France--Huguenots
  d. In Germany & Holland--German & Dutch Reformed
  e. In America--Calvinists from many countries came here and exerted an enormous impact on the American mentality & on our institutions

F. Anabaptism
   1. Description of a group of many sects ("ana" meaning <u>again</u> in Greek--practice of baptism in infancy & again later in adulthood) regarded as radicals or extremists by their contemporaries because:
      a. They were the only ones not only to preach but also to <u>practice</u> complete personal religious freedom, meaning:
      b. The right to interpret religion & the Bible in the light of individual conscience & reason
   2. Natural tendency of Anabaptist groups constantly to split up due to disagreements over Biblical interpretations:
      a. Famous aphorism: the only thing on which they agreed was their right to disagree
      b. Potential extension of this doctrine to the point of anarchy or "antinomianism" (Greek for "against law"), meaning each man to determine his own law in a dangerous justification for free love, murder, & whatever
   3. Usual recruitment from the poor, downtrodden, & uneducated populace of cities & small towns alienated from the social mainstream that persecuted them severely--Calvin described Anabaptists as "those who live pell mell like rats in the straw"[11]
   4. Feature of highly emotional worship-services with singing & dancing & "holy rolling"--yet most Anabaptists pursuing quiet & simple & exemplary lives in communes imitating primitive early Christians--tradition of pacifism & asceticism & suspicion toward powerful government among some Anabaptists
   5. Modern descendants including Baptists, Quakers, Hutterites, Mennonites, & Amish
G. Unitarianism
   1. A Protestant strain close to Anabaptism stressing a denial of the Trinity & the full divinity of Christ--interpretation of Christ as the Son of God but more mortal than immortal, thus facilitating human identification with Christ in a mystical sense
   2. Evolution of Unitarianism by the late-18th century into a highly intellectual faith rejecting the Trinity as irrational and viewing Christ simply as a particularly inspirational human being

Chapter 7   EARLY MODERN EUROPE & THE AGE OF ABSOLUTISM: 1500--1715

I. Introduction
   A. Emergence in Western Europe by the first half of the 1500's of the modern "nation-state"; characteristics of the "nation-state":
      1. A largely centralized form of government ruled by a monarch of a certain dynastic royal family
      2. A professional civilian bureaucracy or administrative system staffed mainly by members of the educated bourgeoisie loyal to the monarch rather than by members of the unreliable nobility usually seeking to weaken national interests while promoting their own local & provincial interests
      3. A legal system of courts attempting to apply uniform laws throughout the entire nation--the king's law representing greater fairness in justice than local aristocratic courts
      4. Armies composed of hired mercenaries replacing feudal levies of lower noblemen (knights)
      5. A national financial system & a treasury to manage taxation, to issue currency, & to monitor royal expenditures
   B. The Era of Religious & Dynastic Wars: 1500--1660
      1. Occurrence during this roughly century-&-a-half epoch of a multitude of devastating & horrifying wars, probably the worst in history thus far because of:
         a. Possession by royal governments of more power & control over the resources of their states
         b. Larger & better organized armies equipped with more terrifying & effective weaponry than ever before
         c. Greater sources of wealth to fight over as the spoils of war--especially colonial empires & world trade
         d. Religious fanaticism unleashed by the Reformation--many massacres ensuing from the demonization of one Christian group by another--religious leaders characterizing each other as followers of Satan & personifications of evil
      2. Development of the first important nation-states in Spain, France, & England--domination of international affairs by the dynastic rulers of those countries during the first half of the 16th century: Charles V., Francis I., Henry VIII.

II. The Age of Charles V.
   A. Charles V. (1519--56) of the Hapsburg Dynasty:
      1. Most powerful figure in Europe during this era--heir to a vast empire comparable to that earlier of Charlemagne, thus causing most other rulers to fear his domination of all Europe
      2. Acquisition of his extensive territorial inheritance by marriage alliances over several generations rather than by military conquest--thus the famous phrase of the time: "Let others wage war; thou, happy Austria, marry."
      3. Territories & lands:
         a. Prestigious title of German (Holy Roman) Emperor (yet exerting little or no authority over the many other German states & rulers) and the traditional Hapsburg lands of Austria (capital--Vienna) in southeastern Germany--both inherited from his grandfather Maximilian I.
         b. Wealthy regions of modern Holland (the Netherlands), Belgium, & Luxembourg (collectively called the Low Countries) plus the lands of Burgundy in central-eastern

            France--all inherited from his mother Mary of Burgundy
        c. Spain & the Latin American Colonies of the New World--
            this era being part of the "Golden Age of Spain" as the
            most powerful nation in Europe--an inheritance from his
            insane mother Joanna (daughter of Ferdinand & Isabella:
            1479--1516)
        d. Existence of the Latin American Empire as the primary
            source of wealth for Spain & Charles after the enslave-
            ment of Aztec & Inca Indians by the conquistadores and
            the confiscation of tons of gold & silver for the Span-
            ish treasury
        e. Direct rule over the Italian states of Naples, Sicily, &
            Sardinia--later conquest of Milan
        f. Appearance of enormous size & awesome strength by this
            empire, yet persistence of many weaknesses
    4. Weaknesses & disadvantages of Charles' empire:
        a. Lack of geographical unity, with lands scattered over
            thousands of miles & impossible to rule effectively
        b. Persistence of different political traditions & instit-
            utions in the many regions & countries
        c. Existence of many languages--Charles once said: "To God
            I speak Spanish, to women Italian, to men French, and to
            my horse--German."
        d. Inclusion of diverse nationalities & ethnic groups with
            little in common with the others
    5. Devotion of his entire reign by Charles to defending his terr-
        itories from a multitude of enemies--perpetual military cam-
        paigns on many fronts & in many countries:
        a. The Ottoman Turkish Empire in the southeastern European
            region known as the Balkan Peninsula--conquest by the
            Turks of Hungary on the German border and two Turkish
            sieges of Vienna during this era--Charles driving back
            the Turks & retaining his possessions after a long
            struggle & a military stalemate
        b. Italy--successful yet costly defense of his territories
            by Charles against French & Italian adversaries
        c. Germany--late wars (1546--55) vs. the Lutheran princes
            organized into the League of Schmalkalden--consequence
            of exhaustive deadlock & failure to reimpose Catholicism
            on Protestants--negotiation of a compromise permitting
            each German ruler to determine the religion of his realm
        d. France--a protracted & expensive dynastic conflict known
            as the Hapsburg-Valois War (religion being no factor
            here in wars between Catholic monarchs) ending with no
            major gains on either side
    6. Abdication of the throne in 1556 by Charles due to fatigue,
        exhaustion, & premature aging--realization that no one man
        could rule the entire empire--thus the decision to divide the
        empire between his brother & his son:
        a. Ferdinand I. (his brother) to receive the German lands of
            Austria plus the title of Holy Roman Emperor
        b. Philip II. (his son) to inherit everything else, includ-
            ing Spain & the New World
B. Francis I. (1515--47) of the Valois Dynasty in France:
    1. The primary adversary of Charles in war & diplomacy often los-
        ing battles but surviving the rigors of war for France

2. A handsome, vain, frivolous, & unscrupulous man of very mediocre abilities--one critic stating the he had "a fatal flaw for snatching defeat from the jaws of victory"
  C. Henry VIII. (1509--47) of the Tudor Dynasty in England:
   1. A renowned ruler having a huge impact on English history and the history of the English-speaking world
   2. His accomplishments--inauguration of the Reformation with the Anglican Church, establishment of a modern national government with administrative departments
   3. Marriage to six wives (two of whom he beheaded) before dying in excruciating misery of syphilis
   4. Commencement of a foreign policy of preserving the balance of power on the European Continent (by attempting to throw English support to weaker states) in order to bring gains or diplomatic leverage to England
    a. Failure by Henry to achieve much by this policy
    b. Yet many successes to follow in the future by others

III. The Age of Philip II. (1556--98)
  A. Philip II.--ruler of Spain during its golden age when Spain was the wealthiest & most powerful nation of Europe
   1. Personality & background--born & raised a Spaniard with a narrow patriotism--bigoted, vain, unimaginative, & lacking in an understanding of men
   2. Manifestation of religious fanaticism--relentless hatred of heresy--belief in himself as the chosen instrument of God & Catholicism
  B. Four goals, objectives, & policies--two international, two domestic
   1. Conquest or domination of Europe, thus a vigorous aggression in the wars of the second half of the 16th century
   2. Restoration of Catholicism as the universal religion, thus requiring the destruction of Protestantism everywhere
   3. Centralization & absolutism in his territories--this policy working fairly successfully in Spain but often failing disastrously elsewhere

   4. Persecution & repression of suspected nonconformists--two groups in Spain being targeted:
    a. Moriscos--Christians of Moorish or Moslem background, or former Moslems who converted to Catholicism after 1492 yet whose devotion to Christianity was always questioned by the Spanish government
    b. Marranos--Christians of Jewish background, or former Jews who also converted to Catholicism under pressure & threat of expulsion and whose faith & fervor was also suspected by the government that often confiscated the property of suspects
    c. Use of the Inquisition--a church court employed to question & torture potential heretics with guilty persons turned over to the government for execution by burning at the stake in a notorious ceremony & act known as the <u>auto-da-fe</u>
  C. The Counter-Reformation Era--this period witnessing aggressive Catholic efforts to restore religious orthodoxy by any means & at any price
  D. Areas of Spanish involvement diplomatically & militarily:

1. Italy--successful yet costly Spanish defense of territories there & domination of most of the peninsula
2. The Mediterranean Sea vs. the Ottoman Turks--generally expensive yet victorious naval conflicts for control of trade, with the Turks remaining a formidable adversary--a renowned Spanish victory at Lepanto in 1571
3. The Netherlands (Holland, or the United Provinces)--a massive & eventually successful rebellion against Spanish rule called the Dutch Revolt (1566--1609): details mentioned below
4. France--Philip's intervention in a French civil war known as the Wars of Religion (1562--98) ending in failure to favor the cause of Catholic fanaticism & to become king of France
5. Scotland--Philip's efforts to strengthen his ally Mary Stuart, Queen of Scots and to promote her as monarch of Protestant England finally resulting in disaster--more details below
6. England--attempts by Philip to invade & conquer England with the Spanish Armada in 1588 bringing catastrophe & opening up the colonies & commerce of the New World to other nations

E. The Dutch Revolt (1566--1609) against Spain
   1. Causes:
      a. Religious--most Dutch people became Calvinist; Spanish rulers were fanatically Catholic and tried to eliminate heresy forcibly & brutally
      b. Political--there were Spanish violations of traditional Dutch provincial liberties & privileges and local governmental powers
      c. Economic--heavy Spanish restrictions & regulations stifled Dutch shipping & seaborne trade
      d. Economic--crushing Spanish taxation alienated the Dutch
   2. Reasons for eventual Dutch victory:
      a. Heroic & dedicated resistance against overwhelming odds inspired by Spanish atrocities in the form of tortures, executions, & property confiscations--consideration of the revolt by most Dutch people as a noble cause & absolute necessity worth any sacrifice
      b. Martyrdom of the Dutch leader William of Orange (called "the Silent") assassinated by hired thugs of Philip II.
      c. Efficient organization by the Dutch resistance groups
      d. Military & financial assistance from England
   3. Results--division & split of the Low Countries that were never completely united on political & religious matters:
      a. The northern provinces of Holland or the Netherlands granted independence from Spain
      b. The southern provinces of modern Belgium (still predominantly Catholic) remained under Spanish control

F. The French Wars of Religion (1562--98)
   1. Occurrence of a civil war between extreme Catholics and the minority Huguenots (Calvinists)
   2. Wish by the French kings & government to maintain Catholicism as the official church in France because:
      a. They were already powerful enough to control some taxes & appointments of the Catholic Church in France (known as the Gallican Church)
      b. Calvinism favored local independence of churches, thus potentially limiting the capacity of national government

              to dominate or manipulate religious matters
   3. Reign during this civil war by three weak & ineffective kings
      under the influence of queen-mother Catherine de'Medici, with
      the national government caught in the middle between extrem-
      ist groups and unable to manage the crisis or restore peace
      or favor the triumph of a moderate Catholic cause
   4. Termination of the Valois Dynasty in 1589 with the death of
      Henry III., provoking a crisis because the heir to the throne
      (Henri de Bourbon, now Henry IV.) was leader of the Huguenot
      armies & cause and thus unacceptable to most Catholics
   5. Conclusion of the wars by the very capable & "good king" Henry
      IV. in two ways:
      a. Personal conversion to Catholicism--more than anything
         else, this ended the conflict & reconciled to his rule
         the vast majority of Frenchmen who could never accept a
         Protestant monarch
      b. Issuance of the Edict of Nantes (1598) granting a limited
         form of religious toleration to Huguenots with permiss-
         ion to worship in and to fortify & garrison for defense
         certain designated cities
   6. Failure of Philip II.'s intervention in French affairs:
      a. His marriage to the last Valois princess in hopes of
         gaining the French throne thwarted by a law favoring
         any heir from the male branch of the family
      b. Demise of the cause of Catholic extremism in France des-
         pite the dispatch of arms, soldiers, & money by Philip
G. England under Elizabeth I. (1558--1603):
   1. Elizabeth I.--one of England's greatest monarchs having a huge
      future impact and possessing a fascinating personality
   2. Refusal ever to marry due to a distrust of men & a wish to be
      independent following the execution of her mother (Anne Bol-
      eyn) by her father (Henry VIII.) as well as an experience of
      sexual molestation as an adolescent
   3. Dynastic status of Elizabeth as the 3rd & last of Henry VIII's
      children to reign, after Edward VI. (1547--53) & Mary Tudor
      (1553--58)
   4. England now envisioning future greatness economically in col-
      onies & commerce--yet these aspirations bringing direct con-
      frontations with Spain, the nation dominating the Americas &
      possessing the most powerful armies & navies in the world:
      a. Unofficial approval by the Queen for English privateers &
         pirates (called "sea dogs") to prey on the Spanish Main
         (Latin American colonies) & to attack treasure ships,
         with most of the booty enriching government coffers
      b. Failure by Philip II. to eliminate Elizabeth with diplo-
         macy & assassination attempts--then a final decision to
         invade & conquer Protestant England with a naval exped-
         ition carrying armies
      c. Decisive defeat of the Spanish "Invincible" Armada in
         1588--this English victory breaking the Spanish monopo-
         ly over the New World colonies & commerce and opening
         the way for involvement of other nations
   5. Achievements of Elizabeth I:
      a. The Elizabethan Settlement (1563)--a compromise developed
         by the Queen in religious matters to make the doctrine &
         theology of the Anglican Church deliberately vague &

general and thus acceptable to a majority of people--a very successful policy in the long term
  b. Creation of a highly efficient & effective national government staffed with able & intelligent administrators & advisors chosen by the Queen
  c. Skillful & proper relations with Parliament--usual domination by Elizabeth, who nonetheless observed its traditional powers over taxation & rights of consultation
  d. Much economic expansion & prosperity during the era
  e. A cultural flowering of Renaissance art & especially literature, partly inspired & encouraged by the Queen--many works by Shakespeare, Marlowe, Jonson, Spenser, etc.
  f. Final conquest of all Ireland (religiously Catholic) after four centuries of only partial English control and many revolts & troubles--this being necessary because of Ireland now posing as a potentially dangerous landing base for powerful enemies of England like Spain & France
  g. Famous rivalry with her beautiful cousin & heir to the English throne--Mary Stuart, Queen of Scots (see below)

H. Scotland:
  1. Existence of Scotland up to this point in history as a separate & independent nation from England with a tradition for hostility toward & intervention in the affairs of each other
    a. Both nations culturally mixed, with the Scots being largely Celtic or Gaelic, and with the English being mainly German & partly French
    b. Backwardness in every regard characterizing Scotland in comparison to England, with closer Continental contacts
  2. Rule in Scotland by the Stuart (sometimes spelled Stewart) Dynasty--marriage by James V. (1513--42) into a powerful French Catholic family, his wife being Marie de Guise & their daughter being Mary Stuart
  3. Background of Mary Stuart:
    a. A beautiful & passionate yet foolish & reckless woman raised & educated in France as a fervent Catholic
    b. Brief marriage to the king of France (Francis II: 1559--1560) till his premature death
    c. Decision to return to Scotland as the rightful queen succeeding her father
    d. Status & position also as heir to the English throne after Elizabeth because of Mary's grandmother (Margaret Tudor) being the sister of Henry VIII.--this fact making Mary Stuart & Elizabeth I. cousins
  4. Conversion of Scotland during the 1550's to Calvinism (Presbyterianism) by preacher John Knox
  5. The reign of Mary Stuart (1561--68) to be brief, turbulent, & controversial--<u>four</u> factors leading to her demise:
    a. Religion--Mary was Catholic; most of her subjects were Calvinists deeply suspicious of their queen
    b. Politics--her policies of centralization & absolutism provoking rebellion from some of the powerful local family-clans of nobility
    c. Status as heir to the English throne--this fact leading to plots & other efforts to stimulate her downfall
    d. Scandalous lifestyle--Mary was indiscreet in her love affairs & probably conspired in the murder of her 2nd

husband (Henry Stewart, Lord Darnley)--then she took one
of the conspirators as her next lover
   6. Deposition & imprisonment of Mary in 1567 by an aristocratic
      revolt--voluntary exile to England in 1568
   7. Her status as a Catholic heir to the English Protestant throne
      now threatening English national security & stability and re-
      quiring her perpetual detention in various manor houses for
      nineteen years
   8. Organization by Philip II. & some English Catholics of four
      different plots to assassinate Elizabeth--failures all
   9. Execution finally in 1587 at the chopping block for Mary after
      Elizabeth succumbing to heavy pressure from Parliament, her
      primary ministers, & the English public
      a. Her death precipitating the sending of the Spanish Armada
         in the next year--1588
      b. Accession of her son immediately to the Scottish throne
         as James VI. and in 1603 as James I. of England--James
         being raised nominally as a Protestant

IV. Economic Theory & Practice
   A. Evolution during this era of the policies & ideas of "mercantilism"
      for the most successful management of a capitalistic economy
   B. Application of mercantilism throughout Europe from 1500 to 1800,
      although precise measures differed from country to country
   C. Primary goal--achievement of national self-sufficiency & economic
      independence, thus promoting prosperity & power
   D. Policies & practices of mercantilism:
      1. A favorable balance of trade, meaning that exports exceed im-
         ports, to be encouraged by protective tariffs on imports &
         bounties on exports
      2. Accumulation of gold & silver (bullion)--regard for precious
         metals as the most basic form of wealth, as a major measure
         of strength, & as the medium of international transactions

      3. Strict economic control & regulation by the central government
         of industry, commerce, & labor--gradual extension of bureau-
         cratic planning & management over many sectors of the economy
      4. Use of colonies or dependencies for materials & markets &
         cheap labor--production within national borders of all com-
         modities necessary for existence
      5. Stimulation of deficiencies in farming & manufacturing with
         governmental subsidies, tax exemptions, monopolies, etc.
   E. Consequences--good & bad:
      1. Great expansion of national economies & world trade, estab-
         lishment & exploitation of European colonial empires abroad,
         and gradual improvements in living standards (especially for
         the bourgeoisie)
      2. Occasional discouragement of economic activity because of gov-
         mental intrusion & suffocation--frequent neglect of local
         needs as well as market forces of supply & demand--elevation
         of the national well-being over the individual welfare

V. The Four Significant Developments of the First Half of the 17th Century
   A. Rapid decline of Spain from greatness to a 2nd-rate power
   B. The English Civil War & Revolution (1640--60), with the consequent
      triumph of Parliament & the constitutional monarchy in England

    C. Establishment of the absolute monarchy in France, resulting from the policies & efforts of Henry IV. (1598--1609) and of ministers Richelieu (1624--42) & Mazarin (1642--61)
    D. The Thirty Years' War (1618--48) in Germany as a major catastrophe

VI. Reasons For the Rapid Decline of Spain
    A. The immense cost of incessant wars in money, men, & material
    B. A major decline in population from eight to five million between 1550 & 1650 because of emigration to the colonies or death in wars
    C. Failure to develop a strong, self-sufficient economy:
       1. Over-reliance on the riches of its American colonies while neglecting the development of domestic manufacturing, the result being a serious trade imbalance & deficit
       2. Too much governmental interference & regulation in some economic sectors, thus stifling certain business enterprises
       3. Permission for only a few merchants with monopolies to profit from the New World commerce--imposition of heavy & unfair taxes on the small number of bourgeoisie
       4. Gross governmental mismanagement of the economy due to rampant corruption & incompetence
    D. The character of the Spanish people as the most un-European of all Western Europeans--preservation of a medieval mentality in a backward & feudal society:
       1. Frequent contempt for the activities of businessmen--prevalence of the popular view that hard work for material wealth was undignified
       2. The most respected occupations in Spain: priest, soldier, nobleman, & peasant farmer (the latter being notoriously lazy)--all four career-types contributing little or nothing to the economy
       3. The most important values & priorities of Spanish civilization directing attention away from industrial & business matters
    E. Regionalism & provincialism--most Spaniards holding a very narrow outlook on the world and extending their greatest loyalty to & identification with local & regional institutions, in spite of a fairly strong central government in Spain
    F. Religious intolerance & fanaticism--the result being repression of all nonconformity & free thought as well as inhibition of modern science & technology
       1. Persistence of the Inquisition as a special ecclesiastic court employing torture to enforce religious & social uniformity
       2. The essence of Spanish civilization symbolized perfectly in Miguel de Cervantes' <u>Don Quixote</u>, its hero being stubborn, impractical, & superstitious

VII. The Thirty Years' War: 1618--48
    A. Causes:
       1. Religious--part of a continuous struggle in almost equally divided Germany between Catholics & Protestants (mostly Lutherans) to dominate or eradicate the other
       2. Political--this war to be the last political & military campaign by German (Holy Roman) emperors of the Hapsburg Dynasty to unify all of Germany under a strong & centralized government & absolute monarchy--resistance coming from hundreds of virtually independent territorial states ruled by princes
       3. Dynastic--the continuation of long-term diplomatic & military

confrontations among the ruling families of the major European states for supremacy in Europe, especially between the Hapsburgs of Spain & Austria and now the Bourbons of France
    a. This war fought exclusively in Germany but eventually involving on one side or the other all the major states of Europe--France, Spain, Holland, Sweden, & Denmark in addition to all the German states
    b. The only important nation not involved being England, in distraction from its own domestic problems & turmoil
  4. Traditional--the normal ambitions & greed of all nations & states for power, riches, & territorial aggrandizement
B. Four phases of the conflict:
  1. The Bohemian Phase: 1618--25
    a. A revolt for religious & political freedom by the largely Protestant Czech people of Bohemia against oppressive rule by the Catholic Hapsburgs of Austria--rapid defeat of the Czechs by the Austrians with horrifying reprisals committed against the Czechs thereafter
    b. These events sparking a general conflagration all over Germany between opposing coalitions & alliance systems with shocking instances of brutality & fanaticism
    c. Thus far, events favoring triumph of the Hapsburg & Imperial cause
  2. The Danish Phase: 1625--29
    a. Intervention by the king of Denmark & his armies on the side of the Protestants & German princes--failure & a quick defeat for Denmark
    b. This period witnessing the zenith of Catholic & Hapsburg Imperial ascendancy with policies of extreme religious persecution & land confiscations
  3. The Swedish Phase: 1630--35
    a. Invasion by Sweden under the leadership of its brilliant king Gustavus Adolphus (the "Lion of the North") & with its superb fighting forces on the side of Protestants & the German princes
    b. Several Swedish victories turning the tide briefly until the tragic death in battle of Gustavus, after which a deadlock or stalemate prevailed between the two sides for several years--neither side capable of completely overwhelming the other
  4. The French Phase: 1635--48
    a. The Catholicism of France now insignificant, as its leaders (Cardinals Richelieu & Mazarin) intervened on the side of the Protestants & German princes and against the traditional Hapsburg foes of France
    b. Religion mattering for nothing in these aspirations by Richelieu & Mazarin to make France the greatest power in European affairs
    c. Final triumph of the excellent French armies with the Swedes & Dutch & Protestants & individual German princes --defeat of the Catholics & the Austrian & Spanish Hapsburgs & the centralization efforts in Germany
    d. Culmination in the Treaty of Westphalia--1648
C. Results of the war:
  1. Emergence of France as the most powerful nation in Europe
  2. Recognition of the political independence of each German ruler

or prince within his territories with power to choose the religion of his subjects--this determining political decentralization & German disunity for over 200 years more as well as religious fragmentation on a permanent basis
3. Catastrophic consequences for Germany--the greatest disaster in its history with the exception of Hitler, Nazism, & World War II:
   a. A severe population decline due to deaths from warfare, disease, & starvation--estimation of 8 million Germans killed, constituting one-third of its entire population
   b. Widespread devastation & destruction of property & entire villages & food supplies--thus a disruption of all society & the whole economy
   c. Infliction of the most suffering on the bourgeoisie (middle class) of society--future weakness of the middle class strengthening political despotism and thus harming the development of representative & democratic government as well as social mobility
   d. Encouragement of callous & insensitive attitudes among Germans after nearly three decades of savage atrocities committed by armies tending to brutalize & dehumanize the population while living off the land
   e. Evolution of certain famous German characteristics in response to the war--an obsession for law & order & personal security at any price (even if costing freedom), and an inclination toward unquestioning obedience to higher authority (in fear that failure to do so resulting in chaos & horror similar to this national calamity)

III. The English Revolution: 1640--60
   A. Introduction
      1. Recognition of the English Revolution of the mid-17th century as one of the _three_ most significant revolutionary movements in all of history, the other two being the:
         a. French Revolution (1789--1815) and Russian or Bolshevik Revolution (1917--21) but _not_ the:
         b. American Revolution (1775--81), which merely constituted a reaffirmation of the principles & ideals of the 17th-century English Revolution--Americans enjoyed only a little more freedom after our Revolution than before--it was more sound than substance, rhetoric over reality
      2. Emergence of Parliament by the reign of the Tudor Dynasty (1485--1603) as a regular, necessary, & permanent part of the English government, with traditional powers of approval over taxation & of consultation over major developments
      3. The 16th-century relationship between Crown & Parliament balanced overwhelmingly in favor of a much more powerful monarchy--that fact to change drastically in the 17th century
      4. Division of Parliament into two houses, with legislation requiring consent of both of them:
         a. House of Lords--hereditary membership for the great noblemen & dignitaries of the realm
         b. House of Commons--unique inclusion of representatives of the urban bourgeoisie & the lower level aristocracy (knights or gentry of the shires)

           c. Elections to Commons far from "democratic" with less than
              5% of the population eligible to vote--yet Members of
              Parliament (MP's) theoretically representing the inter-
              ests of the entire nation
        5. Convulsion of England during the 17th century over two central
           problems: religious, and political or constitutional
   B. Causes:
        1. Political or constitutional--Parliament vs. Monarchy--the
           Stuarts (unlike their Tudor predecessors) openly espousing
           royal absolutism while refusing to cooperate with Parliament
           or to obtain its consent for royal acts
        2. Economic:
           a. Constant indebtedness by the royal government, which re-
              sorted to the collection of illegal taxes and extra-
              ordinary & unfair revenue measures
           b. This era experiencing severe inflation and social & econ-
              omic disruptions due to a volatile capitalist system in
              a state of rapid change or flux
        3. Religious:
           a. Upset of the Elizabethan Compromise by the Stuart kings
              in their favoritism of High Church Anglicans (those de-
              siring a Catholic-like ritual, doctrine, & hierarchical
              organization more easily controlled by the national gov-
              ernment)--pursuit of these unpopular policies by Arch-
              bishop William Laud
           b. Mounting opposition from extreme Protestant (Calvinist)
              groups like English Puritans & Scots Presbyterians de-
              manding local church independence & no royal intrusion
        4. Personal--tactless & uncompromising traits plus inept policies
           of the Stuart kings James I. (1603--25) & Charles I. (1625--
           49) very unpopular partly due to their foreign background
           from Scotland, as the son & grandson of Mary Stuart
   C. Major events of the times:
        1. Decision by Charles I. to reign as an absolute monarch--rule
           without calling Parliament for 12 years--then precipitation
           of an armed revolt in Scotland over religious interference
           by the royal government
        2. Military preparations for the Bishops' Wars of 1639--40 neces-
           sitating much new money & thus the calling of Parliament to
           vote for major tax collection
        3. Short Parliament (April-May, 1640)--a brief meeting with much
           hostility & bitter debates--demands by Parliament of a sur-
           render of royal power--dissolution by Charles yet a continu-
           ation of the crisis
        4. Long Parliament (1640--53, later recalled briefly in 1660 to
           end the Revolutionary Era):
           a. The royal government bereft of funds & financially des-
              perate--only Parliament capable of providing money--
              immediate Parliamentary passage of laws destroying much
              royal authority & limiting monarchical power in 1640--41
           b. Decision by the king to fight rather than capitulate--
              failure of an attempted arrest & seizure of Parliament-
              ary leaders by the king--departure from London to rally
              provincial support & commence the:
           c. Civil War (1642--46): essentially a religious & political
              struggle between King & Parliament whose supporters were

called Cavaliers (many aristocratic dandies served the king as cavalrymen) and Roundheads (the mop-topped, shaggy, Beattle-style haircut of the 1960's [so scandalous & controversial in conservative America] originated with the Puritans, who put bowls over their heads & cut everything else)
   d. Crucial role in the Parliamentary victory of Oliver Cromwell, as the Puritan general forming superb & dedicated fighting units comprised of religious zealots known as the "Ironsides"--defeat & capture of the king by 1646
   e. Foolish intransigence by Charles I. in captivity and his refusal to negotiate with Parliamentary leaders or to make any concessions leading to a radicalization of the events
5. Occurrence of a Revolution & 2nd Civil War (1647--48) resulting from divisions in the Parliamentarians (over religion, a future form of government, & the king's fate) and a power struggle between:
   a. Moderates--Scots Presbyterians & most Anglicans favoring a constitutional monarchy politically (a balance between Crown & Parliament), vs....
   b. Radicals--Puritans (sometimes called Independents or Congregationalists) demanding the supremacy of Parliament politically & a republic (meaning abolition of the monarchy) in government
6. Triumph of the radicals in 1648--defeat on the battlefield of their opponents by Cromwell in August, and elimination of their political enemies in December with Pride's Purge of ninety-six moderate members of Parliament--always the key to victory being control of the army by the Puritans
7. Establishment of the Puritan Republic (1649--53), or the Commonwealth, by only sixty members remaining from the original 500 members of the Long Parliament--now called the Rump Parliament because it still sat as the national government
   a. Trial & execution (January 1649) of Charles I. by the Rump Parliament--the king meeting his death with quiet & courageous dignity which inspired reference to the Shakespearean quote: "Nothing in his life became him, like the leaving it."
   b. Actual existence of the Republic during the Rump Parliament as a dictatorship by a radical but well-organized minority of Puritans imposing its policies with military might on an unwilling English population
   c. A "Reign of Terror & Virtue"--characterization of this period as one of excess & extremism with harsh "blue laws" closing ale houses & prohibiting all forms of worldly pleasure--these measures of puritanical morality were too severe to survive & alienated most Englishmen
8. The Protectorate (1653--58): Cromwellian military dictatorship after his forcible dissolution of the Rump Parliament, followed by brief yet abortive efforts by the "Lord Protector" to rule with newly elected assemblies
   a. Description of Cromwell as a reluctant ruler & unwilling dictator who embodied the only alternative to a return of the Stuarts or the fanaticism of Puritan extremists
   b. Personality of Cromwell: moderate by Puritan standards,

earnest, sincere, patriotic, lacking in great ambition, stubborn yet willing to compromise
      c. Impossibility at this time to achieve his simple desire for relative toleration & constitutional government
      d. Yet intense hatred of Catholicism--Cromwell's invasion of of Ireland earlier in 1649-50 to suppress a rebellion eventually causing the death of more than one half million Irishmen (over one-third of the population)
      e. Death of Cromwell in 1658--misrule & weakness & anarchy under his incompetent son Richard ("Tumble Down Dick")--reconvocation of the original members of the Long Parliament, making the only plausible decision to recall the Stuarts from exile in France
   9. The Stuart Restoration in 1660 with Charles II. (1660--85): monumental agreement by the king to rule with Parliament in a form of government known as "constitutional or limited monarchy", thereby achieving a power balance between Monarchy and Parliament
   10. Appearance during the Revolution of extremist groups:
      a. Levellers--anticipation of political democracy with the advocacy of universal suffrage, progressive taxation, a written constitution, separation of church & state, and protection of individuals against arbitrary arrest
      b. Diggers--early socialists or communists repudiating the existence of private property & unequal wealth
      c. Fifth Monarchy Men (Millenarians)--believers in the imminent 2nd Coming of Christ and utopia on earth
      d. Quakers ("Society of Friends")--extreme yet humanitarian, tolerant, pacifist, anti-slavery Protestants

D. Positive accomplishments & legacy of the Revolution:
   1. Firm establishment of the principle of representative & constitutional government in England
   2. Emergence of a greatly strengthened Parliament possessing the capacity to prevent royal absolutism permanently
   3. Strong promotion of the idea of religious toleration & abhorrence of fanaticism as worthy goals of society
   4. Frequent discussion of basic human freedoms such as speech, press, assembly, & protest as important ideals of the future

E. Persistence of reckless & illegal policies by Charles II. & his brother James II. (1685--88) in unsettling the political & religious arrangements:
   1. Conspiracies by Charles II. throughout his reign either to weaken & dominate Parliamentary opposition or to rule without the body altogether--also he was secretly a Catholic promoting its cause against virulent public protest
   2. Refusal by James II. to work with Parliament, open declaration of himself as a Catholic king over a nation fearfully paranoid toward Catholicism, and birth of his son & heir provoking the Glorious Revolution in 1688

F. Development of two political parties in Parliament during the Restoration Era:
   1. Whigs (known later as the Liberals in the early 19th century)---composed of the great nobility & wealthy bourgeoisie and favoring religious toleration for Protestant minorities (now called Dissenters) and a political balance between Crown & Parliament

            2. Tories (known later as Conservatives by the 19th century)---
               represented the lesser aristocracy of gentry and favored re-
               ligious dominance of the Anglican Church as well as a more
               powerful Monarchy than Parliament
      G. The Glorious Revolution of 1688:
         1. Unity in opposition by the Parliamentary leaders of both part-
            ies to James II.--negotiation with William III. of Orange
            (leader of the Dutch Republic or Holland) & his wife Mary II.
            (James II's elder Protestant daughter by an earlier marriage)
            to occupy the English throne jointly

         2. Flight of James to France without a fight when few supported
            his cause--landing in England by William & Mary to accept the
            terms of Parliament
         3. Immense importance--this royal change being engineered by Par-
            liament with the dual monarchs owing their crowns to Parlia-
            ment--confirmation of Parliament by this Revolution as the
            dominant partner of the two & superior in the Crown in the
            final analysis
         4. Acceptance by William & Mary of the Bill of Rights in 1689:
            a. This document constituting a summary of English constit-
               utional practices that established Parliamentary suprem-
               acy over the Monarchy through control over taxation,
               royal incapacity to suspend laws, guarantees against ar-
               bitrary arrest, and certainty of Parliamentary meetings
            b. However, this English document not resembling the later
               American Bill of Rights, which enumerated basic individ-
               ual freedoms of the citizen

IX. Louis XIV. of France (1643--1715)
    A. Introduction
       1. Perfect personification by King Louis XIV. of royal absolutism
          & the theory of the "divine right of kings", which provided
          religious justification for monarchs exercising unlimited
          political power--thus the belief that God ruled the world
          through these divinely-inspired individuals
       2. Description of this era of the Old Regime as the Age of Abso-
          lutism (1660--1789), the dominating spirit of the times
       3. Classification of the 2nd half of the 17th century as the "Age
          of Louis XIV." because he so impressively ruled the leading
          European nation, France--Louis known as Le Grand Monarque:
          a. Inheritance of the crown at age 4 1/2 in 1643--rule by
             Cardinal Mazarin as chief minister for the first 18
             years until death in 1661--assumption of the reins of
             government thereafter by the King--one of the longest
             reigns of any major monarch in history at 72 years
          b. Famous phrase demonstrating his belief in royal absolut-
             ism: "L'Etat, c'est moi." (I am the State)
          c. Renown as the "Sun King"--just as the sun was the match-
             less celestial body of power & radiance in the heavens,
             so Louis XIV. dominated France soon after that nation
             became the arbiter of all Europe
          d. Description of his reign--long, splendid, prestigious, &
             memorable yet flawed by heavy governmental debts, ignor-
             ed problems, & failure to fulfill its enormous potential

            e. Yet mastery by the King of the entire French state while
               achieving order, stability, & national unity and main-
               taining a balance among turbulent nobles, ambitious
               bourgeois, & oppressed peasants
   B. Personality of Louis:
      1. Lacking in "greatness" because of only average intelligence,
         poor education, & absence of extraordinary talents
      2. Yet effectiveness as a ruler emanating from self-discipline,
         patience, tireless energy & fortitude, a strong physical
         constitution, a handsome demeanor, natural grace & dignity
         (important in an age when public appearances counted for
         much), calm resolution, & devotion to work
      3. His most impressive quality: a willingness to work hard & a
         dedication to his duties as king with a remarkable capacity
         to endure 18-hour work days on a consistent basis
      4. Possession also of an ability to judge men's character & to
         choose competent subordinates & to consider decisions care-
         fully--derivation of enjoyment by the King from the routine
         of council meetings & ceremonious occasions
   C. Limitations on the powers of 17th & 18th century monarchs--possess-
      ion by rulers on only theoretical & not real authority:
      1. Slow communication & transportation facilities--thus the im-
         possibility to implement national governmental policies on a
         short-term basis
      2. Survival of medieval diversities in language (hundreds of dif-
         ferent dialects existed in France alone, making verbal inter-
         changes very difficult), law (more than 100 different local
         codes existed), customs, and traditions (weights & measures,
         coinage)--rendering centralized uniformity non-existent
      3. Persistence of privileged social groups & economic corporat-
         ions retaining feudal rights, immunities, & status which
         could not be violated even by the king--groups such as the
         nobility, clergy, provincial courts & representative assemb-
         lies, and guilds (trade & craft unions)
      4. Governmental incompetence--existence of cumbersome & ineff-
         icient bureaucracies riddled with overlapping jurisdiction,
         red tape, & confusion--Louis tried to rule France through
         four royal councils, none of which functioned properly
      5. Tradition of local governmental independence--customary disre-
         gard by provincial rulers toward centralized authority--real
         influence by national over local or regional government being
         extremely weak
      6. Ignorance & stupidity of monarchs--poor educations & mental
         deficiencies often wrecking the policies of rulers inheriting
         their right to rule
      7. Ironically, 20th century presidents & prime ministers of mod-
         ern democracies exercising more power over their populations
         & nations than did 17th-18th century absolute monarchs, the
         difference being a matter of degrees of efficiency, centrali-
         zation, & capacity of government to command large numbers of
         people through modern technology
   C. Social & class structure--division into three orders or "estates":
      1. 1st Estate--Clergy:
         a. Less than 1% of the population, yet highly privileged by
            paying no direct taxes on land or wealth and by dominat-
            ing the lives & minds of the popular masses

  b. Gallicanism--traditional movement within the French Catholic Church for independence from the Papacy in Rome by extending its initial allegiance to the French monarchy---this "union of throne & altar" reaching its zenith under Louis XIV.
 2. 2nd Estate--Nobility: less than 2% of the French population--two types of noblemen:
  a. Nobility of the Sword--traditional aristocrats with a title & lands traced back many centuries, sometimes to the feudal era when their ancestors customarily fought
  b. Nobility of the Robe--former bourgeois commoners who were newly-created noblemen after serving as administrators, councilors, governors, or royal favorites, or after buying the status of aristocracy with much money
 3. 3rd Estate--Commoners: roughly 98% of the French population & including many professions:
  a. Peasantry--at least 80% of all in society--largely illiterate, overtaxed by government & exploited by the nobility, some owning a little piece of land but most renting or sharecropping or working the land of others--mainly living lives of drudgery & misery
  b. Bourgeoisie--around 10% of the total population--business & professional people exhibiting a wide range of wealth & education, from rich merchants & bankers to governmental bureaucrats & lawyers to skilled artisans & craftsmen (the latter being the vast majority of this group)
  c. Proletariat--roughly 5-10% of society--lower class workers of the cities & countryside lacking land, skills or training, working tools, & steady employment

D. Governmental policies toward the nobility:
 1. Elimination of most of their traditional powers over local & regional government by Cardinal Richelieu (1624--42)--replacement with royal governors (<u>intendants</u>) responsible to the crown & central government directly
 2. Suppression of the last armed rebellions (the <u>Fronde</u>: 1648-53) against the national government by Mazarin
 3. Encouragement of the leading aristocrats by Louis XIV. to reside or visit often his royal palace of Versailles where he consoled them with pensions & gifts & sinecures & impressive yet unnecessary duties while keeping an eye on them & preventing them from organizing opposition from their provinces
 4. Consequences--perpetuation of their social & economic privileges (titles, property, tax-exemptions) with the destruction of their role in provincial government:
  a. Thus the reduction of the nobility to the status of parasites on society and a greater financial burden on the state & on the entire populace
  b. Rising & deepening resentment toward the nobility by the commoners

E. Economy:
 1. Achievement of great economic expansion & general prosperity under the mercantilistic policies of the most brilliant finance minister in French history: Jean-Baptiste Colbert
 2. Accomplishments:
  a. State revenues doubling in 10 years with the elimination

                of much waste & corruption
            b. Construction of an excellent navy & merchant fleet; foundation of overseas colonies & trading companies; establishment of schools to encourage invention & technological education; improvement of roads, canals, & harbors
            c. Stimulation of weak yet necessary industries with assistance from the national government
        3. Results--attainment of great prosperity during the 1st thirty years of Louis' reign and undoubted leadership in European commerce & industry--yet economic decline & loss of dominance to Britain after 1690
        4. Reasons for French economic decline after 1690:
            a. Death of Colbert in 1683--no one else capable of equalling his energy, intelligence, & talent in managing such a complex economy
            b. Too much regulation & governmental interference in some business affairs, thus tending to stifle individual initiative & to impede progress
            c. Ruinously expensive wars, thus a diversion of much investment capital from constructive to destructive purposes--this being the most important cause of decline
    F. Culture:
        1. Rise of France during the 17th century to a position of preeminence in high culture, partly due to generous royal patronage by the King who supported many artists with monetary grants & contracts
        2. Adoption by the remainder of Europe of the French style & taste & standards in manners, clothing, cuisine, language, art, & literature--the magnificent Moliere as well as Racine & Corneille were writing dramas & comedies in this century
        3. European adoption of French as the international language spoken by the upper classes and indispensable to a distinguished social or political or diplomatic career
        4. Construction of the Palace of Versailles, 11 miles southwest of Paris, and movement of the government there from Paris
            a. Rapid emergence as the wonder of all Europe with its grandiose classical exterior, elegant & lavish interior, and massive gardens
            b. A perfect setting for cultural events, ball, & state affairs where the King indulged his love of ceremony & ritual--his dinners & promenades & drives becoming major daily events attended at times by thousands
        5. Long-term disastrous impact on the monarchy of Versailles:
            a. Expensive costs of construction & maintenance contributing ultimately to mounting governmental debts
            b. Isolation of the royal family & court & government from the mainstream of society, especially the people of the Parisian capital:
                (1) The kings symbolically turning their backs on the French masses who paid heavy taxes to support the extravagances of Versailles
                (2) Popular beliefs increasing that the monarchy cared no longer about the suffering of commoners
            c. Encouragement of notoriety resulting from aristocratic waste, frivolity, contempt for the common masses, & immoral behavior with Louis XIV. setting the example of a

                    long succession of mistresses while fathering at least
                    thirty illegitimate children
    G. Religious persecution of minorities:
        1. Pursuit of policies of religious intolerance by the King as an
            extension of his political policies:
            a. Desire by the supporters of absolutism & centralization
                for uniformity in all things, thereby facilitating con-
                trol & regulation & manipulation

            b. Thus the stress by Louis XIV. on uniformity: one king,
                one system of law, & one religion--traditional Roman
                Catholicism
            c. Adoption by the King of the opinion that religious unor-
                thodoxy meant political disloyalty & potential treason
            d. Repression & persecution of several groups:
        2. Jansenists:
            a. Appearance of Jansenism as a reform movement within the
                Catholic Church--its followers called the "Puritans of
                the Catholic Church" for their austere morality & strong
                stand on predestination
            b. Severe criticism of the King's immoral behavior & sexual
                promiscuity with a stress on the human need to obey the
                authority of God when it conflicted with the authority
                of popes or monarchs
            c. Heavy royal repression of Jansenists--destruction of
                schools & churches and harassment of individuals--only
                partial success of this campaign as most Jansenists went
                from open to secret practices of the faith
            d. Existence of the Jansenists always as a small minority
                yet very prominent among business & professional people
                of wealth & education
            e. Persistence of the Jansenists into the next century work-
                ing in quiet yet effective opposition to monarchy & roy-
                al absolutism
        3. Quietists:
            a. Another reform group within the Catholic Church--emphasis
                on mysticism & emotional expression of the faith--most
                followers located at court
            b. Successful suppression by the King
        4. Huguenots:
            a. Prior grant by Henry IV. in 1598 of the Edict of Nantes
                extending religious freedom & full liberties of French
                citizenship
            b. Commencement by Louis XIV. of a campaign of reconversion
                to Catholicism--initial use of verbal persuasion & then
                bribery--later resort to forcible closure of schools &
                churches as well as intimidation by army soldiers
            c. Information of the worst abuses withheld from the King,
                who concluded wrongly that most Huguenots had now become
                good Catholics
            d. Thus the Revocation of the Edict of Nantes in 1685 by the
                King in the belief that legal rights were no longer nec-
                essary for Huguenots
            e. Flight thereafter of several hundred thousand Huguenots
                to other countries including America, taking their bour-

geois talents & skills & energetic pursuits with them
       f. Consequence of the Revocation--economic & social harm for France and enrichment for other nations, thus proving the costliness of intolerance more so than anything else ever done by Louis XIV.
  H. The wars of Louis XIV:
    1. Existence of a state of war during two-thirds of his reign, with the King posing as the international aggressor
    2. General causes of the wars:
       a. Mercantilistic goal of eliminating economic competitor nations by any means
       b. Traditional desires of territorial conquest & expansion
       c. Historic French policy of weakening the rival Hapsburgs of Austria & Spain
       d. Love of military prestige & glory as well as aspirations to dominate all of Europe
    3. An important incentive to war--organization by the Minister of War (Louvois) or French armies into the most efficient, well-equipped, & finest in Europe--development of the first standing army permanently trained, uniformed, & paid by the state
    4. Results of the wars--few gains for France while weakening all nations--heavy debts for the French treasury as well as much misery inflicted on French subjects
    5. The wars themselves--there were <u>four</u> major conflicts:
       a. The War of Devolution (1667-68): fought against Spain in the Spanish Netherlands (Belgium)--French victories followed by a quick peace treaty granting small territorial possessions to France along the northeastern border
       b. The Dutch War (1672-78): directed initially against the Dutch of Holland (the Netherlands or United Provinces)--establishment of a trend in all of the wars of early French triumphs followed by opposition victories and then exhaustion & military stalemate for all
       c. War of the League of Augsburg (1688-97): precipitation by continuous French aggression in western Germany--organization of a coalition to oppose Louis by William III. of Orange (leader of the Dutch Republic & now also King of England)
       d. War of the Spanish Succession (1701-13): the last & most devastating war caused when the dying last Hapsburg King of Spain named as his successor the grandson of Louis XIV. (Philip of Anjou), thus raising the possibility of uniting the thrones & empires of Spain & France
    6. Reasons why Louis XIV. particularly despised the Dutch and wished to destroy Holland:
       a. Envy of their prosperity & wealth--emergence of Holland as the commercial leader of Europe for most of the 17th century--about half of the seaborne trade of Europe by the mid-century carried in Dutch ships--Amsterdam as the banking & financial capital of Europe from 1610 to 1789
       b. Dislike of the Dutch as religiously Protestant and as the most tolerant & free society in all of Europe
       c. Their republican form of government controlled by an oligarchy of wealthy bourgeoisie--not an absolute monarchy
       d. Dutch erection of a tariff against French products in retaliation for French discriminatory taxes against Dutch

                manufactures
        7. Treaty of Utrecht (1714)--the settlement ending the wars of
           Louis XIV. & bring thirty years of comparative peace--terms
           & provisions of the treaty:
            a. Retention of the Spanish throne by Philip of Anjou (now
                Philip II.) on the condition that the crowns & countries
                France & Spain never be united in the same person
            b. Reception as compensation by the Austrian Hapsburgs of
                Belgium plus the Italian possessions of Milan, Naples, &
                Sardinia from Spain
            c. Reward for the Margrave of Brandenburg with bits of terr-
                itory and the royal title of King of Prussia--achieve-
                ment by this northeastern German state of great future
                significance as the unifying nation of all Germany in
                the late-19th century
            d. Reward for the Duke of Savoy (Piedmont) with the royal
                title of King of Sardinia after 1720--achievement by
                this northwestern Italian state of great future signif-
                icance as the unifying nation of all Italy in the mid-
                19th century
            e. Territorial additions by England to its colonial empire
                with the Rock of Gibraltar & Minorca from Spain and with
                Newfoundland, Nova Scotia, & the Hudson Bay region of
                Canada from France--plus the Asiento Agreement with
                Spain: the very profitable privilege to supply the Span-
                ish American colonies with black African slaves
    J. Revolutionary origins in the reign of Louis XIV:
        1. Consideration by many historians of the French Revolution be-
           ginning in 1789 (just three-fourths of a century after the
           Sun King's death) as the most significant series of events in
           the modern world
        2. Origination & roots in the reign of Louis XIV. (in spite of
           its many glories & greatness) of some causes of the French
           Revolution:
            a. Versailles--isolation of the monarchy from the popular
                mainstream; avoidance of the masses & their problems,
                resulting in much resentment in Paris especially
            b. Expensive wars--exhaustion & impoverishment of the nat-
                ion with little compensation, resulting in huge govern-
                mental debts
            c. Policies toward the old feudal nobility--their parasitic
                status contrasted by the rising hatred of them by com-
                moners
            d. Failure to effect fundamental reforms--of the tax system
                as well as governmental institutions

            e. Religious intolerance & persecution--intensification &
                exacerbation of social conflicts leading to future
                attacks on the institutions of royal government & the
                Catholic Church
            f. Alienation of the intelligentsia--most educated French-
                men turning against the royal government & especially
                absolute monarchy

X. Peter the Great of Russia (1682--1725)
    A. Introduction

1. Condition of Russia in the late-17th century as the most backward & barbaric region of Europe, with few & restricted influences from the more progressive Western Europe in terms of social & economic & political developments
2. Manifestation by Russian culture of many Oriental & Middle Eastern elements as well as Occidental or European influences--in spite of the European ethnicity of the Russian people
3. Significance of the Time of Troubles (1598--1613):
   a. A period of civil war, factional rebellion, foreign intervention, anarchy & chaos, and general weakness
   b. Survival of the Russian people & emergence of the new & weak Romanov Dynasty (1613--1917)
4. Pursuit by the tsars thereafter of the policies of centralization & absolutism to convert their theoretically unlimited autocratic powers into real ones
   a. Increasing royal consent for the gradual enslavement of peasant farmers to satisfy demands from the powerful nobility
   b. Consolidation of these trends during the reign of Peter the Great (1682--1725)

B. Policy of Westernization--a massive effort to modernize Russia & to make it a great power by embarking on a crash program of importation & imposition on the populace of Western European knowledge, technology, & ideas
   1. Implementation of this program for Russia by Peter after his personal tour of Europe in 1697-98
   2. Consequence of tremendous & rapid & permanent changes as well as vigorous opposition from many of the illiterate, superstitious, & anti-foreign masses

C. Reforms & changes of Peter the Great:
   1. Introduction of European dress, clothing styles, & social habits--the Tsar himself clipped beards & cut off long sleeves of courtiers' robes--women ordered to leave former seclusion & to mingle with men socially at court
      a. These changes only affecting the nobility class
      b. Yet prevalence of the view of them as shocking assaults on venerated customs
   2. Reorganization of national & local government with the provision for greater centralization--establishment of the first true bureaucracy for Russian national government with councils on the Swedish model to administer various departments
      a. Delineation of the first provinces, with governors for each appointed by the tsar
      b. Conduct of the first census ever in Russian history
      c. Development of the first systematic (and deeply burdensome on the populace) form of taxation
   3. Establishment of secondary schools & technical academies & hospitals--general failure of these institutions as well as government to function competently during Peter's reign due to the inadequate number of educated individuals in Russia
   4. Immigration of thousands of foreigners to practice trades, serve in government, & teach Russians
   5. Creation of a "service" nobility--aristocrats formerly inheriting lands, titles, & serfs without any obligations now required by the Tsar to earn them through service to the state either as officers in the army & navy or as officials in gov-

ernment--grant of titles & lands by Peter also to deserving men of other classes--yet complete dependency by all on Peter
6. Foundation of the first Russian navy (800 ships at his death) and modernization of the armies on European standards of drill, dress, & equipment
7. Destruction of the independent power of the Greek Orthodox Church & its potential threat to tsarist absolutism--abolition of the ecclesiastical leadership position of patriarch in 1721 and replacement of it with a council functioning as a department of state directly under the tsar's authority
8. Promotion of heavy industry such as iron & textiles with government subsidies--negotiation of trade agreements with other nations--construction of canals & public buildings
9. Construction of a new capital city in the Western architectural style to replace the old capital of Moscow--the new city named for the Tsar as St. Petersburg (for seven decades under Communism in the 20th century it was called Leningrad):
    a. Situation of the new capital city on the Neva River near the Baltic Sea for trade & proximity to Western Europe
    b. Reference to the city by Peter as his "Window on the West"--the perfect symbol of his colossal changes

D. The Great Northern War (1700--21)
1. Russian participation in a coalition against the greatest 17th century power in northeastern Europe (Sweden) & its young ruler (Charles XII.--the most brilliant, daring, & erratic monarch of the age but also a military phenom)
2. Famous campaign of 1708-09 in which Russian inferiority of arms overcome by resort to the "scorched earth policy" (later employed successfully against Napoleon & Hitler)--constant retreat & few battles while exhausting the enemy, burning crops & lands to starve the enemy, poisoning wells, etc.
3. Eventual destruction of the Swedish army in summer heat, winter snows & ice, and the final battle of Poltava--Russian acquisition of lands along the Baltic Sea from Sweden
4. Later Russian expansion & conquest during the 18th century of territories along its western borders at the expense of the declining states of Sweden, Poland, & Turkey

E. Results of the reign of Peter the Great:
1. Elevation of Russia to great-power status as one of the top five states militarily in all of Europe
2. Destiny of Russia in the future as culturally & politically much more of a European & not an Asian nation
3. Vast expansion of the powers & authority of the tsars, with the subservience of the nobility to the crown
4. An increase in serfdom & heavy burdens on the peasants plus a strengthening of their bonds of servitude in the form of high taxation, forced labor, & army service--sacrifice of their human welfare & needs always to national aspirations for power & greatness
5. Deep divisions in society still apparent today between:
    a. Westernizers--those supporting the importation of European outside influences as beneficial to Russia (usually true of the nobility & upper classes generally), and
    b. Slavophiles--those regarding foreign elements as harmful & corrupting of the native purity of Slavic Russian culture (often true of the peasant & lower-class majority

generally
c. Intensification of hostilities & cleavages between the
   classes as a result of this divisive issue

Chapter 8   THE OLD REGIME OF 18TH CENTURY EUROPE

I. Nature of the Old Regime
   A. The term "Old Regime" describing the social, economic, & political institutions prevailing in Europe during the 17th & 18th centuries prior to the advent of the French Revolution in 1789, when those institutions were destroyed or greatly modified in Western Europe
   B. Description of society during the Old Regime:
      1. Rural existence rather than urban--most people still residing in the countryside & small villages and not in large cities
      2. Agrarian or agricultural economy rather than a commercial or industrial one--economic domination still of farming over business enterprise
      3. Narrow & provincial rather than cosmopolitan & worldly outlook on life--this being quite understandable when considering the very slow transportation & communication facilities of that time--thus much ignorance of international events & the real world--most people never travelled more than 25 miles from their birthplace
      4. Oligarchical (oligarchy--rule by the few or handful) control of society--domination of all important institutions by a tiny & privileged elite of noblemen, clergy, royal bureaucrats, & wealthy businessmen
      5. Medieval class-consciousness--persistence of a fairly rigid class structure based on hereditary socio-economic status and with little class or social mobility--this being a legacy of a distant past of the Middle Ages or Medieval Era (500--1300)
   C. Class structure--division into three classes, social orders, or "estates":
      1. First Estate--Clergy: less than 1% of the population--conduct of religious functions and possession of enormous influence over the popular masses as well as many social & economic privileges
      2. Second Estate--Nobility: less than 2% of the population--the usually hereditary landed aristocracy also possessing numerous social, economic, & political privileges (such as traditional exemption from most taxes and control of local government & judicial authority)
      3. Third Estate--Commoners: roughly 97-98% of the population and including many professions and socio-economic groups:
         a. Peasantry--at least 80% of the entire population and consisting of small-scale farmers, farm renters, & farm laborers who were almost universally illiterate, overtaxed, & exploited by the upper classes and who lived lives mainly of drudgery & misery on the margin of subsistence
            (1) In Western Europe they were free & occasionally owned a little piece of land, but most peasants worked the land of others on a renting or sharecropping basis
            (2) In Eastern Europe they were virtual slaves with no property & no rights
         b. Bourgeoisie--the "middle class" of business & professional people manifesting a wide range of wealth & education from rich merchants & bankers & investors to government administrators, to lawyers & doctors & university pro-

fessors, to skilled tradesmen, craftsmen, & artisans at the lower level just barely surviving economically
        (1) Around 10% of the entire population--although their numbers were small, the bourgeoisie was the most productive, progressive, educated, & potentially powerful segment of society in Western Europe
        (2) Yet their rise to the top of society was usually blocked by the privileged nobility & clergy, thus creating pressures leading toward the French Revolution
      c. Proletariat--roughly 5-10% of the total population--the unskilled, wage-earning laborers of cities & countryside lacking land, training & education, working tools, and steady employment--their frequent destitution & desperation destined them to play critical roles in modern revutions & upheavals
  D. Appearance of the Old Regime institutions at the beginning of the 18th century as stable, durable, & permanent--yet <u>two</u> forces working throughout the 1700's to undermine, destabilize, & ultimately destroy the Old Regime & its institutions:
    1. Revolutionary economic changes in commerce, agriculture, and industry--the primary impact at this time being in Western Europe, especially England & France & Holland
    2. The Enlightenment--an intellectual movement expressing demands for institutional reforms that culminated in the French Revolution at the end of the century

II. Revolutionary Economic Changes
  A. In commerce:
    1. Occurrence since 1500 of a steady increase in international trade--then in the 1700's there was a tremendous expansion of world-wide trade by Europe due to superior ship construction, navigational improvements, use of marine insurance, & continuous development of overseas colonial empires
    2. Results--higher standards of living (mainly for the upper classes), great wealth for some of the bourgeoisie, and provision of:
      a. Much investment capital for other domestic ventures
      b. Raw materials imported from abroad for manufacturing
      c. Markets for the exportation of surplus finished products
      d. Cheap labor (often slaves) overseas for European needs
  B. In agriculture:
    1. Production of significantly greater yields of food because of technological advances and the introduction of new crops & new growing processes
    2. Beginnings at that time of the trend away from small & self-sufficient plots of land growing a variety of crops, to large farms producing a single crop or specialized crops for a distant & not a local market (this happening mainly in England)
    3. Emergence of a major demographic change--movement of many impoverished farm laborers in England to the cities seeking jobs in the new factories
  C. In industry:
    1. Commencement of the Industrial Revolution in England in the last decades of the 18th century with perfection of the steam engine in the 1770's and introduction of the "factory system"

    2. Features of the factory system--mass production through the use of:
       a. Many laborers employed together in a large workshop
       b. Power-driven machinery (usually steam, but also water)
       c. Assembly-line techniques with a series directly interconnected processes
       d. Labor specialization in one activity
       e. Standardization of interchangeable parts
    3. Impact of industrialization in the late-1700's only on a few industries in England, yet it marked the inception of awesome economic developments with enormous profits & power ultimately for the upper bourgeoisie
    4. Reasons for the head-start & early dominance of England in the Industrial Revolution:
       a. Ready availability of investment capital--banking leadership maintained throughout the 18th century
       b. Possession of vital natural resources--large deposits of easily obtainable coal & iron
       c. Geographical compactness of the island, facilitating the rapid movement of materials & products as well as the construction of a good transportation system
       d. An immense supply of cheap labor, partly created by agricultural advances
       e. A vast overseas colonial empire--in fact, the world's largest, supplying raw materials & markets & cheap labor
       f. Favorable political climate:
          (1) Control of the national government already by the commercial & financial leaders of the upper bourgoisie (sharing power with the old aristocracy)
          (2) Absence of a rigid centralized administrative structure, thus allowing local initiatives by businessmen free of national governmental prohibition
D. Factors in European History preparing Europe for the Industrial Revolution:
    1. Rise of commercial capitalism during the Italian Renaissance commencing in the late-13th century--emergence of a wealthy & influential upper bourgeoisie
    2. Foundation & exploitation by European nations of overseas colonies, empires, & trading posts during the 16th, 17th, & 18th centuries
    3. Economic policies of mercantilism pursued by European nations emphasizing vigorous governmental promotion of economic growth & strength (1500--1800)
    4. Existence for several centuries of a European "competitive state-system"--intense national rivalries stimulating efforts to gain military & economic superiority or advantage
    5. The Scientific Revolution (17th century) and the Enlightenment (18th century)--the disregard for tradition & encouragement of new approaches to the world & its problems by scientists & philosophers assisting in the creation of a society more conducive & amenable to change
    6. The Protestant Reformation (16th century)--some Protestant religions (especially Calvinism) became very influential among the bourgeoisie of Western Europe, stressing such characteristics as hard work, thrift, sobriety, & perseverence:

  a. Exaltation by Calvinism of the pursuit of wealth and the acquisition of material possessions
  b. Regard for prosperity & riches as a sign of God's blessing--thus a strong incentive to capitalism

III. The Enlightenment
 A. An intellectual movement championing reform of all institutions in society, presenting new ideas for solving the world's problems, and providing the ideological foundation for modern democracy, humanitarianism, and beliefs in progress for mankind & the betterment of the world
  1. Background--the great scientific discoveries, knowledge, & inventions in the 1600's inspiring confidence in rational thought, scientific analysis, & natural laws
  2. The Enlightenment thinkers (<u>philosophes</u> in French) then applied those principles to human institutions in an effort to reform & improve society by making it more efficient & logical & fair
  3. Key words: reason, natural law, progress, & optimism--belief that <u>reason</u> would enable the discovery of <u>natural laws</u> regulating all existence (in the erroneous conclusion that the laws of nature predictably governed human institutions and interactions), and their application to society's problems would result in <u>progress</u> & <u>optimistic views</u> of the future
  4. The following are some parts of the Enlightenment reform program in various fields:
 B. Economics:
  1. Introduction of a new program by a group of French thinkers known as the Physiocrats (literally meaning "believers in the rule of nature") headed by Francois Quesnay
  2. Their policies known as <u>laissez-faire</u> (a French term meaning "allow to do", leave alone, live & let live) and in strong contrast & opposition to the prevailing theories of mercantilism in vogue for around three centuries: 1500--1800
  3. Beliefs & policies of L-F:
   a. Few or no governmental regulations, controls, & constraints on the economy--motto: "To govern better, govern less.", meaning the less state interference in the economy, the more prosperous & successful it will be
   b. Free trade, domestically & internationally, uninhibited by governmental interference or taxes or tariffs
   c. Emphasis on competition, with wages & prices determined by supply & demand (the latter called "market forces")
   d. Recognition of land or labor as the main source of national wealth, rather than gold & silver (bullion) as in mercantilism
   e. Regard for the individual (farmer, worker, businessman) as more important than the nation as a whole--this being contrary to mercantilism which raised the state above the individual person
  4. The classic formulation of L-F economics made by Scotsman Adam Smith in <u>The Wealth of Nations</u> in 1776--stress on freedom & competition for all with wealth being created by allowing the economy to be regulated by the "invisible hand" of natural laws and not by government

5. Role of L-F theories in providing the ideological foundation for 19th & 20th century "free enterprise" capitalism, which achieved its highest development in the United States and had a powerful impact on the world--both positive & negative
C. Justice & Law:
  1. Condemnation of slow judicial procedure, unfair laws, & practices such as torture, mutilation, branding, enslavement, and severe labor for punishments
  2. Desire to humanize & simplify legal codes while making punishments fit the degree of crimes
  3. Importance of Italian reformer Cesare di Beccaria, with his three natural laws of justice in his Essay on Crimes & Punishments:
     a. Prevention of crimes more effectively by the certainty rather than the severity of punishment
     b. Aspiration to prevent future crimes by the application of punishment meant to make a lasting mental impression yet leaving no physical harm on the criminal
     c. Goal that trials be held speedily and as soon as possible after the crime
  4. Opposition by Beccaria also to capital punishment, advocacy of rehabilitation systems, and recommendation that crimes be prevented through education
D. Education:
  1. Criticism of church control of education as well as heavy curriculum emphasis on the subjects of theology, Greek & Latin languages, and ancient history
  2. Demands for more consideration of subjects like science, modern languages, & modern history
  3. Impact of Jean-Jacques Rousseau--a reformer far ahead of his time in attacking strict discipline, lesson-drilling through repetition, & harsh punishment in schools--warm support for no discipline or coercion, direct & first-hand learning experiences more than bookishness, and permission for each student to study at his/her own pace
E. Religion:
  1. Advocacy of religious toleration with the rise of anticlericalism--the latter being an opposition to the negative & harmful influence of religious leaders & traditional faiths
  2. Denunciation of religious persecution, discrimination, & fanaticism that led for centuries to hatred, warfare, violence, & destruction of society
  3. Frequent ridicule of dogma & ritual as superstition, ignorance, & folly preventing the progress of humanity
  4. Deism--the religious views professed by most educated people attempting to reconcile traditional beliefs in a supreme being with the knowledge acquired by modern science:
     a. Belief in god as a creator of the universe & natural laws who no longer interfered in its operations or redeemed mankind
     b. Depiction of the universe as a gigantic world-machine with God merely being the Great Mechanic--analogy also to the "Watch and the Watchmaker"
     c. Rejection of some traditional aspects of Christianity--no formal organization, priesthood, uniform body of doctrine, or need to attend church

d. Regard for the Bible as fine literature but not divine
                revelation--perception of Christ by the Deists only as
                an inspirational mortal and not an immortal deity
             e. View of morality as originating with a rational respect
                for humanity & society & the "natural order" rather than
                out of fear for a wrathful & vengeful God
          5. Anticipation by Deism of modern materialism, agnosticism, and
             atheism--most Americans are appalled to learn that most of
             the 18th-century Founding Fathers of the United States were
             Deists (Jefferson, Madison, Franklin, etc.)
   F. Politics & Government--development by numerous thinkers of theories
      on the best form of government & society--four will be mentioned:
       1. John Locke (1632--1702)
          a. English politician & philosopher resolving to write a
             brilliant & compelling defense of the Glorious Revolu-
             tion of 1688 which he entitled <u>Two Treatises on Govern-
             ment</u> (1690)--presentation of arguments logically and
             persuasively:
              (1) Primitive men in an original state of nature were
                  reasonable, had a moral sense, and possessed cer-
                  tain "natural rights"
              (2) Those natural rights were life, liberty, & property
                  (meaning the possession or use of land, for which
                  Jefferson later substituted the "pursuit of happ-
                  iness" in the Declaration of Independence)
              (3) Eventually mankind agreed to form a government by
                  mutual consent of its members (the "social con-
                  tract" between a people & their rulers) in order
                  to preserve the natural rights
              (4) Thus if a ruler or government violated & usurped
                  those rights (as did James II.), the people have a
                  right & a duty to revolt in order to regain them
              (5) This was a bold yet rational justification of rev-
                  olution as a positive force for stability rather
                  than for chaos or upheaval
          b. Renown for these ideas as the "doctrine of popular sover-
             eignty" with their implication that authority ultimately
             resided with the people & not the government, and that
             rulers were responsible for their acts to the general
             populace
          c. Simultaneous impact of these ideas of condemning royal
             absolutism and the theory of "divine right of kings"
             (belief that monarchs could do whatever they wished as
             God's chosen agents on earth & in nations)
          d. However, Locke's ideas <u>not</u> arguing in favor of democracy
             --to him, the "people" meant only that small minority of
             landed & privileged aristocrats with a few wealthy bour-
             geoisie who sat in Parliament--thus an oligarchy
       2. Voltaire (1694--1778)
          a. Recognition of Voltaire (his pen name) as the most famous
             & influential thinker & writer of his day, about whom it
             was first stated that "the pen is mightier than the
             sword"--clarity, logic, & satiric humor were his features
          b. Devotion of his life to a tireless championing of religi-
             ous toleration & press freedom while condemning fanatic-
             ism & persecution--personal belief in Deism

c. Advocacy in government for "enlightened despotism" by a
              philosopher-prince, meaning that he wished to preserve
              absolute monarchy in the person of an educated ruler who
              supported & enacted the reforms of the Enlightenment
           d. Profound mistrust by Voltaire in the capability of the
              popular masses to rule themselves--agreement with this
              view & assessment by the vast majority of thinkers
      3. Montesquieu (1689--1755)
           a. Enormously important thinker who was a great admirer of
              English government & society and who analyzed its supp-
              osed virtues in his work <u>The Spirit of the Laws</u> (1748):
           b. Theory of the separation of powers and the concept of
              "checks & balances"--belief in the division of national
              government into three distinct & fairly equal (in auth-
              ority) branches: executive, legislative, & judicial
           c. The purpose of this division being to safeguard against
              despotism & tyranny and to preserve individual liberties
           d. Belief in powerful local & regional government encourag-
              ing popular participation also with the goal of protect-
              ing basic freedoms from authoritarian national govern-
              ment--this idea later known by the term "federalism"
           e. Obvious & profound impact of these ideas on the American
              Constitution and our entire system of government
           f. Abhorrence by Montesquieu likewise for democracy in his
              conviction that a role in government must be reserved
              only for the small elite of birth & riches
      4. Rousseau (1712--78)
         The most influential thinker on the future world beyond his
         Age of Enlightenment--in his writings he anticipated or fore-
         shadowed many things:
           a. Democracy--true conviction that the entire society should
              be eventually governed by the "general will" (a kind of
              consensus opinion) in which all citizens participated--
              derivation of governmental authority from the consent of
              the governed--this being his ideal rather than a reality
           b. Revolution--famous quotes that "the depositaries of the
              executive power (rulers) are not the people's masters
              but its officers; it (the people) can set them up or
              pull them down when it likes." and "Man is born free,
              and everywhere he is in chains..."
           c. Socialism--advancement of the view that the evils of civ-
              ilization & inequities of humanity were attributable to
              the existence of private property--yet he preferred that
              "the fruits of the earth belong to us all"
           d. Nationalism--expression of the idea that modern nations
              should encourage a sense of membership, community, &
              kinship among their populace as well as responsible cit-
              izenship & active involvement in public affairs
           e. Cultural Romanticism--stress in his writings on the great
              importance of human impulse, spontaneous feeling, emot-
              ional expression, & mystical insight--thus a reaction
              against a perceived excess of rationalism, constraint, &
              balance during the 18th-century Age of Classicism

Chapter 9　　　　　　　　　FRENCH REVOLUTION-NAPOLEON

I. An Outline of the Revolutionary Events and the Succession of Governments
   A. Estates General: May 5--June 27, 1789
      1. Vital demand by the 3rd Estate for a change in the voting method from a "vote by order" to a "vote by head"
      2. Political stalemate & paralysis--eventual defection from the 1st Estate by some parish priests joining the 3rd Estate
      3. Proclamation of the National Assembly on June 17, 1789
      4. Issuance of the Tennis Court Oath on June 20 committing the National Assembly to a written constitution for France
      5. The Royal Session on June 23--the king promising limited reforms but demanding dissolution of the NA & return to the EG legislative organization--persistent resistance by 3rd Estate
      6. Surrender by the king on June 27 and official recognition of the NA--fundamental reforms now possible--this marked a very significant political yet nonviolent revolution with the:
      7. Transformation of the French government from a theoretical absolute monarchy to a constitutional or limited monarchy similar to England
   B. National (Constituent) Assembly: June 27, 1789--September 30, 1791
      1. The July Revolutions: Storming of the Bastille on July 14, 1789--upheavals in provincial towns & cities--the Great Fear
      2. Night of August 4: renunciation of feudalism and abolition of economic & social privileges of the nobility--passage of the Declaration of the Rights of Man on August 26, 1789
      3. Women's March to Versailles: October 5, 1789
      4. Civil Constitution of the Clergy: November, 1789--July, 1790
      5. Reorganization of the courts, provinces, & local government
      6. The Constitution of 1791, providing for the future Legislative Assembly
      7. Flight to Varennes on June 20-21, 1791--an abortive attempt by the royal family to flee the country
   C. Legislative Assembly: October 1, 1791--August 10, 1792
      1. Power struggle between the Feuillants (constitutional monarchists) and Girondists (moderate democratic republicans)
      2. Declaration of war and beginning of an international conflict on April 20, 1792--serious French losses & Allied invasion of the nation directed toward the capital city of Paris
      3. Emergence of the Paris Commune as a rival & threat to the LA Monarchy--the independent city government falling into the hands of radical leaders representing the Parisian lower classes seeking more democratic reforms
      4. The Brunswick Manifesto on July 25, 1792--Allied threat to destroy Paris if the royal family harmed--the capital city gripped by a deep sense of desperation & urgency
      5. Fall of the Monarchy on August 10, 1792--insurrection in Paris overthrowing the LA & king and calling for elections to a new ruling body with authority to prepare another constitution
      6. Temporarily governing the nation between August 10 and the 1st meeting of the National Convention on September 20 was the Paris Commune--key role of Danton on the Executive Council
      7. The September Massacres: Sept. 2-6, 1792, with its critical issue of national security vs. individual personal liberties
      8. Intense wartime preparations resulting in the battle victory "miracle" of Valmy on September 20, 1792

D. National Convention: September 20, 1792--October 26, 1795
   1. Proclamation of the First Republic on September 22, 1792
   2. Trial and execution of King Louis XVI. on January 21, 1793
   3. Appearance of many domestic & foreign problems tending to radicalize Revolutionary events and require drastic solutions
   4. Power struggle between Girondists (moderate democratic republicans) and Jacobins, or the "Mountain" (radical democratic republicans) from September, 1792 to June 2, 1793--ultimate purge of most moderates (Girondists)
   5. Reign of Terror: June, 1793--July, 1794. The Terror was a wartime emergency government imposing drastic measures necessary to survive the crises & to save the nation--purge by Robespierre & his Jacobin faction of former political allies (Indulgents, Enrages, Hebertists) in March & April, 1794--the Terror coming to an end with:
   6. Overthrow & execution of Robespierre & his faction in the Coup of 9 Thermidor (July 27, 1794) by moderate leaders of the Convention, followed by the:
   7. Thermidorean Reaction, a dismantling of the laws & measures of the Terror: July 28, 1794--October 26, 1795
   8. Preparation finally of the Constitution of the Year III. (October, 1795)--to be the future Government of the Directory and marking a return to a moderate or even conservative republic
E. Directory: October, 1795--November, 1799
   1. Domination of the republic by the wealthy bourgeoisie--failure to solve domestic problems yet achievement of military victories abroad, both paving the way for dictatorship
   2. "Conspiracy of the Equals" led by F-N. Babeuf: 1796-97
   3. Treaty of Basel ending war with Prussia & Spain in 1795 & the Treaty of Campo Formio with Austria in 1797 after the brilliant Italian Campaign of Napoleon Bonaparte
   4. Coup of 18 Brumaire (November 9, 1799) overthrowing the Directory and led by Napoleon with a group of conspirators
   5. Preparation of the Constitution of the Year VIII. (December, 1799) creating the:
F. Consulate: December, 1799--December, 1804
   1. A constitutional dictatorship with Napoleon as First Consul & as the undisputed yet very popular ruler of France
   2. Inauguration of many reforms and consolidation of the Revolutionary changes under Napoleonic guidance
G. First Empire: December, 1804--March, 1814
   1. A practical dictatorship following the proclamation of Napoleon on December 2, 1804 as Emperor of the French
   2. Occurrence of almost incessant military campaigns, with numerous triumphs & the conquest of most of Europe followed by defeat at the hands of a coalition of Old Regime adversaries
   3. Brief revival during the Hundred Days (March 20--June 29, 1815) after the escape & return of Napoleon from the Mediterranean island of Elba--final demise in defeat at the Battle of Waterloo on June 18, 1815

I. Introduction
   A. Consideration of the French Revolution (1789--99) as the greatest & most significant of all the "popular & democratic" revolutions in human history inaugurating extensive social, economic, political,

&cultural changes in France that quickly influenced Western Europe and eventually convulsed the entire world:
    1. It was "popular", meaning that a vast majority of the French people actively participated in many of its major events as well as benefitted from their consequences
    2. It was "democratic" from the standpoint of creating a fairer & more equitable society for nearly all French people
  B. The reason why the French Revolution was the most significant revolution of all--its unique occurrence in the most advanced nation in the world at the time, which rapidly made its impact world-wide--no other revolution can make this claim
    1. Existence of France as the center of the Enlightenment, the leader in literature & science, and the wealthiest (equally with Britain) nation in Europe with the largest population under a single government
    2. Role of French as the international language and France as the pacesetter in most new trends, with the world watching developments there closely
  C. Differences between the French & the American Revolution (1775-81):
    1. Popular participation--involvement in the events by most of the French people, yet very few Americans participated or benefitted much from the American Revolution
    2. Role of women--extensive participation in the events by French women as well as discussions about equal rights--not so by American women during our Revolution
    3. Slavery--abolition during the height of the French Revolution, yet perpetuation by the American Revolution
    4. Socialism--inauguration by a French Revolutionary government (as trustee for all the people) of the first policies utilizing national resources for the benefit of all in society---later assumption that socialism involved government ownership of some property or other means of production
    5. Total mobilization of society for survival in a colossal crisis--role of a French government (the Convention) as the first successful model for the entire world of a powerful central government marshalling all of its resources to deal with an unprecedented crisis--resort by all nations in World Wars I. & II. to precisely these same policies
    *6. Provision by the above five factors of an explanation for the awesome & unparalleled impact on & importance to the world of the French Revolution

III. Causes of the French Revolution
  A. Existence for all significant developments in history of both long-term causes (tracing their origins back for centuries or at least decades) and short-term causes (occurring within a few years, months, weeks, or days)--this is especially true of the Revolution
  B. Inequitable class structure--persistence of a feudal stratification of classes in society based primarily on birth rather than on talents or efforts
  C. Legal & financial abuses:
    1. Existence of barbarous judicial practices, unjust punishments, arbitrary governmental powers of arrest & detention, and a legal system favoring the upper-class few over the lower-class multitude

    2. Survival of a taxation system charging no direct taxes on the wealth of the nobility & clergy yet imposing heavy taxes on the land & property of the peasants, the latter being one of occupational groups in society least capable of paying taxes
- Incompetence of government--problems with:
    1. A slow, cumbersome, inefficient, secretive, often inexperienced bureaucracy staffed with political favorites or hereditary appointees
    2. An administrative system impervious to change & intolerant toward criticism & created by terribly ignorant or corrupt ministers and/or monarchs
- E. Influence of the Enlightenment--the reform movement providing the ideas that the Revolution would implement--a great writer after the Revolution paying tribute to its impact: "The Revolution was accomplished in men's minds before they made it the work of their hands."[1]   (Alexis de Tocqueville)
- F. The American Revolution: 1775--81
    1. Most importantly, involvement by France militarily & economically in significantly assisting the American triumph greatly increased the royal governmental debt, thereby hastening the financial drift toward bankruptcy and provoking the calling of the Estates-General & the initial phase of the Revolution
    2. Also, service of the American Revolution as an inspirational precedent for the French people, even while they exaggerated & idealized its impact & extensiveness
- G. Royal family: [lecture material]
    1. King Louis XVI. (1774--92)
    2. Queen Marie Antoinette
    3. Humorous quote by the modern Irish playwright George B. Shaw: "Kings are not born, they are made by universal hallucination."[2]
- H. An economic & financial crisis--the most immediate cause providing the catalyst & triggering the Revolution:
    1. Bankruptcy of the national government--reckless borrowing from private banks & spending during the 1780's resulting by 1787 in a collapse of public confidence in the royal government, a termination of all private loans to it, & an inability to pay even the interest on the national debt
        a. Agreement & consent by the king in the necessity for the collection of new taxes never impose before, which required the approval also of the national representative assembly, or Estates-General
        b. Commencement of the Revolution with its first meeting on May 5, 1789
    2. Worsening economic conditions over nearly twenty years for the wage-earning urban lower classes & rural peasants, devastated by a combination of rising costs of living plus declining purchasing power of their incomes:
        a. Specific problems during the four years prior to the Revolution (1785-89) of crop failures, food shortages, starvation in some areas, urban unemployment, monetary inflation, & massive misery throughout most of France
        b. Results--sporadic riots & civil disturbances, a mounting sense of desperation as well as popular fury directed increasingly against all sources of authority

IV. Early Developments of the Revolution
   A. Lecture material on conversion of the Estates-General into the National Assembly, events leading up to Bastille Day, the four July Revolutions & their consequences, and the Women's March to Versailles in October, 1789
   B. Origination during the Revolution of our political terminology and the political spectrum:
      1. Introduction of our word-usage to describe political views and positions--basis on one's attitude toward "change" in society & the world, "democratic change" desiring more fairness and equality for more people, & "oligarchic change" pursuing no change or less change and thus a perpetuation of wealth, privilege, & status--below is the political spectrum:
      2. Radical....Liberal....Moderate....Conservative....Reactionary
         (LEFT WING)   (RIGHT WING)
         a. Moderate--view of balancing some democratic change with an oligarchic maintenance of tradition
         b. Liberal--view advocating fairly steady democratic change more than the preservation of oligarchic tradition
         c. Conservative--view supporting only very slow democratic change while emphasizing the maintenance of oligarchic tradition
         d. Radical--view favoring very rapid democratic change to the disregard of all oligarchic tradition
         e. Reactionary--view opposing all democratic change for the total preservation of oligarchic tradition
      3. Thus, association since the French Revolution of Right Wing views with preserving the status quo and perpetuating wealth, status, & privilege; and of Left Wing sentiments with the advocacy of greater equality & a more democratic society
      4. Classification throughout all of history (even today) of the vast popular majority as "conservative", because:
         a. Most individuals are psychologically insecure, fear the unknown, & are "creatures of habit" who conform to social values & institutions even when such conduct is harmful to them
         b. Most persons are ignorant of the world's realities & how they affect everyone
         c. Most people seek <u>advantage</u> over others, thus providing the primary explanation for human prejudice, stereotyping, & scapegoating--by putting others down, we elevate ourselves while projecting greed & selfishness
   C. Contribution to the world by the Revolution of the famous slogan: Liberty, Equality, (Liberalism & Democracy), Fraternity (Nationalism & the Brotherhood of Humanity):
      1. Liberalism to most Europeans during the 1st half of the 19th century meant:
         a. Abolition of social & economic & political privileges for the nobility & clergy
         b. Extension of greater civil liberties (basic freedoms of speech, press, assembly, ballot) to more people
         c. Introduction of national representative assemblies (such as Parliament in England) to help govern nations and to serve the interests of commoners
         d. Either constitutional (or limited) monarchies or republics as governmental forms, not the traditional absolute

            monarchies where the popular masses possessed no defense
            against tyranny
      e. Granting of written constitutions, to document the rights
         of people as well as the definite powers of government
  2. Nationalism to most Europeans during the 19th century meant:
      a. Independence from foreign domination for many peoples
      b. Unification of states in Germany & Italy into nationhood
      c. Cultural & political autonomy, signifying self-determin-
         ation or semi-independence for certain ethnic groups or
         nationalities ruled by a different yet dominant power
      d. Respect for diversity in language, customs, & cultures
     *e. Patriotic feelings within a country of community & to-
         getherness & common values & necessity for shared sacri-
         fices, with the consequence of greater social cohesion
         as well as cooperative efforts in solving problems---
         Revolutionary France was the first society to witness
         the benefits of this phenomenon
  3. Expansion of these ideas increasingly throughout Europe & the
     World in the 19th & early 20th century
D. Inauguration by the Revolution of a long struggle between Democracy
   and Institutional Religion:
  1. Existence of the Catholic Church & religion in general as a
     highly conservative institution & ideology wedded to tradit-
     ion, authoritarianism, non-change, & the Old Regime--thus the
     popes declared war on the French Revolution & its principles
  2. Later ensued the "alliance of throne & altar"--a coordinated
     campaign by monarchs & religious leaders to thwart advances
     by liberalism & democracy (something <u>not</u> so apparent here in
     America, making us very unique in the world)
  3. Conservative impact of religion:
      a. The popular masses taught to accept their suffering as
         the will of God, thus constituting a device for the rul-
         ing class to keep the downtrodden fatalistically resign-
         ed to acceptance of their miserable lot in life
      b. Religion encouraged unquestioning obedience & deference
         to higher authority, whether it be God in heaven or pol-
         iticians or clergymen on earth
      c. Focus of lower-class attention on achieving salvation in
         the hereafter discouraged them from trying to improve
         conditions in this world of the here-&-now
E. Advent of the "principle of armed popular insurrection":
  1. Modern celebration of Bastille Day (July 14, 1789) as the 1st
     & best example of the masses of people rising up with weapons
     to resist tyranny & oppression and to defend moral principles
     by force & coercion if necessary, with the consequence of the
     popular movement spreading all over the nation thereafter
  2. Captivation of the world imagination by that event ever since
     and emulation in many modern revolutionary "days"
  3. Frequent use of this theme of fighting on barricades & in the
     streets, as in the classic novel <u>Les Miserables</u> by Victor
     Hugo (now a Broadway musical)
  4. Popular belief in the necessity of resorting to violence & un-
     lawfulness for the purpose of pressuring or overthrowing the
     government, the ultimate goal being the creation of a more
     democratic society & a better world
  5. Remembrance of these uprisings <u>not</u> as individual acts of viol-

ence for personal profit, but as collective movements for the betterment of all
F. Summary of the reforms of the National Assembly:
  1. Writing of the Constitution of 1791--the most progressive and liberal document in the world:
     a. Grant of certain civil liberties to all French people
     b. Yet extension of voting rights only to about half of all Frenchmen, with only 50,000 men elligible to hold political office (out of a total population of 25 million)
  2. Abolition of special social, economic, & political (called feudal & manorial at the time) privileges associated with the Old Regime
  3. Establishment of a uniform & relatively democratic system of courts promising equality for all before the law
  4. Reorganization of the provinces (now called "departments") and foundation of local government providing for the popular election of local officials
  5. Elimination of much unnecessary wealth & power of the Catholic Church (details mentioned below) in the CCC
G. Civil Constitution of the Clergy (CCC):
  1. A crucial piece of legislation passed by the National Assembly in June, 1790 combining government policies toward the Catholic Church and toward the national economic & social woes
  2. Provisions & measures of the CCC:
     a. Government confiscation of Church landed property & some material wealth, with the plan to sell the land in order to pay off governmental debts
     b. Issuance of paper currency (known as <u>assignats</u>) using lands as collateral or security to pay off governmental debts--the money being worth 2 billion francs--possibility of citizens to collect the circulating paper money & to exchange it for landed property
     c. Results--a significant redistribution of land with most property acquired or "bought" by the bourgeoisie & well-to-do peasants
     d. All Church officials (priests & bishops) to be paid by the government and elected by local & regional populations--this seemingly democratic reform was truly revolutionary because it:
        (1) Transformed clergymen into civil officials responsible initially to the French people & government
        (2) Stripped the pope of effective authority over the French clergy, thus running counter to the entire Roman Church tradition as an independent ecclesiastical institution & monarchy (the pope)
        *(3) Achieved a greater unity or combination of Church & State in France than ever before (and a drastic difference to our American separation of the two)
     e. Governmental requirement of the clergy to swear an oath of loyalty to the state & of acceptance of this new settlement--following their consciences & instructions from the pope, a majority of clergymen (55%) refused & thus recorded their opposition to the Revolution (known in the future as refractory or non-juring priests)

3. Consequences of CCC--beneficial & disastrous:
   a. Temporary stimulation of the economy and an eventual democratic redistribution of land to more people
   b. Long-term depreciation of the paper currency to the point of worthlessness through governmental mismanagement:
     (1) Production of excessive amounts of money (more than was covered by land) & failure to remove it from circulation by the government when exchanged for land, the results being:
     (2) Runaway inflation, a loss of public confidence in the money & in the government, and a continuation of economic uncertainty & financial crisis
  *c. Most disastrously, the alienation of some devout Catholics (most Frenchmen were still practicing Catholics) forced to choose between loyalty to the Revolutionary government or to the Catholic Church, but not to both
   d. Unavoidability & inevitability of this conflict in many ways, and the beginning of a history of hostility between French Democracy & Catholicism not ending until after World War II.

H. Reasons why the Revolution moved in a more Leftward or radical direction during the first four & a half years:
1. The King--his untrustworthiness, hatred of the role as constitutional monarch, refusal to work with political leaders, and outright treason
2. Mutual hostilities between the Revolution & Catholicism over the CCC
3. Economic troubles & turmoil--governmental failure to deal effectively with these problems
4. Demands by the Parisian lower classes for democratic reforms unfulfilled by the early governments
5. Threats by right-wing extremists (royalists & clericals) to destroy the Revolutionary gains
6. War with Europe (declaration in April, 1792)--initial unpreparedness & defeats creating mounting pressures for drastic measures
7. Power struggles--rivalries among different political parties & factions & groups encouraging greater expectations & a rising willingness to implement radical action

J. Use of lecture material to cover the Overthrow & Fall of the Monarchy on August 10, 1792, the September Massacres, the Battle of Valmy, and first meetings of the National Convention

K. Girondists vs. Jacobins in the National Convention:
1. A power struggle between Girondists (moderate democratic republicans) and Jacobins (radical democratic republicans) in the Convention pushing the Revolution in a leftward direction
2. Differences (ideological & practical) between the two:
   a. Girondists defending the interests of the provinces--Jacobins catering to the desires of the city of Paris--thus the big city vs. the rural & small-town countryside
   b. Girondists representing the wealthy bourgeoisie--Jacobins drawing support from the lower middle class & proletariat (<u>sans-culottes</u> of Paris)

   c. Girondists favoring a decentralized form of government with many checks & balances and federalism--Jacobins wanting a highly centralized & all-powerful national government in Paris to solve huge problems
   d. Girondists urging a laissez-faire, free enterprise economy with the sanctity of private property--Jacobins demanding governmental controls & activism & some activities anticipating modern socialism
  3. Interestingly, a common origination of most leaders & major members of both Girondists & Jacobins in the upper middle class--thus the Jacobins not coming from the socio-economic stratum that they represented, this fact causing failure of communication & their eventual downfall
  4. Yet emergence of the Jacobins by mid-1793 as the only truly effective political faction or group capable of governing the entire nation & surmounting its enormous challenges because of their:
   a. Preservation throughout the Revolution of a nationwide party organization featuring an extensive network of affiliates in the provinces linking the capital city with the outlying towns & rural communities
   b. Thus facilitation of their establishment of the most powerful & vigorous & popular government in all of history

V. Reign of Terror: June, 1793--July, 1794
 A. Attainment by the Revolution of its highest point as well as its most dramatic & radical phase
 B. Assumption by the National Convention in Paris of the role of a wartime emergency government adopting extreme & severe measures to deal with a colossal crisis threatening to destroy all of the progress & reforms achieved thus far by the Revolution
 C. Reasons why the French people tolerated & mostly supported the extremism & severity of the Terror--confrontation by France with a desperate life-and-death struggle for survival:
  1. Foreign invasion--nearly all of Europe at war with France
  2. Civil war--royalists & dissidents in some regions in rebellion
  3. Economic instability--major problems with chronic inflation & scarcity of vital commodities
  4. Assurances of the temporary longevity of the measures until the crisis ended & the Republic was stabilized
  5. Power struggle for control of France--existence of threats by traitors & counter-revolutionaries to destroy the Revolution
 D. Measures of the Terror:
  1. War--a draft or conscription law (<u>levee en masse</u>) of all unmarried men aged 18 to 25, and total mobilization of all people & all resources in society for contributions to a winning effort
  2. Civil war:
   a. Establishment of a supreme political police organization known as the Committee of General Security (similar to the FBI) for hunting & arresting traitors
   b. Creation of the Revolutionary Tribunal to try counter-revolutionaries, and use of the guillotine for execution of a total of over 20,000 during the Terror
  3. Economy:
   a. Imposition of wage & price controls, known as the <u>maximum</u>

        b. Rationing of scarce commodities and requisitioning of food & essential supplies from farmers & businessmen by the national government
        c. Extraction of forced loans from some wealthy citizens
        d. Progressive taxation--efforts to collect higher rates on higher incomes
        e. Passage but <u>not</u> implementation of the Law of Ventose in the spring, 1794 permitting the confiscation of property of the Republic's enemies for redistribution to the poor
    4. Social & cultural measures:
        a. Abolition of slavery in the colonies--February 4, 1794
        b. Censorship of the press, to prevent the undermining of public confidence in the government
        c. Creation & introduction of the metric system (based on the decimal system of numbers) for weights & measures-- meaning the liter, gram, & meter
        d. Religion--discouragement of traditional faith & closure of some churches--promotion by the main leader (Robespierre) unsuccessfully of Deism as the official government religion, known as "Worship of the Supreme Being"
        e. Establishment of a new calender beginning on September 22, 1792 (proclamation day of the 1st Republic), with the months of the old Christian calendar renamed and the weeks lengthened into ten days
        f. Drastic changes under Revolutionary influence of clothing styles, forms of address, names of people & places, music themes, architectural features, theater productions, & all popular amusements--frequent inspirational references to ancient Rome (with its republic) & ancient Greece (with its democracy)
    5. All general problems:
        a. Foundation of a powerful national government with a high degree of centralization, concentrating all important authority in the National Convention in Paris
        b. Creation of an executive cabinet selected from the majority of deputies in the National Convention to serve as the chief instrument or body providing executive leadership--the Committee of Public Safety, also known as "The 12 Who Ruled"
        c. Appointment of "representatives-on-mission" as deputies with special powers dispatched from Paris to the provinces & armies to review the actions of leaders and generals
E. Results of the Terror:
    1. All things considered, great success in surmounting the crisis and saving the Revolutionary gains
    2. Expulsion of foreign armies from French lands by the end of 1793, with Republican forces now on the offensive
    3. Intensification of patriotic pride & nationalistic spirit-- greater willingness of citizen-soldiers representing a democratic-republican society to fight & die for their cause
    4. Defeat or containment of all internal revolts
    5. Stabilization of the economy
    6. Yet also creation of a Revolutionary governmental dictatorship more powerful & effective at coercion & curtailment of personal freedom than any government thus far in all of history

      7. Abatement of the national crisis leading to calls for an end to the measures by some people
- F. Final power struggle among the Jacobins & other radicals:
    1. Domination of the Committee of Public Safety & the Convention by Maximilien Robespierre & his faction of Jacobins
    2. Purge by Robespierre in September, 1793 & in March, 1794 of former allies who were leftist groups of radicals urging more extreme policies:
        a. Enrages, or "Fanatics"--true socialists & members of the proletariat earlier pressuring for the economic measures
        b. Hebertists--violent & anticlerical champions of more egalitarian reforms, prominent in the Paris Commune
        c. Elimination of these true spokesmen & leaders of the city sans-culottes leaving the Parisian masses leaderless, confused, & alienated from the Jacobin government of the Convention
        d. Destruction also by these purges of the urban power-base on which the Jacobins earlier rose to the top, and which had been the motivating spirit of the entire Revolution
    3. Arrest & execution by Robespierre for treason in April, 1794 of Danton & his rightist faction of former allies known as the "Indulgents"
    4. Personality of Robespierre--a very idealistic, puritanical, impractical, & self-righteous lawyer & bachelor & dreamer nicknamed the "Incorruptible"
    5. Belief by Robespierre in June-July, 1794 in the possible attainment of the "Republic of Virtue" (a utopian society of citizens possessing moral purity, lofty ideals, selfless patriotism) necessitating more purges to "purify" society & the government
    6. Combination & unity of Robespierre's opponents in desperation to defend themselves & to resist his personal dictatorship
    *7. Coup of 9 Thermidor (July 27, 1794)--arrest & detention of Robespierre and 22 members of his faction--their execution on the following day marked the end of the Terror and a significant turning point in the Revolution irrevocably toward conservatism
- G. Thermidorean Reaction: July, 1794--October, 1795
    1. Experience during this aftermath of the Terror of a return to moderation & normality and away from extremism
    2. A dismantling of the machinery of the Terror by the remaining Convention delegates--abolition or weakening of its institutions--repeal of its laws in response to popular opinion
    3. Occurrence of a counter-revolutionary White Terror in southern & western France as conservatives murdered thousands of Jacobin supporters & those profiting earlier from the Revolution
    4. Repeal of the Terror's economic laws causing severe popular suffering & ineffective demonstrations against the government
    4. Eventual preparation of the Constitution of the Year III. (1795) providing for the Government of the Directory
    5. Suppression of the final uprising in Paris against the government during the Revolution--the right-wing royalist Insurrection of 13 Vendemiaire (October 5, 1795), in which the young artillery officer Napoleon Bonaparte rose from obscurity to fame

I. Directory: October, 1795--November, 1799
   A. Continuation of the 1st Republic yet under a moderate to conservative upper-bourgeois republic with a bicameral legislature, an executive of five Directors, separation of powers, and restricted voting & officeholding rights favoring the wealthy
   B. Trends & developments:
      1. A four-year era of drift, inconsistent policies, and general non-accomplishment for the government
      2. Political corruption, profiteering, & unpopularity
      3. An era socially of frivolity, extravagance, dissipation, cynicism, & disillusionment
      4. Chaos in government--annulment of some elections, violations of the constitution, purge of several Directors, and illegal deprivation of seats for numerous legislators
      5. Frequent conspiracies & plots against the Directory, the most famous being the "Conspiracy of the Equals" organized by Francois-Noel (called "Gracchus") Babeuf in 1796-97---failure, arrest, & execution yet his ideas & goals anticipated the communism of Karl Marx and Vladimir Lenin:
         a. His most important doctrinal principle--the seizure of a national government by a small, secretive, tightly-knit, conspiratorial group ruling dictatorially until the uneducated masses were capable of governing themselves
         b. Proposed policies--all land to be owned by the state, governmental control of food distribution, all people to live in rural communes & not cities, abolition of religion & the arts, and each individual to receive according to his/her needs & not according to abilities
      6. Achievement of numerous military victories abroad, mainly by Bonaparte in Italy in 1796-97, as the only positive accomplishment of the period:
         a. Demonstration by Napoleon of brilliance, daring, versatility, & military genius in a long series of spectacular victories capturing the popular imagination & stirring an international sensation as perhaps no other hero-figure had in all of history
         b. Emergence of a striking contrast in the public perception between the often corrupt, unstable, & incompetent Directory government and the young, handsome, vigorous, charismatic, & multi-talented Bonaparte
      7. Napoleonic seizure of power with a group of conspirators in the Coup of 18 Brumaire (November 9, 1799), overthrowing the Directory

VII. Napoleon Bonaparte (1769--1821)
   A. Rule as 1st Consul or as Emperor for nearly 15 years (1799--1815) as ordinarily a very popular dictator:
      1. Acceptance by the French of his despotism & their loss of civil liberties because of a strong desire for stability & order in social, economic, & political life
      2. Accomplishment of these things by Napoleon generally very well
   B. Early battle successes in war:
      1. Victory over the Austrians at Marengo in 1800 terminating the 2nd Coalition of European nations against Revolutionary France and bringing four years of peace
      2. Greatest triumph of Napoleon at Austerlitz in 1805 over Russia

& Austria in a strategic & tactical masterpiece crushing the 3rd Coalition
3. Destruction of Prussia at the battles of Jena & Auerstadt in 1806 and defeat of Russia at Friedland in 1807, thus vanquishing the 4th Coalition
4. Attainment of Napoleon's zenith of power & prestige in the Treaty of Tilsit (1807) with Tsar Alexander I.--domination of most of Continental Europe by Bonaparte & France
5. Later defeat of Austria again in 1809 at Wagram ending the 5th Coalition against France

C. Accomplishments & reforms of Napoleon:
   1. Final pacification of a civil war in western France (the Vendee) and restoration of domestic tranquility & stability--termination of the internal lawlessness & chaos surviving somewhat as a legacy of the Revolution
   2. Restoration of economic strength & prosperity--the currency stabilized, national debt consolidated, budget balanced, public works financed, fairness of taxation granted, Banque de France (central bank) established, trade expanded, business confidence revived with the consequences of impressive economic growth & prosperity for nearly a decade
   3. Foundation of a highly centralized, very efficient, & well-organized national government (probably the best so in the world) with the bureaucracy open to all men of ability, and under the general supervision of the Council of State
   4. Codification of all French laws into one system called the Code Napoleon--embodiment of many Revolutionary principles such as "equality before the law for all" yet in combination with some of the best concepts of the Old Regime--recognition of this as his greatest accomplishment and still in modified use today
   5. Concordat of 1801:
      a. An "agreement" with the Papacy permitting the official & legal return of Catholic institutions & practices
      b. Yet preservation of the Revolutionary confiscation & sale of Church lands to private citizens--commitment by the French government to pay for clerical salaries & other Church expenses--thus still a unity & combination of Church & State, not a separation
      c. Guarantee of the principle of "freedom of worship"
      d. Grant by Napoleon (an atheist) of a decent measure of religious toleration as well as civil liberties to Jews--thus being the first European ruler to do so
   6. Reconstruction & reorganization after conquest of the many states of Germany & Italy into a few (from over 300 in Germany to about 30, and from around 15 to 3 in Italy)--role of this consolidation of being the first & most important step toward political unification in the late-19th century
   7. Establishment of a secondary school system--the consummation of a Revolutionary ideal
   8. Dissemination (through the medium of his military campaigns) of Revolutionary principles & ideals (liberty, equality, fraternity) to the remainder of Europe & afterward to the world

D. Reasons for the downfall of Napoleon:
   1. Military involvement in Spain & Portugal with the Peninsular (Iberian) Wars (1808--14):

a. Provision of the first highly effective demonstration of
      the devastating impact of guerrilla warfare in its role
      of draining the Napoleonic Empire of manpower, re-
      sources, & morale--Napoleon later called it "my bleeding
      wound"
   b. Nature of guerrilla (meaning "little war" in Spanish)
      warfare--use of unconventional, irregular methods of
      hit-&-run tactics with a recognition of no rules or reg-
      ulations and with fighters posing as normal citizens &
      wearing no military uniforms & employing any means to
      harm or harass or sabotage the enemy
2. Inordinate & insatiable ambition as well as decline in physical capabilities of Napoleon--the results being some disastrous decisions and an eventual overextension of the empire
   beyond his capacity to control it
3. The Continental System--his policy of closing European ports
   to British shipping & commerce in an effort to destroy the
   British economy--consequences:
   a. Economic hardships on the European Continent and alienat-
      ion of subjugated peoples & nations
   b. Precarious occupations of other countries in addition to
      more wars in an effort to apply this policy
   c. Impossibility & failure in enforcement with many violat-
      ions of the policy
4. Failure to develop a navy & to control the seas and thus to
   strike at France's most relentless & formidable enemy and the
   organizer & financier of as well as participant in all Six
   Coalitions of European states against the Revolution &
   France: England--colossal French naval defeat at Trafalgar in
   1805 at the hands of an English fleet under Horatio Nelson
5. Estrangement with Pope Pius VII., a segment of the French
   clergy, & some devout Catholics because of Church policies of
   interference, manipulation, & repression
6. Occasional disloyalty & frequent incompetence of his relatives
   in the Bonaperte family--his four brothers & three sisters
   were mostly an emotional & financial burden to Napoleon
7. Invasion of Russia in 1812--destruction of the Grande Armee of
   a half million men because of the geographical enormity of
   land, the enemy strategy of retreat with the "scorched-
   earth policy", summer heat, and especially winter ice & sub-
   zero temperatures
   a. Defeat in Russia followed by the formation of the 6th
      Coalition including most of the European nations
   b. French forces overwhelmed in 1813-14 by superior numbers
      in Allied armies--occupation of France & Paris in April,
      1814--abdication by Napoleon & exile to island of Elba
8. Inadequacy of his subordinate officers in the final campaigns
   as death & injuries over many years required the replacement
   of talented veterans with less experienced & able officers
9. The Hundred Days & Battle of Waterloo on June 15, 1815--the
   triumphant yet brief return of Napoleon culminating at Waterloo and marking an end to the Revolutionary Era with the
   Bourbon Restoration and the final exile & death in 1821 of
   Napoleon on the south Atlantic island of St. Helena

VIII. Congress of Vienna--1815
   A. Introduction--the defeat of France & Napoleon by nations representing conservatism, monarchy, aristocracy, & clericalism led directly to a peace conference in Vienna for the purposes of:
      1. Redrawing the map of Europe according to Old Regime standards
      2. Strengthening governments against a recurrence of Revolutionary movements domestically & internationally
      3. Creating a stable world order & system
   B. Leaders of the Congress:
      1. Metternich--host of the conference, foreign minister of Austria, the chief figure in European diplomacy for the next 33 years, a gifted statesman, the primary spokesman of conservative forces, & the most influential diplomat at the meeting
      2. Castlereagh--British foreign minister working to restore the international balance of power for the benefit of Britain
      3. Tsar Alexander I. of Russia--eccentric & enigmatic ruler vacillating between humanitarian idealism & unscrupulous realism during the negotiations
      4. King Frederick William III. (1797--1840) of Prussia--a person of few ideas & little influence
      5. Talleyrand--foreign minister of the newly restored Bourbon regime in France--an experienced, brilliant, & clever diplomat who shrewdly maneuvered to secure the best possible peace for his defeated nation
      6. Representation of all other European nations & states by leaders & statesmen playing little if any major role in the proceedings
   C. Principles guiding the final settlement:
      1. Legitimacy--meaning the restoration of crowns & borders to their pre-1789 & thus French Revolutionary conditions--these "legitimate" monarchs & dynasties deserving to return to their traditional states after often being unseated earlier by Revolutionary forces
         a. Separate branches of the Bourbon family restored to thrones in France, Spain, & Naples--Austrian Hapsburgs to Milan in Italy--the Popes to Rome & the Papal States--the House of Orange to the Netherlands
         b. Minor families returned to many smaller states within Italy and Germany
      2. Containment of France--a successful effort to prevent future French expansionism & aggression against neighbors (France having been the most powerful Continental nation economically & militarily for nearly two centuries) by strengthening most of its border states:
         a. Unification of Belgium with Holland (Netherlands), grant to Prussia of a significant area of the Rhineland, enlargement of Switzerland, reward of Piedmont-Sardinia with Genoa--all acting as buffers against expansionist ambitions of France
         b. Punishment of France by returning it to the frontiers of 1790 & by imposing on it a large indemnity payment and an occupation army until 1818
      3. Compensation--victorious nations in the wartime coalition rewarding themselves with territorial acquisitions:
         a. Prussia took two-fifths of German Saxony, Russia took half of the old kingdom of Poland, Austria took Venetia

        & the Illyrian Provinces, & Sweden took Norway from Denmark
- b. Britain rewarded itself with trade concessions plus the colonies of Malta, Ceylon, & the Cape of Good Hope (the future South Africa)
4. Suppression of liberalism & nationalism--the conservative aspiration to discourage, thwart, & hopefully destroy those convulsive forces of the French Revolutionary Era
    - a. Germany, or former Holy Roman Empire:
        - (1) Division of Germany for many centuries into a decentralized conglomeration of over 300 virtually independent political states with the Hapsburg dynasty of Austria as titular figurehead
        - (2) Consolidation by Napoleon into around thirty states --now German patriots & liberals wanting the creation of one unified German nation
        - (3) Establishment by the Congress instead of a German Confederation composed of 39 independent states under Austrian leadership with a weak national assembly in the ceremonial capital of Frankfurt
    - b. Italy:
        - (1) Denial by the Congress of patriotic aspirations by Italians for national unification & freedom from Austrian domination
        - (2) Fragmentation of Italy into around ten states, with Austria ruling directly over Milan & Venice and possessing major influence elsewhere
        - (3) Existence of only Piedmont-Sardinia as an independent state & very significant as the future unifier
    - c. Austria:
        - (1) The empire most vulnerable to the future problems of restive & alienated ethnic minorities seeking cultural or political independence or autonomy
        - (2) Ethnicity of the Austrians as a German people, yet containment by their empire of many Slavic nationalities such as Czechs (Bohemians), Slovaks, Poles, Ukrainians, Serbs, Croats, Slovenes, and Rumanians
        - (3) In Milan & Venice--habitation by Italians
        - (4) Emergence presently of the Hungarians (Magyars) as the largest & most problematic minority nationality in this Hapsburg Monarchy, whose demands for political concessions could not long be delayed or resisted--thus the cause of much future trouble
    - d. Poland--rule over most of this region by Russia, yet differences between Poles & Russians existing in language, popular culture, historic traditions, & religion (Catholicism vs. Greek Orthodoxy)
    - e. Finland--domination also by Russia after the Congress (gained from Sweden) yet varying from Russians in language, popular culture, history, & religion (Lutheranism)
    - f. Belgium--unity with Holland yet differences existing with the Dutch of the Netherlands in:
        - (1) Economy--industrial vs. commercial & agrarian
        - (2) Demography--urban Belgium vs. mainly rural or small town Holland

                (3) Culture & language--a mixture of French & German
                    dialect vs. only a German dialect & culture
                (4) Religion--Catholic vs. Protestant (Calvinism)
            g. Balkan Peninsula:
                (1) Control & rule over nearly all of southeastern Europe by the Ottoman Empire (Turkey), which was religiously Islamic or Moslem and culturally & linguistically Middle Eastern
                (2) Often harsh & repressive authority in the Balkans over Christian Europeans such as the Greeks, Macedonians, & Slavic peoples (Bulgarians, Rumanians, & Yugoslavs--Serbs, Croats, & Slovenes)
            h. Ireland--Occupation & control entirely by England since the 16th century--yet uniqueness of the Irish people & alienation from their overlords in popular culture (Gaelic or Celtic) and religion (predominantly Catholic)
    D. Results of the Congress of Vienna:
        1. A massive political reconstruction of Europe more successful than most in preventing future wars among the great powers:
            a. Occurrence of no major conflict involving the great powers until the 1850's (Crimean War: 1854-56)
            b. No general involvement of all the major nations again until 1914 with the beginning of World War I. (1914-18)
        2. Yet doom of the Vienna settlement eventually to failure:
            a. Existence of no effective & permanent means to enforce its decisions
            b. Greed & selfishness guiding the national leaders more often than international principles
            c. Refusal by a more progressive England after 1820 to cooperate with the more conservative Continental powers
           *d. Most importantly, the impossibility to suppress indefinitely the ideas & movements of liberalism & nationalism all over Europe--actual intensification as time passed
        3. Continuation of the Quadruple Alliance including England, Austria, Russia, & Prussia into the post-war years as an extension of the wartime coalition for the purpose of maintaining peace & safeguarding the settlement (England quit in 1820 but France joined in 1818)
        4. "Concert of Europe"--agreement by the representatives of the great powers to hold periodic conferences to consider measures for the maintenance of the Vienna settlement

IX. Revolutionary Movements of the 1st Half of the 19th Century
    A. Revolutions of the 1820's:
        1. In 1820-21: Spain, Portugal, Naples (Two Sicilies), & Piedmont-Sardinia
            a. These movements following a common pattern of army mutinies led by generals & officers against repressive regimes--brief success, with support from the bourgeoisie, proletariat, & educated elite (still a small minority)
            b. General failure in all except Portugal, where a constitutional monarchy & some reforms were preserved by British threats against conservative-power intervention
        2. Decembrist Revolt of 1825 in Russia--total & tragic failure to pressure the Tsarist regime for democratic reforms

  3. Greek War of Independence: 1821-29--victory for an independent nation of Greece from Turkish rule, with popular sympathy and later naval & military assistance from England, France, & Russia--the latter nation breaking with Metternich over this issue
B. Revolutions of 1830:
  1. France--destruction of the Bourbon Dynasty & ascendancy of Louis Philippe, Duke of Orleans as constitutional monarch after the "three glorious days" of fighting on the barricades & in the streets of Paris, founding the July Monarchy
  2. Belgium--attainment of national independence from Holland & constitutional government following an uprising & war of liberation
  3. Poland--rebellion against Russia achieving brief victory followed by reoccupation & horrible repression in 1833
  4. Germany & Italy--uprisings in small states ending usually in failure or few reforms
C. Revolutions of 1848-49: the most formidable & extensive chain of revolutionary movements in the history of the Western World
  1. France--popular insurrection establishing the 2nd Republic (1848--52) which was so beset with divisions & difficulties that it succumbed to the popular dictatorship of Louis Napoleon Bonaparte (entitled Napoleon III. and nephew of the great Napoleon I.) in December, 1851
  2. Germany--all states experiencing upheavals (including Prussia & Austria) with demands for democratic reforms & greater unification of Germany into one nation:
    a. Initial victories ending in near total defeats
    b. Efforts toward unification at the Frankfurt Assembly culminating in complete & comical collapse
  3. Italy--similar uprisings as in Germany for liberalism & national unification, (the latter under the leadership of the monarchy of Piedmont-Sardinia)--eventual failure everywhere
  4. Austria, or the Hapsburg Monarchy--four separate movements, all of them later destroyed by the imperial armies:
    a. Vienna--a temporarily successful uprising in the capital city for a constitution & liberal reforms
    b. Italian states of Lombardy (Milan) & Venetia (Venice)--independence movements against foreign domination
    c. Hungary--demands by the Magyars for political & cultural autonomy (semi-independence, or greater freedom & control over such matters while remaining inside the state)
    d. Bohemia, or the Czech lands--similar demands for political & cultural autonomy following an armed uprising in Prague--eventual suppression by Austrian troops

Chapter 10
KARL MARX & MARXISM

I. Introduction
   A. In all probability, no other thinker has had a greater impact on the modern world than Marx:
      1. While his theories & predictions are regarded by thoughtful & informed scholars today as erroneous, contradictory, & fundamentally flawed, nonetheless...
      2. He was also very correct about many historical developments in his past & present, and he exerted a profound influence on the way we view & interpret our world
      3. Proclamations by statesmen & economists declaring that Marxism in our world is dead must be greeted with skepticism & amusement; the ideas & impressions of Marx will be alive & very relevant as long as capitalism, injustice, & exploitation exist
   B. Ironically, both Karl Marx & Jesus Christ shared in common a Jewish background, a wish to improve the lives of oppressed people (Marx in this life, Christ in the afterlife), the regard of themselves as radical troublemakers by the establishments of their day, and a disapproval of the modern movements utilizing their names
      1. According to the Synoptic Gospels, Christ was non-violent & pacifistic, apolitical, contemptuous of material wealth, and mindful of & compassionate toward suffering people--thus exceedingly different from the typical contemporary "Christian"
      2. Likewise, Marx would have vehemently opposed the policies of 20th-century communism
   C. It is appalling that few Americans know ANYTHING about Marx and Marxism:
      1. Most people cannot distinguish between Karl Marx on the one hand and Groucho, Chico, Harpo, Zeppo (the straight guy in the films), & Gummo (never appeared in the movies) on the other hand
      2. However, this is untrue of Doc Barry's students (if they intend to pass the next exam)

II. Early Years of Marx (1818-83)
   A. Born in the Prussian Rhineland city of Trier to a prosperous, upper bourgeois Jewish family whose father converted to Christianity for professional reasons & assimilation purposes--early education in the thought of the Enlightenment & as a skeptic in religion
   B. Acquisition of an unusually rich intellectual background:
      1. Excellent educational preparation at several of the best universities in the world--study of many subjects at Bonn & Berlin before earning a doctorate in philosophy at Jena in 1841
      2. German philosophy--absorption of ideas from the most impressive thinkers (such as Darwin) of his age, many of whom were Germans--Goethe, Herder, Fichte, and especially Hegel
      3. French social thought & doctrine--residence in Paris (1844-48) amidst the most stimulating intellectual ferment of the age on the subjects of socialism & class conflict
      4. English political economy (the study of how governmental decisions & policies affect economic developments)--the remainder of Marx's life after 1849 spent in exile from the Continent (due to his revolutionary activities in 1848-49) in Eng-

land as often a lonely, embittered, & alienated man, but in the vanguard nation of industrialism
    5. Intellectual development of Marx into a deeply knowledgeable person in all of the most advanced theories & practices as well as on contemporary events, thus making him one of the best educated individuals of his era
  C. Enormous significance to Marx of the year 1848:
    1. Publication in January of his most famous work, The Communist Manifesto, predicting political upheaval & class warfare between proletariat & bourgeoisie
    2. Occurrence soon after in February in Paris the French Revolution of 1848 that in subsequent months swept throughout most of Europe, fulfilling Marx's earlier predictions and seeming to prove the basic correctness of his theories
    3. Later analysis by Marx brilliantly in two publications in 1852 of the reasons for proletarian defeat in Paris during the "Bloody June Days" of 1848 as well as in other revolutions: poor leadership, lack of effective organization, betrayal by the lower (petite) bourgeoisie, & ignorance of realities
  D. Role of Friedrich Engels (1820-95):
    1. Lifetime collaboration with Marx beginning in 1844 of this German friend from a wealthy capitalist family with business interests in Britain
    2. Future regard for their writings & research as often inseparable partly because of fundamental agreement & common purpose
    3. Yet possession by Marx of the dominant personality & a more forceful prose writing style, thus explaining why he has received the lion's share of credit
  E. Marxist ideology--generalizations:
    1. Like all great thinkers, Marx changing his beliefs over several decades as ideas evolved & matured with experience
    2. Emphasis in this study on his basic principles & opinions after the early 1850's & for the last three decades of his life
    3. Existence of very little originality in his core beliefs, with Marx borrowing most of his ideas & theories from other people & sources while twisting & modifying them to fit his own interpretations & views--thus being a matter of:
    4. Eclecticism--drawing ideas & inspiration from various sources & lacking in originality of conception
    5. Consequently, combination by Marx of numerous ideas & theories of others with his own penetrating perceptions into a powerful & persuasive body of ideology

III. Ideology of Marxism--Seven Basic Principles:
  A. Materialistic conception of the world--only matter in motion & in evolution truly exists; the spiritual world exists only as a figment of the imagination--espousal of these views earlier by various thinkers in the late-18th & early-19th centuries
  B. Dialectical interpretation of history:
    1. Creation of this theory & explanation of history by the great German philosopher G.W.F. Hegel (1770--1831), whose influence was pervasive in contemporary German universities
    2. View of history as a "process of social evolutionary change through a series of conflicts between antagonistic or opposite forces & movements & trends resulting in a new & better world"--to Hegel, these opposites & their consequences were

    expressed by the terms:
     a. Thesis--the established order of life
     b. Antithesis--the challenge to that old order
     c. Synthesis--the result, being a new & better world that then becomes the thesis against which an antithesis would arise--this process to proceed interminably throughout human experience, in Hegel's opinion
 C. Dialectical materialism--this was Marx's combination of the two previous points into his own version or modification of Hegel's theory of history--Marx and Hegel differed on <u>two</u> essential points:
  1. Hegel believed in the existence & supremacy of <u>ideas</u> in determining events in the world; Marx believed only in the importance of the <u>material</u> world--famous quote by Marx: "Philosophers have merely given different interpretations of the world; the point is to change it."
  2. Hegel believed the dialectical would be an endless process in history; Marx believed the dialectical would end finally in the triumph of communism--Marx's prediction for the dialectical was:
   a. Thesis--capitalism & the bourgeoisie (mode of production)
   b. Antithesis--exploitation & industrial poverty & the proletariat, eventuating in revolution (socio-economic class divisions & conflict)
   c. Synthesis--a classless & communist society

*Belief by Marx in <u>three</u> "laws of history":
 D. Economic determinism--the idea that economic activities & institutions & conditions dominate & control all other human ones and destine events & developments in history
  1. Marxian reference to the "mode of production" (the methods used & the human relations involved in making & distributing products & things) as the most important element in history--Marx stated: "The mode of production in material life determines the general character of the social, political, and spiritual processes of life."
  2. "Determinism"--a belief that occurrences are shaped by a series of antecedents & impersonal forces beyond human control or volition
   a. This materialistic & secular interpretation reflected Marx's great confidence in science--belief that he had discovered natural laws governing society (like his Enlightenment predecessors), just as Newton exposed gravitation as the force that moved the universe
   b. The religious version of determinism is called "predestination" and explains all happenings as a matter of divine intervention, with humans having no free will or control over their own destiny
 E. Class struggle--conviction by Marx that the laws of social development & the dialectical process unfolded in continuous conflicts throughout history between the rich & poor, haves & have-nots, the exploiters & exploited that shaped the outcome of human affairs--identification of the class struggle by Marx as having been:
  1. Freemen vs. slaves in Ancient times, nobility vs. serfs in Medieval times, guildmasters vs. journeymen in Early Modern times, and bourgeoisie vs. proletariat in 19th-century Modern times

        2. Actually, in point of fact, Marx was mistaken in his perception of history--while there were only a few & very rare instances of Marxist class struggles between upper & lower class...
        3. There had been a constant struggle for power <u>within</u> the small ruling upper-class elite of kings or emperors and landholding aristocracy and religious leaders--the exploited masses had remained passive, obedient, & subservient
    F. Inevitability of communism--the destruction of capitalism was an inexorable & unavoidable consequence (and not a thing of chance) because historical & human developments guided by deterministic natural laws were leading in only one direction--no different than a solar eclipse, it was natural & predictable & inevitable
*Separate from the previous six principles was the idea of the:
    G. Labor theory of surplus value (profit)--this was partially borrowed from Adam Smith & other classical economists, who proposed the labor theory of value--thus, in the opinion of Marx:
        1. The value of a commodity should be determined by the labor of the person producing it, so that...
        2. Workers should receive most of the profits from sales, yet did not, due to the unfairness of the "wage system"
        3. Industrialists & factory managers were a parasitic breed undeserving of the enormous profits derived from their exploitation of laborers
        4. Capitalism prevented the correction of these wide disparities between employee wages and employer profits, because of the:
            a. Irresistible human impulse of greed, selfishness, & the wish to dominate & manipulate other humans
            b. Necessity to compete against business rivals by the purchase of new technology & superior processes

J. The Marxian Analysis of the Future
    A. Portrayal by Marx of the coming of communism as the "spectre haunting Europe"--his scenario seems terribly simplistic today, yet it was compellingly logical to many educated people a century ago
    B. The sequence of occurrences:
        1. With no controls on a laissez-faire economy, cutthroat competition among businessmen would leave fewer & fewer wealthy capitalists at the top (thus a "shrinking bourgeoisie") and more & more propertyless proletarians at the bottom with worsening conditions of unemployment
        2. The nature of industrial capitalism was to replace labor with machines whenever possible, the consequence being problems of mounting overproduction & underconsumption (workers having little purchasing power) & massive misery
        3. Result--a popular revolution seizing the central government & establishing a <u>temporary</u> "dictatorship of the proletariat" in order to inaugurate the "permanent revolution" of communism:
            a. Interestingly, this was <u>not</u> to be accomplished by firing squad executions or terrorism or excessive coercion
            b. Instead, while private landed property would be abolished immediately, other forms of wealth would be gradually eliminated through high income taxes & inheritance limitations
            c. Eventually, social classes & tensions would vanish and international peace would emerge--the state (powerful

central government) would "wither away" as no longer being necessary and authority would be invested at the local level in small, self-sufficient communities applying the principle of "from each according to his abilities, to each according to his need"
       4. How the revolution was to be organized & led:
          a. Belief by Marx intially, before the Revolutions of 1848-49, that the national government could be seized in a coup d'etat by a small & dedicated body of revolutionaries who would then rule for the ignorant & unprepared masses of proletariat & peasants (what Lenin, Trotsky, Mao, & Castro later did)
          b. Final conclusion by Marx, however, after the Revolutions of 1848 and by roughly 1852, that the masses over a long period of time must be educated & made conscious of their destiny & task of preparing for a truly <u>popular</u> revolution and not one effected by a <u>tiny group</u> of elite leaders or a vanguard of superiors

V. Fallacies & Weaknesses in Marxist Ideology
   A. Belief in historical determinism & natural laws guiding human affairs--the vast majority of historians & social scientists reject the notion that mankind has no free will or control over his destiny, and that events are driven by forces beyond human influence
   B. Inability to appreciate the power of non-economic factors & institutions such as religion & spectator sports & family & popular culture with its examples of music, literature, the arts (and now radio & television & computers):
      1. All of these motivate & entertain people while distracting them from their focus on the drudgery or unpleasantness of jobs & work
      2. Quite obviously, materialistic explanations are sometimes inadequate for understanding the world
   C. Oversimplification of human nature by stereotyping motives, interests, and people:
      1. The bourgeoisie was regarded as fundamentally selfish, greedy, corrupt, & doomed because capitalism inevitably made them that way
      2. The proletariat was regarded as fundamentally decent, beneficent, virtuous, & capable of perception because of their exploitation by capitalism
      3. Marx never did understand the proletariat whom he had devoted his life to helping, for <u>two</u> reasons:
         a. He came from an upper-bourgeoisie background socio-economically which blinded him to the realities of lower-class existence
         b. Even while living in desperate poverty for two decades in London, Marx almost never socialized with uneducated, lower-class sorts--instead of working for money, he went nearly every day for study & research to the Reading Room (library) of the British Museum, sitting always at seat #G-7
      4. Marx failed to realize that the proletariat preferred to benefit from capitalism & to become middle-class rather than to destroy the entire system

D. Failure to foresee general social improvements & rising standards of living, that reconciled many formerly lower-class people to the capitalistic system--these better conditions resulted from:
  1. Machines & modern technology increasingly making available higher-quality products at reasonable & declining prices to more & more people, consequently elevating proletarians to bourgeois status (the French term <u>embourgeoisement</u> describes the process of becoming more middle class)
  2. National governments more inclined to intervene in economic matters with protective laws & regulatory practices to curb the excesses of free enterprise capitalism (especially after the extension of voting rights to the proletariat in the late-19th century)
  3. Later generations of capitalists being somewhat less inhumane & callous and more enlightened toward worker problems
  4. More powerful labor unions generally pressuring for positive advances during the 20th century in wages, working hours, factory conditions, health benefits, etc.
E. Underestimation of the power of nationalism, which became <u>the</u> most influential & pervasive ideology in the modern world--it undermined & emerged as more predominant than the class-consciousness being glorified by Marxists

I. Marxist Predictions That Failed
  A. Anticipation of the occurrence of future communist revolutions in advanced, highly urbanized, & industrialized states with large percentages of a proletariat class:
    1. In fact, they happened in backward, rural, & underdeveloped nations with tiny percentages of proletarians
    2. To Marx, the least likely European nation to experience a successful communist revolution was Russia!
  B. Achievement of a "classless society" emphasizing sharing, equality, & fairness after the communist revolution--actually, there was the persistence of a wealthy & privileged elite of bureaucrats & party members at the top of society
  C. The "withering away" of a powerful central government as eventually unnecessary after playing a dominant role in forging the new communist society--obviously not so, as the states in communist countries became even more powerful than before (until collapsing from incompetence & exhaustion, as did the Soviet Union in 1989)
  D. Fate of the "dictatorship of the proletariat":
    1. Marx ultimately envisioned a vague kind of workers' democracy in local, small, self-sufficient communities without oppression or social distinctions--in fact, Marx described the state as the "organized power of one class for oppressing another" and assigned it only a temporary role in the new & better world of the future
    2. Yet Lenin, Stalin, Mao, & Castro established totalitarian dictatorships by a small, elite, exclusivist group--in this sense, Marx's so-called disciples did not fulfill but betrayed the aspirations of their prophet

VII. Accurate Observations by Marx
   A. Prediction of the downfall of "free enterprise" capitalism in the late-19th century:
      1. Cutthroat, unrestricted, & uncontrolled competition drove out most real competitors and resulted in modern monopolies, cartels, or trusts that still dominate many major sectors of our contemporary economies
      2. Today wages & prices are only partially determined by "market forces" of supply & demand--also shaping them are governmental policies & decisions, labor union pressure, and <u>mainly</u> the arbitrary wishes of a handful of very rich & powerful corporate executives who dictate numbers while ignoring or at least seeking to avoid "market forces" altogether
   B. Observation of religion as the "opiate of the masses" used as a tool by the ruling classes to maintain the status quo & to keep the downtrodden in their position of inferiority
      1. Expression of these opinions first by the ancient Greek philosophers over 2,000 years before Marx
      2. Yet he publicized & popularized these views while demonstrating their applicability throughout history
   C. Perception of the tremendous transformation-power of industrial capitalism in effecting enormous change--almost no one understood as did Marx just how revolutionary its long-term consequences would be, and even he underestimated them

VIII. Positive Impact of Marx & Marxism on the World
   [the initial five in this listing were not originated by Marx but greatly publicized & popularized]
   A. Stress on a materialistic understanding of the world--Marx forced serious scholars to seek realistic, practical, rational, down-to-earth explanations for problems
   B. Application of "scientific" methods of exhaustive research, accumulation of evidence, and factual quantification to prove points & to ascertain knowledge in the study of society--this approach often called <u>positivism</u>
   C. Recognition of class conflict as very influential & important in explaining events in the modern world
   D. Emphasis on economics as an awesome force in affecting & shaping almost everything that occurs in our world
   E. Establishment of an appreciation for the processes of history resulting from evolutionary change, growth, & development
   F. Foundation of the social sciences as separate fields of study, such as sociology, economics, psychology--initial development by Marx of the "idea of alienation" (the withdrawal or separation or isolation of a person or group from the social mainstream) as a unified social theory

Chapter 11   19TH CENTURY EUROPE: NATIONAL DEVELOPMENTS

GREAT BRITAIN

I. Introduction
   A. The history of the 19th century can be understood as the expansion & spread throughout the world of English institutions (Parliament, Common Law) and French ideas (democracy, nationalism)---thus the immense importance of both nations to an understanding of the modern world
   B. Development by both Britain & France of representative & democratic governments, but usually in different ways:
      1. British tradition stressing gradual, evolutionary change through peaceful & non-violent reform--a preparatory period of education, political discussion, agitation, & campaign to be followed by the passage of bills in Parliament
      2. French tradition often featuring revolutionary upheaval & destruction of governments to achieve sudden & dramatic change--yet both nations experiencing the opposite methods as well
   C. Geography--the island nation of Britain ("Britannia" is the Latin term), sometimes known as the United Kingdom or the "U.K.", consisting for many centuries of four regions or "nations" or kingdoms: England, Wales, Scotland, & Ireland
   D. Recognition of Britain in the 19th century as the most powerful nation in the world--sources of power & wealth:
      1. Leadership in the Industrial Revolution until the last two decades of the century when overtaken by Germany & the U.S.A.
      2. Rule over the world's largest colonial empire
      3. Maintenance of the world's most powerful navy
      4. Dominance of international trade
      5. Possession of a small & fairly good professional army employed only in the colonies to preserve the empire
   E. Evolution during this century from an aristocratic & oligarchical society into a more democratic one--importance of numerous political, social, economic, & assorted other reforms:
II. Political Reforms
   A. Extension of voting rights gradually to larger segments of the population in local elections & national ones (House of Commons):
   B. Elections to Commons were far from "democratic", with roughly 15% of the male population eligible to vote by virtue of landownership & payment of substantial taxes
      1. 1st Reform Bill of 1832--grant of franchise or suffrage (voting rights) generally to the bourgeoisie, thus doubling the electorate to around one-third of all males--passage by the Liberal Party (known as Whigs prior to the 1830's and representing great noblemen & especially wealthy urban bourgeois)
      2. 2nd Reform Bill of 1867--grant of the vote mainly to urban workers without property--another doubling of the electorate to two-thirds of males--this considered a drastic gamble & "Leap in the Dark" by the Conservative Party (known as Tories before the 1830's & representing mainly rural landed interests of the mainstream aristocracy) and its leader Benjamin Disraeli
      3. 3rd Reform Bill of 1884--extension of the vote to rural laborers without land, thus including nearly all males--passage by the Liberals under the leadership of PM William Gladstone

4. 4th Reform Bill of 1918--grant immediately after WWI. of the vote to all males over age of 21 & all females over 30--since so many men had died in war, leaders feared that women would control government if allowed to vote equally--belief also that young women were too impulsive & irrational to vote intelligently
5. 5th Reform Bill of 1928--grant of the vote to all men & women over 21, thus total voting equality

C. Inclusion in each Reform Bill of reapportionment--assignment of greater representation to electoral districts growing in population as industrialized cities) and elimination of "rotten" boroughs depopulated districts) & "pocket" boroughs (controlled by local noblemen)

D. Parliament Act of 1911--termination of the traditional absolute veto of the House of Lords over legislation passed by the Commons (laws needing approval of both Houses) and grant of a delaying or suspensive veto--capability of the Lords now to vote down a law twice in two years after passage in the Commons; on the third passage in the Commons, the Lords could do nothing & the bill automatically became law

E. Catholic Emancipation of 1828-29--grant of the right to vote & hold political office to the religious minority of Catholics--extension of similar rights to Jews in 1858

III. Social & economic & educational & other reforms (to be lectured on in class):
A. Reform of the Criminal Code in 1820's removing some antiquated laws
B. Partial repeal of the Combinations Acts (earlier prohibiting formation of craft unions)--allowance in the 1820's to organize but not to strike or to pressure for collective bargaining
C. Introduction in the 1820's of the 1st professional police force for London known as "Bobbies" & named for reformer Robert Peel
D. New Poor Law of 1834--shift from an old system of local & decentralized & "outdoor" relief to a new system of national & centralized & "indoor" relief in notorious poorhouses--controversial sponsorship by the Liberal Party & bourgeoisie
E. Repeal of the Corn Laws in 1846--conversion of the economy to a free basis by abolishing high tariff taxes on grain importation, thus significantly lowering food prices & stimulating exports
F. Factory Acts--featuring a landmark act in 1833 providing for government inspectors to enforce laws for 1st time
G. General Education Act of 1870--beginning the gradual establishment over 21 years of a nearly national & free & compulsory educational system at the elementary level
H. National Insurance Act of 1911--provision of compulsory health insurance & unemployment compensation--the 1st of several social welfare measures to be paid for with progressive taxation

IV. Victorian Morality
A. Description of the code of behavior & lifestyle & values pursued by the bourgeoisie during 19th century--named for Queen Victoria (1837-1901) who personified it
B. Primary objective--to present an impression of total superiority to others by the psychologically insecure middle class, who are still a numerical minority of all society
C. Main features & characteristics:
1. Importance of appearances, formality, & public display
2. Stress on respectability & decent or proper manners

3. Paternalistic & condescending attitudes toward unfortunates, with charity & compassion reflecting a sense of duty
   4. Public avoidance of emotional & irrational behavior, thus demonstrating self-discipline & control
   5. Acceptance of hypocrisy--feigning to be what one is not
   6. Repression publicly of sexual desires & refusal to discuss such matters in public--constant emphasis on being a lady or gentleman

FRANCE

. Introduction
   A. Famous comments on the significance of the history of France:
      1. Admission by British historian Arnold Toynbee in his huge <u>Study of History</u> that "France perhaps approaches nearer than any other national state to being co-central and co-extensive with the whole of our Western Society."[1]
      2. Declaration by Frenchman Jacques Fauvet that "France, like a microcosm, reproduces the problems of all humanity."[2]
      3. Its 19th-century experience was most truly reflective & indicative of the difficulties & struggles of a people attempting to establish a democracy
   B. Statement by historian Paul Gagnon that: "By 1814, France had a new society but had not yet found a political system to govern it. Unlike the English and American Revolutions, the French Revolution left no single political tradition to its heirs."[3]
   C. Emergence instead from the French Revolutionary & Napoleonic Era (1789--1815) of <u>four</u> political traditions each with its supporters and programs:
      1. Ultra-Royalism--absolute monarchy and the Old Regime of narrow privilege, social hierarchy, and clerical control of thought & education
      2. Constitutional Monarchy--political compromise of royal predominance with representative parliamentary institutions in the hands of a conservative group of educated & wealthy citizens known as "notables" (rich bourgeoisie & aristocrats)
      3. Jacobin Republicanism--bourgeois democracy (the Jacobins being "radical" republicans during the 1st Republic) dedicated to anticlericalism, nationalism, & liberalism with a willingness to countenance social & economic reforms to benefit the lower classes
      4. Bonapartism--a curious & unique mixture of national & military glory, political authoritarianism, economic development, and opportunities for all--thus a kind of popular dictatorship emphasizing progressive reforms for the benefit of all
         a. Existence of Bonapartism as a combination of some conservative policies & principles <u>and</u> some liberal ones
         b. Example of the universal attraction & popular romanticism surrounding the "man on horseback" (military commander)
   D. Consequent characterization of 19th-century French politics & government as displaying factionalism, instability, divisions over highly emotional issues, numerous governmental changes, frequent failure to accomplish fundamental reforms, and long periods of moderation followed by crises causing polarization into the "two Frances" of Left & Right extremes

E. Procession of 19th-century French governments:
  1. Bourbon Restoration: 1814--30
     a. Constitutional monarchy of Louis XVIII. (1814-24) and Charles X. (1824-30) under the Charter of 1814--conservative governments increasingly moving to the Right
     b. Violations of the constitution in 1830 in the form of press censorship, reductions in voting qualifications, & restrictions on civil liberties resulting in the July Revolution of 1830 and the...
  2. July (Orleanist) Monarchy of Louis Philippe, Duc d'Orleans (cousin of the last king & a separate branch of the royal family): 1830--48
     a. Another constitutional monarchy promising moderation & reforms initially yet never delivering & increasingly inclined also toward conservativism & repression
     b. Failure to effect reforms, violations of the constitution, and mounting economic & social misery during a depression of the late-1840's resulting in the Revolution of 1848 in February and the...
  3. 2nd Republic: 1848--52
     a. Appearance of cleavages between moderate & radical factions of 1848 revolutionaries leading to workingclass alienation and a proletarian uprising in Paris with the "Bloody June Days" that were quelled savagely
     b. Creation of a liberal constitution with universal manhood suffrage--yet failure to prevent the election of a very conservative National Assembly conniving to restore the monarchy, and the...
     c. Election of an ambitious adventurer with a legendary & popular name (Louis Napoleon Bonaparte--nephew of the great emperor) as first president of the Republic
     d. Seizure of power with support of loyal army units by LNB on December 2, 1851 and establishment of the...
  4. 2nd Empire of Napoleon III.: 1852--70 (the 1st Napoleon had had a son--called Napoleon II. by some supporters--who died in 1832 at age 21 without ever ruling anywhere)
     a. A veiled dictatorship with the emperor as chief of state ruling with the assistance of a relatively weak legislature usually packed with "official" candidates winning elections manipulated by government bureaucrats
     b. Achievement of enormous popularity during the 1st decade of his reign with the accomplishment of many positive projects & reforms
     c. Declining health of the emperor, rising criticism from the opposition, and finally defeat & capture during the Franco-Prussian War of 1870 resulting in the...
  5. 3rd Republic: 1870--1940
     a. Impressive longevity despite its birth in the midst of foreign & civil war and despite its shaky instability & numerous vicissitudes for the first three decades
     b. Gradual acceptance of bourgeois democracy by the majority of Frenchmen

II. Napoleon III. & the 2nd Empire
  A. Accomplishments of his reign:
    1. Modernization of Paris--emergence of the city as it appears

today under a massive construction program providing work for the unemployed--directorship of Baron Georges Haussmann
- a. Replacement of many crooked & narrow streets with the sweeping boulevards of today
- b. Creation of the most spacious, elegant, & beautiful European capital city of its day (or of our own day as well)

2. Cultural revival--Paris regaining its position as the world center of art, literature, music, fashion, & diplomacy under the stimulus of the national government
3. Impressive economic expansion & prosperity in response to governmental promotion & encouragement, especially during the first decade (1852-62):
   - a. Modernization of large-scale & heavy industry--production doubling, railway mileage increasing sixfold, & steam power usage rising fivefold
   - b. Authorization of the 1st investment banks (such as Credit Mobilier) to lend much money for business projects, and many deposit banks (such as Credit Lyonnais) for individual transactions
   - c. Governmental organization & sponsorship of railroads, steamships, & telegraph lines by private enterprises--thus completion of a basic transportation system making possible a truly national market
   - d. Foreign trade tripling
   - e. In spite of great gains, persistence of France as a nation of small businesses under family ownership adhering to luxury trades & old methods of handicraft skills with little machinery--thus industrial production falling behind that of Britain & Germany
   - f. Decline also in the population growth-rate below that of other major nations
4. Gains & improvements for all classes in society:
   - a. Advances especially for the upper bourgeoisie, yet progress also for all in the middle class
   - b. Significant benefits for peasant farmers due to cheap transportation systems & access to markets--official favoritism also for the conservative Catholic Church
   - c. Fewer gains for proletarian workers--yet benefits from rising wages, lower unemployment, organization of insurance companies, public construction of tenement houses, & relaxation of laws prohibiting labor unions
   - d. Permission granted to form labor unions for the purpose of mutual assistance but not of fomenting strikes

B. The "Liberal Empire": 1860-70
1. Always incomplete success with the methods used by Napoleon to maintain total control: arrests, deportation, manipulation of elections, censorship of the press
2. Popular response to these practices with mounting resentment, pressure, & unpopularity
3. Thus a slow abandonment of repressive measures after 1860 with efforts to conciliate liberals--later attempt by Napoleon to establish himself as a constitutional monarch toward the end of his reign--reasons for these new policies:
   - a. Powerful tradition in France of representative government & liberalism--desires by the vast popular majority for certain civil liberties & free elections

            b. Premature aging & failing health of the Emperor--incapacity to rule directly
            c. Increasing inability of the government to reconcile so many discordant elements in society--in other words, existence of numerous & deep socio-economic divisions
            d. Strong opposition by many bourgeoisie & the lower classes generally to heavy Church influence in the regime
        4. Liberal concessions after 1860:
            a. A general amnesty for political prisoners
            b. Free discussions in the legislature of proposals from the throne--sessions open to the public--allowance of opposition parties to form & to campaign for elections without governmental harassment
            c. Grant of freedom of the press & assembly in 1867--permission in 1869 for the legislature (Corps Legislatif) to propose laws and to criticize & vote on the budget--thus the opposition parties winning 45% of the total vote in the 1869 elections
            d. Plan by Napoleon in 1870 to introduce the democratic principle of "ministerial responsibility" in the legisture when war caused his downfall
            e. Yet persistence of the determination by republicans & socialists to destroy this government--attitude of Napoleon that such hostility posing a threatening menace to his survival as ruler
            f. Decision by the Emperor to gamble on dangerous wars in order to regain his popularity & prestige
    C. Wars of Napoleon III.
        1. Bonapartism almost inevitably meaning military & national glory to the French--enhancement of Napoleon's regime by early victories in wars & campaigns, but ultimate destruction by later defeats
        2. Crimean War: 1854-56
            a. A bizarre conflict fought by France, Britain, & Ottoman Turkey against Russia on the Russian Black Sea peninsula of Crimea--main cause of the war in the constant Russian pressure on & aggression toward the rapidly declining Ottoman Turkish Empire
            b. This diplomatic debate & quandary over what to do about the collapsing Turkish state due to minority-nationalities problems, governmental incompetence, internal decay, & assaults from European neighbors known as the "Near Eastern Question"
            c. Results of the war--Allied victory despite incredible ineptitude & blunders on both sides--attainment by Napoleon III. of his zenith in power & prestige at the war congress in Paris
        3. Franco-Austrian War of 1859
            a. French negotiation of an alliance with Piedmont-Sardinia for war against Austria & a consequent attainment of the political unification of Italy
            b. Involvement also of devious desires by Napoleon to control the momemtum of events & thus to replace Austrian domination of Italy with a strong French presence there
            c. Existence of romantic notions by Napoleon as well--origination of the Bonaparte family as Italians from the is-

                    land of Corsica--thus sincere espousal of the cause of
                    Italians as an oppressed nationality
                d. Early triumphs in 1859 liberating northern Italy--then
                    negotiation of a premature treaty with Austria because
                    of heavy battlefield casualties, his inability to guide
                    Italian events, & the anger of French Catholics over the
                    Pope's loss of territories in central Italy to the unif-
                    ication movement
                e. Rapid departure of Napoleon from Italy except for a garr-
                    ison of French soldiers left in Rome to protect the Pope
                f. Reward for this brief war with the border territories of
                    Savoy & Nice as compensation from Piedmont-Sardinia
            4. Mexican Venture: 1861-67
                a. A foolish enterprise in response to Napoleon's conviction
                    that the tiny Mexican aristocracy (favorably influenced
                    by French culture & commercial ties) might sustain the
                    rule over Mexico of a French regime & small French army
                b. Exploitation of a power vacuum & chaos in Mexico by Nap-
                    eon to dispatch a French expeditionary force--capture of
                    Mexico City in 1863 & emplacement on the throne of Aus-
                    trian Archduke Maximilian
                c. Response by the Mexican masses of resentment, hostility,
                    & rebellion into civil war
                d. Eventual abandonment of the venture by Napoleon & the re-
                    call of his troops due to pressure & protest from the
                    U.S.--Maximilian captured & shot in 1867
                e. Disastrous consequences owing to the expensiveness of the
                    expedition as well as its hopelessness & stupidity
            5. Overseas Empire--extension of influence in Algeria & North
                Africa, Indochina, & the Pacific Islands--establishment of
                the 2nd largest empire in overseas possessions to Britain
            6. Franco-Prussian War: 1870-71
                a. Debacle ("collapse") at the warfront along the eastern
                    border with Germany as the French armies were defeated &
                    surrounded--surrender & capture of Napoleon with one of
                    his armies--later exile to Britain & death there in 1873
                b. Insurrection in Paris & proclamation of the 3rd Republic
                    on September 4, 1870, yet continuation of war with Ger-
                    many by the provisional government
                c. Siege of Paris (September, 1870--January, 1871) by encir-
                    cling German armies for four months until capitulation
                    after heroic efforts, severe suffering, & the death of
                    60,000 to smallpox alone
                d. Negotiation of an armistice on January 28, 1871--occurr-
                    ence of national elections in February to chose a per-
                    manent French government & to decide on war or peace

II. 3rd Republic: 1870--1940
    A. Birth of the republic in the midst of a foreign & civil war
        1. Elections for a new National Assembly waged over the issue of
            war or peace, with republicans & radical Parisians naively
            campaigning for a continuation of fighting, but with conser-
            vative provincials & monarchists favoring immediate peace
            at any price--a huge victory for the latter due to war-weari-
            ness & exhaustion

        a. Election by the NA of Adolphe Thiers as temporary president (1871-73) and a clever, intelligent, moderate, tactful, & veteran politician
        b. Negotiation of the humiliating Treaty of Frankfurt with a now-unified Germany surrendering areas of the provinces of Alsace-Lorraine, paying a huge indemnity, & suffering an occupation army briefly
        c. The loss of Alsace-Lorraine quickly becoming the key issue that would lead to future war & the impossibility of peace between France & Germany
        d. Plans by the conservative majority in the National Assembly sitting out at Versailles to restore the monarchy
        e. Provocation by these events & other punitive measures against the city of Paris of a massive uprising in Paris & the establishment of a new city government (the Commune) proclaiming itself autonomous & in rebellion against the rest of the nation
    2. Paris Commune--a civil war between the National Assembly representing the conservative provinces and the Paris Commune representing the liberal & republican city
        a. Occurrence of another siege of the city for nine weeks & 62 days (March 27--May 28, 1871) ending in defeat for the Communards in savage fighting
        b. Fearful destruction of property & life with parts of the city burned, hostages murdered, and 20,000 killed & many thousands more deported, executed, or sentenced to years of hard labor
        c. Propagation by Marx later in his writings of a myth that the Commune constituted a class-conscious & Marxian socialist movement--incorrectness of this myth in the fact that most Communards were simply lower bourgeois, anticlerical, patriotic republicans
        d. All of these events (German war, siege of Paris, peace treaty, & civil war) known collectively as the Terrible Year
    3. Rapid economic recovery & restoration of social stability during the next several years under the leadership of Thiers
B. Establishment of a definitive form of government
    1. Critical split in the monarchist majority of the National Assembly between supporters of the two dynastic branches--Bourbons (Legitimists) & Orleanists, each with a candidate for the throne
        a. A compromise plan to allow the childless & elderly Bourbon candidate (Comte de Chambord) to ascend the throne first wrecked by his stubborn insistence on ruling as an absolute monarch with no constitutional constraints
        b. This absolutist notion unacceptable to the Orleanists & the vast majority of French people
        c. Election by NA of a new president--Maurice de MacMahon (1873-79), an old general & conservative monarchist chosen to hold government together long enough for the monarchists to unite in another compromise--that development never occurred
        d. Subsequent elections to the NA returning a solid moderate republican majority that finally wrote a constitution

2. Constitution of 1875
   a. Bicameral legislature--a Senate chosen indirectly by regional electoral bodies, & a Chamber of Deputies elected directly by universal manhood suffrage--all legislation requiring passage of both houses, but nothing more
   b. Election for seven years of a president jointly by both houses of the National Assembly sitting together only for this occasion
   c. No mention of the practice & principle of "ministerial responsibility" (requirement that the true executive branch, meaning prime minister & cabinet, come from the majority in the legislature)--this point to be decided by the:
3. Crisis of Seize Mai (May 16, 1877--date for the calling of elections to resolve a constitutional crisis):
   a. Dismissal by President MacMahon of a premier (French title for prime minister) who was a republican & replacement with a monarchist having no support in the Chamber of Deputies--vote of no confidence by the latter with consequent governmental paralysis & stalemate
   b. Decision by MacMahon to call parliamentary elections as a popular referendum on the issue of ministerial responsibility, with a republican victory signifying yes and a monarchist triumph meaning no
   c. Victory by the republicans & acceptance by the president of a true parliamentary system with the practice of ministerial responsibility
   d. Solidification of this republican government in 1879 with MacMahon's resignation & his replacement by a moderate republican and with election victories in the Senate

C. Characteristics of politics in the 3rd Republic:
   1. A multiplicity of parties compelling coalition or bloc governments of cabinets or ministries
   2. Instability & impermanence of those ministries, with the average life expectancy of only one year fefore falling from power & necessitating the formation of a new cabinet that could win a majority vote in the Chamber of Deputies--yet many of the same politicians usually serving on many cabinets
   3. Overemphasis on compromise with many mediocre leaders fearing & opposing brilliant or controversial politicians because the latter often caused cabinet defections & led to downfall in a loss of the parliamentary majority
   4. Avoidance of controversial issues for the same reasons above
   5. Domestic & foreign weakness in dealing with fundamental problems
   6. Personal rivalries & petty competitions plaguing governments
   7. Existence of formidable opposition to these bourgeois republicans on the Left from socialists, & on the Right from monarchists & clericals & Bonapartists--yet constant maintenance of a majority of legislative seats by this group of weak & flabby bourgeois parties forming cabinet governments
   8. Appropriate application to these politicians of a famous phrase--very often "democracy breeds mediocrity"

D. Scandals & crises of the 3rd Republic--a series of major challenges causing disrepute, humiliation, & destabilization of government:
   1. Boulanger Affair

a. Emergence during the 1880's of Georges Boulanger as a very popular, handsome, ambitious, & charismatic army general and then in 1887 minister of war
   b. Saberrattling calls for war with Germany earning him the nickname of "General Revenge"--retirement from the military and entrance into politics in 1888
   c. Existence of an opportunity for an overthrow of the government in January, 1889 after sweeping a by-election in Paris--friends urging him to seize control illegally with loyal local regiments--refusal when his nerve failed to equal his bombastic rhetoric
   d. Retaliation by the government in launching an investigation of his shady & compromised background--flight of the General to exile in Belgium, where he committed suicide in 1891 on the grave of a former mistress
2. Various revelations of political graft, corruption, racketeering, favoritism, and distribution of spoils leading to severe criticism of the political system and inspiring right-wing scandal-sheet newspapers to refer to the 3rd Republic derisively as "la gueuse", meaning the filthy slut or whore
3. Panama Scandal
   a. Bankruptcy in 1889 of a private company attempting to build the canal--subsequent revelations of proof that government ministers & deputies accepted bribes for supporting the shaky company with votes of governmental subsidies & concessions
   b. Implication of several prominent bankers & financiers with one of them committing suicide--public furor & outrage when no legal action taken against the major participants
4. Death of President Felix Faure in February, 1889 from a stroke suffered in the rear of a limousine while his dancehall girlfriend performed fellatio (oral sex)--rumors abounded that he expired with a smile on his face and that never in history had such a "blow" been struck for French democracy
5. Dreyfus Affair--the most serious & formidable crisis facing the 3rd Republic, known as "the shame & glory of France"--(to be lectured on in class)

E. Political structure of the 3rd Republic:

President--a figurehead & ceremonial leader

Premier & Cabinet of Ministers--true executive branch

Chamber of Deputies, with a weak Senate--legislature

Frenchmen--electorate

UNIFICATION OF ITALY

I. Introduction
   A. Strong appeal among Italians of liberalism & nationalism in this century, meaning unification of the 8-10 relatively small & weak states into one Italy with an end to foreign (Austrian) domination and the establishment of democratic government
   B. Description of this movement with the term <u>Risorgimento</u>, or "regeneration", "resurgence", "resurrection"--much popular support for these objectives yet existence of formidable obstacles to its achievement
   C. Emergence of the leadership of the constitutional monarchy of Piedmont-Sardinia as the only truly independent Italian state willing to risk war for the cause
   D. Obstacles to Italian unification and reasons for the necessity of assistance from an outside power:
      1. Disunity of Italy into numerous small & weak states incapable of defeating Austria by themselves--direct Austrian rule over the northern provinces of Lombardy (Milan) & Venetia (Venice) and easy intimidation of all opposition elsewhere
      2. Opposition to Risorgimento by the petty rulers governing most of the Italian states--selfish wishes to maintain their power & status with Austrian backing
      3. Disagreements between liberals & nationalists over the extent & degree of democratic reforms
      4. Divisions among nationalists over the future unified state of Italy--thus a lack of common goals (see below)
   E. Three schools of thought appearing by the 1840's:
      1. Leftists favoring a democratic republic--known as the "Young Italy" movement under the inspirational leadership of Giuseppe Mazzini (1815-72)
      2. Moderates favoring unity under the dominance of the constitutional monarchy of Piedmont-Sardinia
      3. Rightists favoring a federation of Italian states under the presidency of the pope and with defense from the Piedmontese army--retention by each state of a monarch & constitution

II. The Unification Movement
   A. Great significance of the leadership of Count Camillo di Cavour as premier of P-S from 1852 until (with slight interruption) his death in 1861--a brilliant statesman & clever diplomat guiding the cause to completion
      1. Impressive support & cooperation from King Victor Emmanuel II. (1849--78) of the dynastic House of Savoy
      2. Implementation by Cavour of a series of reforms in P-S
      3. Realization of the necessity of military support for Italian unification from an outside power to expel Austria--negotiation of a secret alliance with France & Napoleon III. in 1858
      4. Extension also of clandestine assistance to the recently organized National Society--an underground group operating all over northern Italy and preparing for armed popular insurrections in various states in favor of unity under P-S
   B. Provocation of war with Austria in 1859--military intervention by France followed quickly by defeat of Austria & then Napoleon's duplicitous & unilateral conclusion of peace after winning for P-S only Lombardy but not Venetia
   C. Successful uprisings throughout northern & central Italy in 1859 concurrently with the war in Modena, Parma, Tuscany, & much of the

      Papal States--popular votes of approval in plebiscites for annexation to P-S in late-1859--completion by January, 1860
  D. Celebrated expedition in May, 1860 of the revolutionary & romantic adventurer Giuseppe Garibaldi with his 1000 volunteer Redshirts to to help liberate & annex Sicily & Naples--total triumph by September, 1860
  E. Announcement of the establishment of the Kingdom of Italy by an Italian Parliament in March, 1861--yet without Venetia (still a possession of Austria) and the city of Rome (the Pope's last bit of territory under the protection of French troops)
  F. Acquisition of Venetia as a by-product of an Italian alliance with Prussia against Austria in the Austro-Prussian War of 1866
  G. Addition of Rome in 1870 with the departure of French troops during the Franco-Prussian War--proclamation of Rome as the new Italian capital after 12 years of sporadic conflict & complex diplomacy

UNIFICATION OF GERMANY

I. Introduction
  A. Leadership of Prussia & its prime minister (chancellor) Otto von Bismarck in the defeat of Austria & the unification of the remaining 38 German states into modern Germany
  B. Character & capabilities of Bismarck--awesomely talented & intelligent, aristocratic family background, brilliantly self-educated, massive physique with a large head & sizeable gray eyes & bushy eyebrows, unscrupulous, ruthless, & opportunistic
    1. An ardent nationalist who despised liberalism and loved tradition & conservatism & the Prussian monarchy of the Hohenzollern Dynasty--service in government over many years
    2. A diplomatic genius, clever maneuverer, & proponent of <u>Realpolitik</u>--a modern version of Machiavellianism
  C. Constitution of 1850--a very conservative document granted by the monarchy to preserve its domination of government while creating the illusion of some democracy
    1. Preservation by the monarchy of an absolute veto over legislation as well as the authority to choose the cabinet without the principle of ministerial responsibility
    2. Possession by the lower legislative house (Reichstag) of only the authority to vote on the budget & to approve or reject new taxes but not to initiate laws--circumvention of democracy by a complex method of elections favoring the rich
  D. Precipitation of a constitutional crisis upon the appointment of Bismarck as chancellor in 1862:
    1. Wish by Bismarck to expand & modernize the military and to construct more railroads (for swift movement of the armies)-- thus the necessity of a major increase in taxation
    2. Demands on the Reichstag for more taxation--adamant refusal by the Reichstag in spite of Bismarck's famous "Blood & Iron" Speech on how the great issues of the day will be resolved
    3. Response by Bismarck--illegal collection of higher taxes by the governmental bureaucracy and expenditure without parliamentary approval for four years until 1866
    4. Profound unpopularity for Bismarck--frequent dissolution of the Reichstag, suppression of newspapers, indictment of opponents, yet successful build-up of the armies

II. Wars of Unification
   A. Employment by Bismarck of clever diplomacy & warfare to achieve the unification of Germany--existence of only Austria as the German state sufficiently powerful to prevent this accomplishment--yet necessity to negate the opposition of other nations such as France & Russia--thus the requirement of very shrewd & flexible diplomacy
   B. Wars of Bismarck:
      1. Danish War of 1864--manipulation of nationalist sentiments in Austria & elsewhere in the other 38 German states for a war against Denmark for control of two Danish provinces (Schleswig-Holstein) inhabited predominantly by ethnic Germans--easy German victory followed by joint sovereignty over S-H
      2. Austro-Prussian War of 1866, or Seven Weeks' War--provocation of a conflict deliberately by Bismarck against all other German states--spectacular triumphs with relative facility
         a. Negotiation of a lenient peace with Austria in hopes of its future neutrality against France--elimination of Austria from involvement in other German affairs
         b. Conquest of all north German states and unity into a confederation of Germany under Prussian domination
         c. Survival of only four south German states (especially Bavaria) outside the unified Germany--basis of their resistance on religious differences (Catholic instead of the Protestantism of northern & eastern Germany) and on traditional cultural & diplomatic ties with France
      3. Franco-Prussian War of 1870-71
         a. Rapid & total defeat of France by the German armies
         b. Decision by the south German states to join the rest of Germany peacefully rather than risk the wrath of Bismarck by armed resistance
         c. Proclamation of the 2nd Empire of Germany at Versailles in January, 1871 under William I. (1861--88)
III. Dangerous Implications of Bismarck's Career
   A. Anticipation of future danger to the world in his methods & means:
      1. Resort to force & illegality--ready use of anything in order to achieve his goals
      2. Massive build-up of the military--emphasis on conscription & modern weaponry
      3. Persecution of minorities & political enemies--harassment & bigotry toward Catholics & socialists
      4. Successful defense of monarchy, elitist privilege, & conservatism in general
   B. Emergence of German nationalism as the most dangerous form in the world by its incorrect glorification of Germans as a physically & mentally superior & "master race", or <u>Herrenvolk</u>
   C. Predilection of Germans to blame their historical weaknesses, divisions, & problems of the past on neighboring nations such as France & Poland & Russia

THE HAPSBURG MONARCHY OF AUSTRIA

I. Central Problem
   A. Eventual death of the Austrian Empire after World War I. because of its inability to solve the problem of alienated minority nationalities seeking autonomy or independence

B. Domination of the empire for many centuries by the Austrian Germans
      ruling over a multitude of other ethnicities who became in the
      19th century increasingly nationalistic & resistant toward oppres-
      sion, exploitation, & insensitivity
   C. Ethnic composition in 1867--23% German or Austrian, 19% Hungarian
      or Magyar, and 55% Slavic and including the Czechs, Slovaks,
      Poles, Ukrainians, Rumanians, Serbs, Croats, & Slovenes
   D. Imminent collapse after the wartime defeats in 1859 & 1866 compell-
      ing the dominant Austrians & the Hapsburg Emperor Franz Josef
      (1848--1916) to negotiate a power-sharing agreement with the sec-
      ond largest nationality, the Hungarians or Magyars, who were very
      unique ethnically & different from Germans & Slavs
II. Compromise of 1867, or <u>Ausgleich</u>--creation of the Dual Monarchy of
    Austria-Hungary, and an administratively divided empire with an auton-
    omous German western half ruled from Vienna and an autonomous Hungar-
    ian eastern half governed from Budapest, with each having its own
    parliament & government
   A. Preservation of imperial unity in four areas: an emperor of the
      Hapsburg Dynasty, the military, foreign affairs, and the economy
      in the form of a customs union
   B. Yet persistence of dissatisfaction & alienation among the Slavic
      minorities--greater strength of the forces pulling apart the em-
      pire than the forces holding it together
   C. Achievement by the Ausgleich of only a temporary rather than a per-
      manent solution to the nationalities problems of the Hapsburg
      Monarchy

                              RUSSIA

I. Introduction
   A. Survival of royal absolutism & autocracy & Old Regime circumstances
      longer than anywhere else in Europe
   B. Continuation throughout the 19th century of Russia as the most
      backward & barbaric & primitive of all the major nations of Europe
   C. Yet emergence of signs of collapse by the mid-19th century under
      the reactionary Tsar Nicholas I. (1825-55)--major pressures on his
      son to reform & liberalize the terribly antiquated society
II. Reforms of Alexander II. (1855-81): [elaboration in class]
   A. Emancipation of serfs in 1861--40 million of them consisting of
      nearly 90% of the total population--arrangements made for their
      peasant communities in the future to own land
   B. Establishment of local self-government--known on the provincial &
      district level as <u>zemstvos</u> and consisting of delegates from all
      classes: landowners, peasants, townspeople
   C. Reorganization of the judicial system--new courts on the Western
      model of jury trials, publicly open proceedings, personal rights
      to choose a lawyer, better-trained judges, & recognition of the
      principle of equality before the law
   D. Reduction of press censorship
   E. Allowance to travel abroad
   F. Greater official consideration & leniency for persecuted minorit-
      ies such as Jews, gypsies, & non-Russian ethnicities
   G. Extension of more academic freedom in the universities

Consequences--much unrest & disorder, heavy criticisms from all sides, & formation of extremist societies--assassination of the Tsar followed by horrifying repression under his son & successor Alexander III. (1881-94)

Chapter 12   THE NEW IMPERIALISM THROUGH WORLD WAR I. (1870--1920)

I. The New Imperialism
   A. Basic definition of "imperialism"--the conquest, colonization, domination, and/or exploitation of one people or nation and their lands & resources & labor by another people or nation
      1. Occurrence of this phenomenon all over the world throughout the thousands of years of human history
      2. Existence especially within Europe among its peoples & nations
   B. Manifestation of <u>two</u> phases of European imperialism toward the non-European world:
      1. Early period beginning in the late-15th century and ending in the 19th century--known as the "old" Age of Imperialism
      2. The "New Imperialism" of the late-19th & early-20th centuries: 1870--1920
   C. Differences between the Old & New Imperialism--the following being true of the New Imperialism:
      1. Involvement of imperialism as a major issue in political life:
         a. It was a subject of universal & fiery debate in this age of increasing democracy and representative government--importance now placed on open discussion & popular opinion in elections
         b. Earlier all decisions were made arbitrarily by monarchs & their advisors & a few wealthy businessmen
      2. Greater economic pressures on politicians & governments from businessmen & bankers & capitalism generally to acquire colonies for markets & raw materials & cheap labor & financial investments
         a. Imperialism usually promoted & supported by the upper bourgeoisie yet generally opposed by the lower-class masses of working people, whose influence over major decisions was slight in comparison to the former
         b. Competition among the powerful industrial nations for imperial conquests causing & intensifying numerous international crises
      3. Nationalism--heightened intensity now for the procurement of colonies as a reflection of national greatness & glory and patriotic pride, even when territories became expensive burdens & a drain on European treasuries
      4. Military advantage--heightened intensity in the New Imperialism for the acquisition of territories for their strategic location and future wartime considerations
      5. Humanitarian idealism--more intensity than before for the naive & misguided belief in the beneficial consequences resulting from the imposition of "civilized" European ways on "uncivilized & inferior & barbarian" non-European peoples--example of Rudyard Kipling's reference to the "white man's burden" toward brown, black, yellow, & red-skinned peoples
      6. Participation of new nations:
         a. Old Imperialism nations included Portugal, Spain, Britain, France, & Holland (the Netherlands)--but now joined & rivalled by:
         b. New Imperialism nations of Germany, Italy, Belgium, the United States, Russia, & Japan

7. Involvement of new areas of the world in European conquests:
   a. Africa--scene of the most spectacular rivalry & activity
      (1) Prior to 1870 Europeans mainly occupied only trading posts along the western coast--African interior remained largely unexplored
      (2) In the 20 years after 1870 nearly all of Africa was devoured by the European powers
      (3) Native Africans exceedingly vulnerable to conquest due to often primitive conditions & fatal fragmentation into many diverse & warring tribes
   b. The Far East & Southeast Asia:
      (1) China was an ancient, thickly populated, & highly civilized empire with a tradition for centralized government & efficient bureaucracy, yet by the late-19th century it was incompetently ruled & politically chaotic & technologically backward--thus susceptible to European penetration
      (2) Military coercion was used by European nations to extract from the Chinese government special trading agreements, extraordinary privileges, & control over certain ports along the eastern coast at the mouths of important rivers
      (3) These small but lucrative areas under direct European rule known as "spheres of influence"
      (4) However, the vast hinterland regions of China remained independent & largely unoccupied by Europeans and not annexed by foreign nations
   c. Pacific Island groups such as Melanesia, Polynesia, Micronesia, the Hawaiian Islands, etc.
   d. Near or Middle East--all under the nominal control of the Ottoman Empire of Turkey yet disintegrating rapidly during the 19th century and constantly attracting major diplomatic attention concerning its future fate ("Near Eastern Question")--occupation by Britain & France of some of its regions & territories after World War I.
   e. South & Central America--not subjected to conquests during the New Imperialism--most of its states won independence from Spain & Portugal in the early 19th century--yet persistence of the traditional intimidation & interference in domestic Latin affairs by the U.S.A. as the "Colossus of the North"
D. Reasons for European domination of the non-European world, or factors of European superiority in relation to non-Europeans:
   1. Modern science & technology--its mastery being the factor most decisively distinguishing European from non-European civilizations
   2. Large-scale & efficient organization, especially in governmental & military bureaucracy--a legacy from the Roman Empire
   3. Application of more practical & rational methods of thought--use of reason or logic as a legacy of ancient Greece
   4. More adaptability & openness to change--an emanation of the previous points
   5. Higher development of capitalism, with its emphasis on expansionism, greed, & acquisitiveness

    6. A more powerful native or non-European tradition of authori-
       tarianism, with its unquestioning obedience to whatever ruler
       lords over the "inferior" popular masses
 E. Nations and colonies of the New Imperialism
    1. British Empire--it was already the world's largest empire and
       would continue to grow more rapidly & extensively than the
       empires of other nations--possession by 1815 of India, Aus-
       tralia, New Zealand, Canada, & Cape Colony in southern Africa
       a. Two types of colony in the British Empire:
          (1) Colonies of settlement--areas where large numbers
              of Europeans went on a permanent basis to develop
              & live on the lands--examples of Canada, Austral-
              ia, New Zealand, & South Africa
          (2) Colonies of exploitation--areas where small numbers
              of whites went on a temporary basis mainly as ad-
              ministrators, military officers, or businessmen to
              rule & supervise the natives--examples of India &
              most of the other African & Asian territories
       b. Application in the "colonies of exploitation" of the
          "system of indirect rule":
          (1) British allowance of native tribal leaders to re-
              main as nominal rulers of various areas under a
              British governor & other officials
          (2) British ban on war & slavery among the natives, yet
              local native laws & customs & religions usually
              left intact
          (3) British use primarily of a few British administrat-
              ors (Resident Magistrates--RM's) to live among the
              native chiefs & to supervise local activities
          (4) In this way, about 1000 British administrators in
              1900 directly ruled 220 million Indians & 60 mill-
              ion more indirectly in various princely states
       c. Eventual formation of the British "Commonwealth of Nat-
          ions"--after an unsuccessful revolt in 1837 against
          British rule in Canada, Lord John Durham of Parliament
          studied the problem of colonial desires for independence
          (1) Issuance in 1839 of his famous Durham Report recom-
              mending ultimate independence with reservations
              for the colonies--this meant granting autonomy, or
              the official title of "dominion status", and join-
              ing the <u>Commonwealth</u>
          (2) Provisions of "dominion status":
              (a) Self-government for the colony through an
                  independent parliament for domestic matters
              (b) Expectation of colonial acceptance of British
                  foreign policy
              (c) Contribution of colonial soldiers to British
                  armies during wartime
              (d) Colonial commitments to retain trading & econ-
                  omic ties to Britain
          (3) The above provisions not spelled out formally until
              the Statutes of Westminster in 1931, yet dominion
              status extended to Canada in 1867, Australia in
              1901, South Africa in 1910, & New Zealand in 1914

    2. French Empire--the 2nd largest in area, yet possessing little territory suitable for European settlement
    3. European conquests in Africa:
       a. Britain--Egypt, Sudan, Kenya, Uganda, Rhodesia (now Zimbabwe), South Africa, Nigeria, & the Gold Coast
       b. France--French North Africa (Algeria, Tunisia, Morocco), West Africa (Chad, Mali, Niger, Mauretania), the French Congo (four states today including Ivory Coast), and the island off the eastern coast known as Madagascar
       c. Germany--Namibia (Southwest Africa), Tanzania (East Africa), & the Cameroons
       d. Italy--mainly worthless areas of Libya, Somaliland, and Eritrea
       e. Portugal--Angola & Mozambique
       f. Belgium--occupation of Zaire (Belgian Congo), a resource-rich region nearly ninety times the size of Belgium
       g. Only two African nations maintaining independence from foreign rule:
          (1) Liberia--a small republic established by American antislavery groups as land for emancipated black American slaves (few ever went there)
          (2) Abyssinia (now called Ethiopia)--a mountainous and backward state--the Abyssinians were the only African people to defeat European invaders in battle--the Italians beaten at Adowa in 1896
    4. European conquests in the Far East & Pacific Islands:
       a. Britain--rule over Burma, Malaya (including Singapore), & the Chinese ports of Hong Kong & Shanghai & Canton
       b. France--subjugation of Indochina (Vietnam, Laos, Cambodia) plus certain ports in China
       c. Holland, or the Netherlands--the very lucrative island group known as Indonesia
       d. Germany--the Chinese region of Kiaochow Bay, part of New Guinea, & some Pacific islands
       e. U.S.A.--occupation of the Philippines, Hawaii, & Samoa in addition to Cuba, Puerto Rico, & the Panama Canal Zone plus the purchase of Alaska from Russia in 1867
       f. Russia--constant encroachments along its Central Asian borders with China, Persia, & Turkey
       g. Japan--seizure from China of the island of Taiwan (Formosa), Korea, & special concessions in the province of Manchuria
    5. European occupations in the Middle East--seizure of many former territories of the defeated & splintered Ottoman Turkish Empire at the end of World War I. by Britain & France
F. Reasons for the rapid rise to greatness of Japan after 1853:
    1. A strategic geographic location for trading with Asian continental markets in exchange for export products--a similar situation to Britain in Europe
    2. Emergence of an ambitious middle class with an aggressive business leadership in promoting industrialization & power
    3. Existence of a large supply of cheap labor generally submissive to authority

4. Possession by the Japanese people of certain favorable characteristics: self-discipline, energetic & hard-working attitudes, efficiency & good organization, willingness to sacrifice for the group or community, appreciation for knowledge & learning--in this respect, somewhat like the Germans in Europe
   5. Very successful adaptation of European technology & science to traditional Japanese institutions--thus a reflection of the Japanese traits of flexibility & willingness to change

II. Causes & Background of World War I. (1914--18)
   A. Introduction
      1. In the general & long-term & underlying causes of World War I. all nations of Europe shared some blame for their encouragement of belligerence
      2. Yet overwhelming responsibility for its specific & short-term causes rested with an aggressive, militaristic, & expansionist Germany pressuring for a conflict it believed winnable
   B. General & long-term & underlying causes:
      1. Failure & inability of the great powers in their adjustment to drastic shifts in the balance of power during the late-19th century
         a. Unification of Germany & Italy bringing radical changes in international affairs with the elimination of many small & independent states previously used as pawns or compensation in diplomacy & war
         b. A unified Germany & Italy now competing in all areas against the other major nations
         c. German predominance militarily & economically shifting the center of European power from Western Europe (meaning France) to Central Europe
         d. Gradual collapse of the Ottoman Turkish Empire in the southeastern European region known as the Balkan Peninsula--earlier reference to the Ottoman Empire by a Russian tsar as the "sick man" of Europe whose fate stirred debate & conflict for over a century
         e. Emergence of some Slavic ethnicities in the Balkans as independent nations from Turkey after wars--Serbia & Rumania by 1778, Bulgaria in 1908--persistence of these states as small, weak, & outraged that many of their fellow ethnics still lived under Turkish or Austro-Hungarian rule--earlier independence for Greece in 1829
         f. Wish by greedy neighbors of Turkey such as Austria-Hungary & Russia to weaken its empire & seize its territory
         g. Constant assertion of extravagant claims by most European nations on the bordering territories of other nations
      2. Nationalism & racism:
         a. Possibility of nationalism being a positive & good force when stimulating cultural creativity and promoting cooperation, common effort, social cohesiveness, & ethnic pride
         b. Yet possibility also of being a negative, harmful, & ugly force when leading to intolerance, bigotry, ignorance, & conflict

    c. All states guilty of fanatical patriotism, with German nationalism being the most extreme & aggressive & ambitious & dangerous
    d. Threat of Pan-Germanism as a form of "racism" (although Germans are merely one nationality among many comprising the Caucasian race, and not a separate race by themselves) in its erroneous belief in cultural, intellectual, & physical superiority and in its expansionist demands that all Germans everywhere (even those living in neighboring countries) must reside under the government of Germany
    e. Dangers also in Pan-Slavism as a racist view among the Slavic nationalities of Eastern Europe, with Russia posing as leader & protector & "big brother" of the less numerous Slavic ethnicities such as Serbs, Croats, Slovenes, Czechs, Slovaks, Rumanians, Bulgarians, & Poles
    f. High intensity of nationalism likewise in Britain, Italy, & France--the latter promoting a "revenge movement" (<u>revanchisme</u>) for the return of Alsace-Lorraine
    g. Reputation of the Balkan Peninsula as the "powderkeg of Europe" due to its potential volatility & explosiveness in sparking huge crises--nationalistic desires among small Slavic states & peoples (especially Serbia) for independence or territorial expansion at the expense of more powerful neighbors (Austria-Hungary & Turkey) possessing Slavic minorities
3. Economic rivalry between Britain & Germany for markets, raw materials, & industrial productivity--a new German challenge at the turn of the century to the old English predominance in commercial & business enterprise, with all of Western Europe now industrialized
4. Imperialism--the struggle for possession of all available colonies & outposts overseas intensifying international tensions and the prospects for war
5. Armaments race:
    a. Universal establishment of enormous conscripted standing armies with millions of civilians in reserve--development of modern weapons featuring the machine gun as well as massive naval destroyers
    b. German construction in the early 20th century of a powerful navy capable of challenging British superiority on the seas
    c. Maintenance of this weaponry for the sole purpose of destroying people & property & nations, not for the purpose of collecting dust--comment earlier by Napoleon: "You can do everything with bayonets except sit on them."[1]
    d. Thus the existence of an armaments race as the natural incentive for war, especially when leaders & generals believing their military possessed an advantage of superiority over adversaries that might diminish in the near future
    e. This precise conclusion drawn in 1914 by the German military high command, in the belief that Germany had the immediate choice between "world power or decline"[2],

meaning that 1914 was the best time to use military superiority for victory & domination of Europe--delay to result only in enemies gradually catching up
6. Alliance systems:
   a. Emergence of two main alliance systems during the four decades prior to 1914 with the ostensible purpose of preserving a balance of power and of preventing one nation or group from threatening the general peace
   b. However, commitment of each state by these agreements & treaties to assisting its allies in case of an aggressive war launched by an opposing nation
   c. Consequence--an isolated conflict in one region of Europe easily spreading & becoming a general conflagration & involving every nation tied by alliance to others
   d. Triple Alliance (1882)--Germany, Austria-Hungary, Italy
      (1) A diplomatic effort by Bismarck to isolate France, working while he maintained friendly relations with Russia in a Reinsurance Treaty
      (2) Allowance of that treaty to lapse by Kaiser Wilhelm II. & his officials after Bismarck's dismissal in 1890, thus leaving Russia isolated but seeking an alliance with & assistance from France
   e. Triple Entente ("entente" meaning <u>understanding</u> in French)---Britain, France, Russia
      (1) Signing of a secret military convention in 1894 between France & Russia, followed by the Entente Cordiale in 1904 between Britain & France and a similar agreement in 1907 between Britain & Russia
      (2) Existence of the Triple Entente <u>not</u> as a formal treaty of alliance but as merely a suggestion of mutual willingness to ally in case of war
      (3) Function particularly of the Anglo-French Entente as a sort of general & gentleman's agreement that both believed it could count on
      (4) Maintenance by Russia separately of agreements with the small Slavic Balkan states (above all, Serbia) promising military assistance against an attack by Austria-Hungary
      (5) Thus setting the stage for 1914--Serbia provoked A-H, Russia promised support to Serbia, Germany totally backed & even pressed A-H, etc.
7. Weak, incompetent, &/or unimaginative leadership
   a. Sufferance of all nations great & small in varying degrees from the ignorance & inflexibility of their politicians--willingness of most statesmen to go to war simply for the purpose of defending national "honor" & "prestige" & "glory" and escaping "humiliation"
   b. Preference by many leaders of military confrontation & saberrattling rhetoric to face-saving compromise
   c. Disastrous personality of German Emperor Wilhelm II., who was childishly immature, impulsive, poorly educated, arrogant & conceited, bombastic & tactless in speech yet vacillating & confused in decision-making

d. Contradictions of Germany:
   (1) Impressive possession of the most powerful army in the world, the 2nd largest navy, an awesome industrial & economic complex, a model society of efficiency & organization & discipline & orderliness, a role of leadership in technological & scientific innovation, and some of the finest schools & universities in the world
   (2) Yet possession also of a government run by a reckless & foolish emperor, fumbling mediocrities, weak incompetents, & unimaginative functionaries--none of whom could control or reason with an independent & aggressive military establishment
   (3) Brilliant description of this contradiction by modern historian Paul G. Halpern, who portrayed pre-1914 Germany as: "A highly efficient locomotive racing full speed down the tracks with no one at the controls."[3]
8. Series of international crises heightening tension: 1905--1914
   a. Two Moroccan Crises (1905-06, 1911) between France & Germany--aggressive yet unsuccessful German challenge to French desires for a protectorate there--British support for France resulting in the conclusion of a compromise
   b. Berlin-to-Baghdad Railway (1908)--culmination in a halting & thwarting of the potential German development of this project by British fears of inordinate German influence in the Balkans & the Middle East
   c. Annexation of Bosnia-Herzegovina in 1909 by Austria-Hungary in violation of international treaties:
      (1) Bosnia-Herzegovina was a former territory of Turkey populated by Serbs & Croats yet granted to A-H in 1878 by an international congress <u>only</u> to administer temporarily & <u>not</u> to possess outright
      (2) Exploitation by A-H in 1908 of Turkish domestic turmoil & global diplomatic confusion to annex B-H as its own
      (3) Diplomatic confrontation between A-H and Serbia, the latter demanding the Serbian people & lands of Bosnia-Herzegovina--weakness of Russia (Serbia's ally) due to internal problems, with the result of Serbian loss of claims and Russian humiliation
      (4) Fatal promise by Russia to Serbia never to back down again in another Balkan crisis--fatal support of Germany for a weak yet expansionist A-H
   d. Turko-Italian War (1911-12)--Turkish loss of Libya in North Africa to Italy, setting off:
   e. Two Balkan Wars (1912-13)
      (1) Final disintegration in the first of nearly all of the Ottoman Empire in the Balkans to the benefit of Serbia, Montenegro, Bulgaria, & Greece
      (2) Fight in the 2nd war over the territorial spoils of the 1st war, with the recognition of independent Albania & further humiliation for Serbia by A-H

C. Most immediate & short-term cause of war--assassination of Archduke Franz Ferdinand, heir to the throne of Austria-Hungary by Serbian terrorists on June 28, 1914 in Sarajevo, Bosnia
   1. Austrian resolve to destroy the Serbian threat permanently-- dispatch of an ultimatum so severe (including an Austrian investigation of the crime in Serbia itself) as to make acceptance impossible--rejection by Serbia
   2. Critical German promise from the outset of full & unqualified support (the infamous "blank check") for Austrian policy toward Serbia even if it meant war--further German encouragement & pressure for a hardline approach to end the Slavic problem forever
   3. Commitment by Russia to assist Serbia--order by the tsar on July 29-30 of partial & then full mobilization for war under the assumption that backward Russia needed more time than others for mobilizing
   4. Fatal assertion on July 31 by the German military leaders of total control over foreign policy, thus ending any possibility of diplomatic flexibility
      a. Declaration by Germany of war on Russia on August 1 after its refusal to cease mobilization
      b. Declaration by Germany of war on France on August 3, with German armies invading neutral Belgium
      c. British commitment to war on August 4 following the German violation of Belgium neutrality

III. World War I.
   A. Introduction
      1. Recognition of World War I. (August 1, 1914--November 11, 1918) as a catastrophe shaking the foundations of Western Civilization, destroying empires, killing millions of people, costing hundreds of billions of dollars, devastating economies, and modifying societies permanently
      2. A disruption of the world so serious that it rendered post-war stability impossible and paved the way for economic depression in 1929, fascist totalitarianism, communism in Russia, & World War II. commencing in 1939
      3. The two belligerent sides:
         a. Central Powers--Germany, Austria-Hungary, Turkey, and Bulgaria (1915)
         b. Allies--Britain, France, Russia (out by March, 1918), Italy (declaring neutrality in 1914 & then entering the war after negotiations & enticements), the U.S.A. (April 1917), Serbia, Rumania, Greece, and Japan (entering the war only to seize German colonies in the Far East & not getting involved in Europe at all)
   B. Advantages & disadvantages in 1914:
      1. Allies:
         a. Superiority in total population & material resources (mainly due to the British Empire)--thus the longer a war raged, the better were Allied chances of victory
         b. Greater industrial production, especially in coal & iron
         c. Control of the seas, with Britain possessing the most powerful navy & largest merchant fleet--imposition of a

            naval blockade on Germany throughout the war, as a tra-
            ditional weapon utilized in the past by the British
         d. More highly developed propaganda techniques, probably be-
            cause of their earlier possession of a freer press with
            greater powers of argumentative persuasion--Allied pub-
            licity on the war as a "moral crusade" after German per-
            petration of numerous atrocities against civilians
   2. Central Powers:
         a. Possession by Germany of the most efficient & powerful
            army in the world, with unified military planning & ad-
            ministration and greater cooperation with its partners
         b. A higher state of preparedness initially for war
         c. Use of the same language by Germany & Austria-Hungary
         d. Psychological advantage of being militarily on the offen-
            sive & carrying the war to their enemies--no combat ever
            fought on German soil, only on Allied land
         e. Geographical advantage of Germany & A-H being side-by-
            side, thus having shorter interior lines of communicat-
            ion and being able to move men & supplies more easily &
            quickly--very wide physical separation for the Allies
C. Early stages of the war:
   1. Schlieffen Plan--the German strategy for winning a two-front
      war simultaneously & rapidly in 1914 against Russia in the
      east and France & Britain in the west:
         a. Projection of the Plan for a minimum defensive force in
            the east against the inefficient & incompetent Russian
            armies to keep the enemy at bay temporarily
         b. Intention to concentrate the brunt of German armies in
            the west for a massive offensive knock-out of the small-
            er yet very tough & professional French armies
         c. Thus the first priority of the Plan being the destruction
            & defeat of France as the most formidable German foe--
            conviction that Russia could be easily beaten later
         d. Execution of the Plan against France employing the feint
            of a major offensive attack along the Alsace-Lorraine
            border while most of the German armies effected an en-
            velopment or flanking maneuver to the north through Bel-
            gium to encircle & trap British & French forces
         e. Involvement by the Plan of a German invasion of Belgium &
            violation of the 1839 international treaty of Belgian
            neutrality, which German foreign minister Bethmann-
            Hollweg now referred to as "a scrap of paper"[4]
         f. Eventual failure of the Plan when Allied forces halted
            the German offensive 12 miles from Paris in the 1st Bat-
            tle of the Marne (Sept. 5-9, 1914) and subsequently
            pushed the Germans back further
         g. Probable doom of the Plan to failure regardless of how it
            was executed--yet contributing to its failure definitely
            was a decision by the commander (von Moltke) to weaken
            the German armies on the northwestern flank in France by
            diverting some units to the eastern front in defense
            against a surprising yet ultimately harmless Russian
            offensive, following Russia's fairly quick mobilization
         h. Thereafter, occupation by the armies on the Western Front

        of positions facing each other along lines stretching hundreds of miles from Switzerland to the English Channel in northeastern France
- D. Features of warfare on the Western Front:
  1. A "war of position" rather than a "war of movement", with the opposing armies digging trenches and placing in front of them barbed wire & other impediments to prevent breakthroughs--in the middle between the armies was the "no man's land"--use of heavy artillery to bombard enemy positions
  2. Futility of a conflict of <u>attrition</u>, meaning a process of wasting away, exhausting, & weakening through usage---defensive strategies & weaponry had surpassed offensive capabilities of destroying the enemy
  3. Employment for the first time extensively in modern warfare of certain weapons:
     a. Machine gun--a rapid-fire device for mowing down millions of men during suicidal charges
     b. Poison gas--introduction by the Germans, yet effectiveness quickly negated by invention of the gas mask
     c. Airplanes--used primarily for reconnaissance
     d. Tanks--their appearance very late in the conflict helped to penetrate lines & fortifications, while hastening an end to the war
     e. Submarines--application by the Germans in the Atlantic to break the naval blockade & to starve Britain into submission
  4. Incompetent & unimaginative generalship throwing away millions of lives senselessly in massive offensives with heavy casualties & no meaningful successes--evocation of Talleyrand's famous quote that: "War is much too serious a thing to be left to the military."[5]
- E. Descriptions of the major war-fronts:
  1. Western Front--lecture material in class
  2. Eastern Front:
     a. Hopeless situation for Russia--unprepared for a serious war in 1914 with an incompetent government & army officer corps, poorly trained & equipped soldiers, a very backward & inefficient society, a feeble transportation system, and little industry
     b. Colossal defeats of the Russians by the Germans in 1914 at Tannenberg (August 26-30) and Masurian Lakes (September 6-15) costing more than 100,000 casualties & 200,000 prisoners
     c. Russian loss of a million troops by the end of 1915, followed by disastrous offensives in 1916 & 1917--total collapse becoming only a matter of time:
        (1) March Revolution of 1917--destruction of the tsarist regime & establishment of a provisional democratic government perpetuating the unpopular war
        (2) November Revolution of 1917--seizure of power by the Bolshevik Communists who negotiated a December armistice & then a humiliating treaty ending the war for Russia by March, 1918

3. Italian Front:
   a. Existence of Italy also as a very weak participant in the war--famous defeat of the Italians by Austro-German forces in 1917 at Caporetto in northeastern Italy--stabilization of the front only with assistance from French & British troops
   b. Persistence of Italy as more of a liability than an asset to the Allied war effort
4. Balkan Front:
   a. Serbia completely defeated by Austria in 1914, as was Rumania in 1916
   b. Launch very late in the war in 1918 by Anglo-French forces of a successful offensive from Greece on Bulgaria & Austria-Hungary
5. Gallipoli Campaign (February, 1915--January, 1916):
   a. Location of Gallipoli in the region of Turkey along the narrow waterway known as the "Straits" connecting the Mediterranean with the Black Sea
   b. Origination of this campaign as the idea of Winston Churchill (1st Lord of the Admiralty) and an effort by British colonial forces to secure that key Turkish territory
   c. Main objective--to gain control of this access to the warm-water Black Sea ports of southern Russia, thus enabling the Allies to supply desperately needy Russian armies with war materials & food
   d. Results--failure mainly due to errors in planning & execution, with the British losing 100,000 casualties
6. Middle East:
   a. British aspiration to weaken Turkey severely by encouraging & aiding rebellions by the suppressed Arab peoples of the Turkish Empire seeking autonomy or independence
   b. Inspiration of this campaign for the exploits & leadership of Thomas E. Lawrence (renowned as "Lawrence of Arabia")
   c. British invasion & conquest of Palestine in 1917---issuance by the British government of the Balfour Declaration promising to favor the establishment in Palestine of a national homeland for Jewish people all over the world, thus a fulfillment of the goal of Zionism
7. Colonial Fronts--all German colonies except one (East Africa) easily overrun by British, French, & Japanese forces
8. War at Sea:
   a. Battle of Jutland (May, 1916)--the only naval confrontation between the British & German fleets, resulting roughly in a draw yet leaving the British still in control of the seas as the German fleet retreated to its harbor & never again emerged to challenge the British
   b. German response to the British blockade with the development of submarines (U-Boat, or "unterseeboot" in German) sinking much Allied shipping by early 1917 with devastating effectiveness

        (1) German declaration in February, 1915 of limited submarine warfare sparing the ships of neutral nations such as the U.S.A. except in accidents
        (2) Later declaration in February, 1917 of unrestricted submarine warfare targeting <u>all</u> shipping, with German hopes high for a quick victory by depriving Britain of food & starving it into submission
        (3) Development by the Allies of shipping convoys, depth charges, & submarine detection devices to combat the German submarines successfully

9. Home Fronts--transformation of the lives of noncombatants with drastic changes & radical policies, to an extreme extent that no previous war in history had
    a. Censorship of the press, restrictions on civil liberties, & suspension of habeas corpus
    b. Imposition of conscription (the "draft") requiring all able-bodied men to serve as soldiers--volunteer armies were out of the question
    c. Economic planning & management & regulation by powerful national governments--rationing of scarce commodities--a temporary end to free enterprise, laissez-faire policies & practices in favor of sacrifices for national survival
    d. Financing of the war by massive government borrowing, heavy national debt, and high taxes
    e. Tremendous changes in the role of women:
        (1) Necessity for females to work in factories & businesses as replacements for male soldiers at the war fronts--thus the departure from the home of middle as well as lower-class women
        (2) Emergence of this trend as a permanent phenomenon following the death or mutilation of millions of male soldiers
        (3) Establishment of voting rights for women in several countries soon after the war in recognition of their contributions

Chapter 13   INTER-WAR EUROPE: 1919-39

. Identification of this 20-year interlude of European History as one of
   the saddest, most tragic, most problem-filled, and most psychologically
   depressing periods that a person can study
I. The Problems, Difficulties, & Nightmares of this Era:
   A. Deep anguish & pain in all countries over the death, destruction, &
      horror of World War I.
   B. Social, economic, & political chaos & instability everywhere as a
      result of the Great War--truly the world would not recover from
      World War I. until after World War II. in the 1950's
   C. The Great Depression of 1929--a near total collapse of the world
      economy enduring for a decade until the commencement of World War
      II. and leaving at its zenith more than half of all people either
      unemployed or part-time & insufficiently employed
   D. Emergence of the threat (sometimes real, sometimes imaginary) of
      Communism in Russia to destroy bourgeois capitalism & democracy
   E. Rise of totalitarian Fascism with its stress on militarism, dictat-
      orship, & elitism
   F. Profound emotional pessimism over the abundance of problems and the
      irrevocable approach during the 1930's of World War II.--common-
      ness during this interlude of the incidence of suicide, as many
      people made the decision not to confront a terrible future
II. Examination of four topics in this segment of material: the Treaty of
    Versailles ending World War I., the Russian Revolution, the general
    nature of Fascism, and the crises leading to World War II.

                    TREATY OF VERSAILLES

. Introduction
   A. Peace conferences being held from January 18 to May 7, 1919 in sub-
      urban chateaux of Paris--most famously Versailles, which became
      the location of the most important meetings & the final signing
   B. Ascendancy of great popular hopes & expectations for a permanent
      peace as well as a better future world:
      1. The war witnessing the apparent triumph of democratic govern-
         ment with victory for France, Britain, Italy, & the U.S.--
         defeat conversely for authoritarianism with the destruction
         of four monarchies in Germany, Austria-Hungary, Turkey, and
         Russia
      2. Generation of much optimism & idealism centering on the peace
         program of American President Woodrow Wilson and his Fourteen
         Points for a moderate & permanent peace
      3. Yet doom of the treaty to tragic failure
   C. Existence of formidable impediments to the making of a permanent
      peace:
      1. Occurrence of the conferences during the immediate aftermath
         of war (1918-19)--a period of major turmoil, disorder, &
         local conflicts--all of eastern & central Europe experiencing
         chaos & confusion, minor wars, & weak provisional governments
      2. Persistence of extreme nationalistic feelings in all countries
         with narrow patriotic intensity now greater than ever before
      3. Wartime propaganda fueling hatreds, fears, & popular demands
         in Allied nations for vengeance against Germany

  4. Extravagant diplomatic commitments made by Allied nations during the war--earlier promises of territorial compensations & adjustments rendering a moderate peace impossible
  5. Continuation of traditional diplomatic habits of duplicity, deception, opportunism, & selfishness by statesmen--these things to be expected after the horrors & losses World War I.
II. The Major Statesmen
 A. Dispatch of delegates to Paris by the 30 nations involved directly or indirectly in the war except Russia--defeated nations taking no part in the deliberations but merely notified of the final terms & told to sign or return to war, which was impossible
 B. All important decisions made by three great leaders with minor assistance from a fourth, the Italian premier
 C. Woodrow Wilson--U.S. President elected as a Democrat in 1912 & 1916
  1. Born & raised in Virginia, son of a Presbyterian minister, educated at Princeton with a PhD in political science & history, professor & then president at Princeton, elected Governor of N.J. with the reputation as a reformer & progressive
  2. Highly intelligent & very well-educated, a shrewd politician and brilliant & inspiring leader as well as successful reformer & generally benevolent man
  3. Possession also of significant character flaws resulting partly from his Scots-Irish ancestry (from Ulster), deep religiosity, & Southern background:
   a. Belief in & promotion of white racial supremacy
   b. Self-righteous & intolerant conviction in his own moral & intellectual superiority
   c. Capability of being foolishly stubborn, uncompromising, sanctimonious, impractical, simplistic & bigoted
   d. Much ignorance of the world beyond the shores of America
   e. Thus truly a tragic figure playing a critical role in causing the Versailles Treaty to fail
  4. The 14 Points--Wilson's peace program issued in 1917 with American entrance into war & seeking to eliminate all those problems that earlier led to World War I.:
   a. Open & not secret treaties & agreements--an obvious reaction to the pre-1914 alliances
   b. Freedom of the seas at all times--something violated during the war by both Britain & Germany
   c. Removal or lowering of tariff barriers to international trade
   d. Reductions in armaments
   e. Self-determination for subjected nationalities, with the right to live under a government of their own choosing--especially applicable in Eastern Europe & the Near East
   f. Adjustments in colonial systems by taking more account of the interests of native peoples
   g. Formation of a general association of nations (the future League of Nations in 1920) for the purpose of guaranteeing political independence & territorial integrity of all nations--several concessions & deals made by Wilson in order to secure approval of this goal
  5. Inspiration by the 14 Points of much popular enthusiasm & optimism all over the world as well as a hastening to the end of the war

  D. Georges Clemenceau--premier of France from 1917 to the end of war
    1. Fiery & controversial leader nicknamed the "Tiger" aggressive-
     ly prosecuting the war & driving the nation heroically to
     triumph--tough disposal of enemy politicians & soft defeat-
     ists--aged 78, white-haired, walrus-mustachioed, eloquent
    2. Main goal--French security from future German invasions, by
     keeping Germany economically weak if necessary
    3. Direction of sarcasm & cynicism toward Wilson & his 14 Points
     as unrealistic, impractical, & impossible to implement:
     "Fourteen? The good Lord has only Ten."[1]
  E. David Lloyd George--prime minister of Britain after 1915--an excel-
    lent organizer & pragmatic politician playing the role at Ver-
    sailles of compromiser & moderator between Wilson & Clemenceau
  F. Vittorio Orlando--prime minister of Italy, playing only a minor
    part & often angry when Italian national interests not satisfied
  G. Use of intrigue, pressure, trickery, & compromise in the negotiat-
      ions & decisions--necessity for Wilson to accept harsher terms--
    Versailles to be an arbitrary peace imposed by the victors on the
    disaffected vanquished
II. Primary Provisions of the Treaty
  A. Toward Germany:
    1. Return of Alsace-Lorraine to France, & of Belgium to independ-
     ence after wartime German occupation
    2. Separation of the Saar Basin (a rich coal-producing region
     near the French border) from Germany for 15 years under sup-
     ervision by the League of Nations--coal from the area during
     those 15 years going to France in compensation for wartime
     damage--then a plebiscite to be held in the region to deter-
     mine its future status
    3. Demilitarization of the Rhineland--no allowance for German
     soldiers, arms, or fortifications in a belt 30 miles wide on
     the east bank of the river, with the possibility of Allied
     occupation for 15 years
    4. Loss of its overseas empire to various Allied powers
    5. Disarmament--limitation of the German army to 100,000 men and
     restriction of navy vessels in number & size--prohibition on
     the possession of submarines & military planes
    6. Reparation payments for damage done to civilian property dur-
     ing the war--the exact amount left indefinite at Versailles--
     Germany to pay $5 billion yearly until 1921 when final deter-
     made & set at $30 billion to be paid over 30 years:
     a. No precedent in history for such a huge indemnity
     b. Predictions by economists that Germany could never pay
      the full amount
     c. Consequence of the payments disrupting, weakening, & de-
      stabilizing the post-war German economy
    7. Article 231: the "war-guilt" clause--requirement that Germany
     accept sole responsibility for starting a war of aggression:
     a. Appearance of this measure as unnecessarily severe & vin-
      dictive to many people of all nationalities during the
      inter-war era, thus later encouraging Allied weakness in
      response to Hitler's violations of the Treaty
     b. Yet subsequent confirmation & documentation of the pre-
      dominant role of the German military staff in provoking
      the 1914 conflict by German historian Fritz Fischer in
      his research & writings of the 1950's

B. Toward Austria-Hungary:
   1. Dismemberment of the old Hapsburg Monarchy & Empire--creation of the two separate & small independent states of Austria & Hungary
   2. Establishment of the nation of Czechoslovakia, including the Czechs of Bohemia & Moravia plus the Slovaks
   3. A doubling in size for Rumania with its acquisition of Transylvania (the real Prince, not Count, Dracula--known as Vlad Tepes the Impaler--was from the province of Wallachia and not Transylvania)
   4. Extensive expansion of a relatively small Serbia into the large state of Yugoslavia, to be more commonly known during the inter-war period as the "Kingdom of the Serbs, Croats, & Slovenes"
   5. Reconstitution of the nation of Poland after its total disappearance from the map earlier in 1795 when its territories devoured by Prussia, Austria, & Russia--ironic & lucky defeat in World War I. of all three nations (Germany, A-H, Russia) possessing Polish peoples & territories
C. Toward the Baltic Region:
   1. Recognition of national independence for the former Russian territories of Lithuania, Latvia, & Estonia in 1920
   2. Achievement of independent nationhood also for Finland, as a former possession of the Russian Empire now uniquely set free in 1918 by Soviet dictator V.I. Lenin partly because of his great admiration for the Finnish people
D. Toward Turkey:
   1. Loss of all European territories except a small area around the city of Constantinople
   2. Surrender of many regions inhabited by non-Turks--Armenia becoming independent--Syria & Lebanon going as mandates (defined below) to France, and Palestine & Iraq going to Britain
E. Toward former German colonies--the Mandate System:
   1. Application of trusteeship under the authority of the League of Nations yet effectively conferring ownership on Britain or France or Japan
   2. Emphasis on the main duty of the ruling power as the preparation of these colonies for eventual independence & democratic self-government, with the League supposedly conducting periodic inspections to guarantee fulfillment of the terms
   3. Yet treatment of these colonies by the European powers as their own possessions to do with them whatever they pleased
F. Covenant, or Charter, of the League of Nations--provision for the commencement of its operations in January, 1920--existence as a weak & ineffective body with its primary purpose being the arbitration of international disputes

IV. Reasons For the Failure of the Versailles Treaty
   A. Total exclusion of Russia from the proceedings--this being a deliberate effort by the Allies to ostracize the radical Communist regime--yet provision of excuses for Russia in the future not to respect the Treaty settlement and the Western nations
   B. Humiliation & alienation of Germany--acquisition of immediate discredit by the new German democratic republican government for its acceptance of the "dictated treaty", or Diktat--popular German identification of democracy with the "betrayal of 1919"--thus an

additional problem to the already formidable difficulties of the shaky Weimar Republic (1919--33)
- C. Inconsistent & often impossible application of self-determination for subjected nationalities--persistence afterward of sizeable minorities still residing in nations with dominant majorities & posing serious problems--especially so in central & eastern Europe
- D. The "Balkanization of Europe"--replacement especially of the immense Austro-Hungarian Empire in southeastern Europe (the Balkan Peninsula) with the creation of numerous weak, small, & discontented nations incapable in the future of resisting the great powers of Germany in the west & Soviet Russia in the east--all of this the disastrous consequence of imperial disintegration
- E. Weakness of the League of Nations--no capacity to enforce the decisions of the Treaty--domination of the League by the great powers of the Allied wartime victory yet generally ignored by them
- F. Return of the United States to isolationism:
    1. Emergence of America as a great power during the war--realization by Wilson of the need to play an active role in international affairs
    2. Adamant refusal by Wilson (a Democrat) to accept modifications of the Treaty by the Senate (under Republicans) in response to rising popular isolationism in the country
    3. Incapacitation of Wilson by a stroke in September, 1919 as he embarked on a national tour to persuade the people of internationalism & global involvement--out of office by 1921
    4. Rejection of the Treaty twice by the Senate--American refusal to request membership in the League or to participate in world affairs in a meaningful way, thus acquiescing later in fascist aggression during the 1930's
- G. Fundamental cause of failure--the destruction & destabilization of the world & its institutions by the war, which uprooted or wrecked every society & economy & government in the Western World--impossibility of achieving a permanent peace or of preventing a more horrifying war of the future

THE RUSSIAN REVOLUTION: 1917-21

. Introduction
- A. Role as one of the greatest & most significant revolutionary movements in all of history, inaugurating major political, economic, & social changes both within & outside Russia
- B. Background to Revolution:
    1. Existence of Russia throughout the 19th century as the most backward & primitive of the major nations of Europe that was barely touched by the Scientific Revolution, Enlightenment, & Industrial Revolution
    2. Yet governmental embarkation in the early-1890's on a crash program of social & economic modernization & development that continued till 1914--an effort to strengthen the nation & the Romanov regime, but not including political reforms
    3. Results of some significant strides in industrialization & urbanization and in programs of turning over more land to individual small-scale farmers
    4. Consequent experience after 1890 of progress in its rapid transition from a backward feudal society & economy to a modern one in the throes of an industrial revolution

5. Accompaniment of these quickening changes by economic dislocation, popular suffering, social unrest, & political repression by the tsarist regime
   6. Condition of Russia on the eve of war & revolution as an explosive & volatile society with enormous problems--but its crisis being caused by a dynamism of growth & rapid adjustments rather than by decline or decay or continued backwardness

II. Causes of Revolution
   A. Increasing alienation of the popular masses from a government and ruling upper class refusing to inaugurate fundamental & meaningful reforms
   B. Deep social & class antagonisms between an upper class of aristocratic landowners & wealthy bourgeoisie and a lower class of:
      1. Urban proletariat living & laboring in subhuman conditions on abysmally low wages
      2. Peasant farmers shackled by primitive tools & methods, insufficient land, overpopulation, heavy taxes, frequent famines & plagues, aristocratic exploitation, & governmental corruption
      3. Lower bourgeoisie of shopkeepers & skilled workers vulnerable to unpredictable & turbulent economic times
   C. Governmental incompetence, personified perfectly in the royal family:
      1. Tsar Nicholas II. (1894--1917): lacking in intelligence, education, & common sense--narrowminded--stubborn & vacillating
      2. Tsarina Alexandra--stupid & ignorant & superstitious as well as beautiful & frivolous--domineering toward her weak husband--her obsession with the fragility of their hemophiliac son leading to her complete reliance on:
      3. Gregori Rasputin--a dissolute, unscrupulous, filthy, & probably deranged mystic & monk partially curing the hemophilia with hypnosis & thus gaining total control of the parents--a power-hungry control of government (1911-16) until his assassination
   D. Disastrous defeats in the Russo-Japanese War (1904-05) exposing the instability & ineptitude of the regime and precipitating a brief & abortive Revolution of 1905:
      1. Introduction by the Tsar of a few reforms that were mostly abolished later with a passing of the crisis
      2. Inauguration of a national representative assembly known as the Duma (1906-17) lacking truly democratic elections, possessing very limited authority, & not practicing ministerial responsibility as a real parliamentary system

III. The Opposition Parties
   A. Organization of three opposition parties with specific programs of actions & aims toward the tsarist regime--formation during the two decades preceding the Revolution
   B. Constitutional Democratic Party, or Kadets, or KD's--composition by moderate & liberal bourgeoisie favoring a constitution, civil liberties, parliamentary government, free public education, & further agrarian reforms--leader Paul Milyukov
   C. Social Revolutionary Party, or SR's (1901):
      1. Representation of peasants & condoning the use of terror & assassination

  2. Goal of destroying tsarist autocracy, seizing the landed estates of the aristocracy, & distributing free farms to each peasant family
  3. Desire for decentralized government & locally autonomous communities--willingness of the SR's to cooperate & collaborate with other leftist groups to promote gains
 D. Social Democratic Party, or SD's--the Marxist revolutionary party organized in 1898 and depending on proletariat support & wishing to destroy the regime through mass action & strikes
  1. Momentous party meetings in exile in 1903 in London & Brussels causing a split & dissension over organization & goals
  2. Division between Bolsheviks (literally in Russian meaning "majority" because of their victory in one congress vote) and Mensheviks (literally meaning "minority", although they had more supporters throughout the party than their opponents)
  3. Differences between the two:
   a. Literal meaning--Bolsheviks, "majority"; Mensheviks, "minority"
   b. Leadership--Vladimir Ilyich Ulyanov (code name N. Lenin) for the Bolsheviks; George Plekhanov for the Mensheviks
   c. Organization--Bolsheviks favoring a dictatorially controlled, small, & strictly disciplined party under a central committee; Mensheviks wanting a democratically organized party with a loose confederation of autonomous local groups open to all
   d. Cooperation with others--Bolsheviks desiring no cooperation initially with other groups, thus going it alone; Mensheviks wishing to work with Kadets & SR's
   e. Ultimate attainment of power--Bolsheviks (as orthodox Marxists) envisioning bloody revolution & dictatorship; Mensheviks (as revisionist Marxists) anticipating the achievement of power through peaceful democratic means such as elections
V. The Two Revolutions of 1917
 A. Catastrophic setbacks in war caused by incompetence of military officers, lack of modern arms & adequate supplies, flawed battle tactics & strategy, governmental corruption & ineptitude, and poor organization of society & military
 B. March Revolution of 1917 (February on the old unreformed Russian calendar)
  1. Strikes & bread riots in the capital city of Petrograd (March 8-15) spreading to other urban areas--workers joined by soldiers in unified movements against war & shortages & inflation
  2. Abdication of the Tsar on the 15th and complete collapse of the national, regional, & local governments of the Old Regime
  3. Uniqueness of this revolution being spontaneous, leaderless, & anonymous--all radical leaders either in exile or in jail
  4. Formation of <u>soviets</u> all over Russia--local & regional councils of workers, peasants, & soldiers assuming control of government in a grand experiment with democracy
  5. Designation of the Duma in Petrograd as the provisional national government of Russia--political dominance in the Duma by the moderate bourgeoisie & the Kadet Party
  6. Confrontation by the Duma & Kadets with huge problems:
   a. Lack of experience in exercising true political power

      b. Absence of popular support & deep roots in a society still overwhelmingly rural & agrarian in nature
      c. Inheritance of war, poverty, economic collapse, & social chaos & disintegration
7. Loss of much popularity & support by the Duma over <u>two</u> critical issues:
      a. Refusal to legalize immediate governmental confiscation of aristocratic lands for quick redistribution to land-hungry peasants--Duma concerns about legal rights, proper land surveys, & financial compensation for owners
      b. Continuation of the war on the side of the Allies--yet desires by most people for immediate peace due to national exhaustion & hopelessness
8. Return of Lenin from exile in Switzerland in the spring, 1917 & immediate proclamation of the Bolshevik program for Russia in his April Theses: land, bread, peace, & "all power to the soviets"--a simple yet effective appeal to the uneducated
      a. Explanation of Bolshevik success in its leadership being pragmatic, flexible, realistic, opportunistic, & unscrupulous in pursuing power
      b. Accurate description of the Bolsheviks as a conspiratorial group of mainly Marxist intellectuals predominantly from the very small middle class, although representing the tiny proletariat class of only 1% of all society
      c. The big three leaders--Lenin (V.I. Ulyanov), Trotsky (Leon Bronstein), & Stalin (Joseph Djugashvili)
      d. Realization by Lenin of Bolshevik weakness & their need for allies--temporary alliance with some leftist SR's to assist them--persuasion of Lenin by the brilliant & incisive Trotsky of the possibility of an early seizure of power in a Marxist revolution toppling the weak Duma
9. Eventual deviation by Lenin from the original ideas of Marx, thus rendering the modern expression "Marxist-Leninist" as a contradiction in terms, or oxymoronism:
      a. Marx believed in the success of a communist revolution in backward Russia only after the achievement of world revutions elsewhere--Lenin hoped to achieve communism in Russia first and, if necessary, alone
      b. Marx urged his followers not to cooperate with other parties in seeking power--Lenin effected an alliance with the SR's for a brief while
      c. Marx anticipated only a temporary governmental dictatorship & centralization before eventually establishing decentralization & local democratic communes--Lenin probably foresaw a long-term or permanent & personal centralized dictatorship
      d. Marx believed in the necessity of a long transitional period of bourgeois capitalism in creating industrial exploitation & a large proletariat class--Lenin came to believe in an immediate seizure of power & the forging of a desirable society by an awesome communist regime
      e. Marx recommended that there be no retreat from communism toward capitalism--Lenin would make concessions to capitalism when communist policies failed & threatened the survival of his regime

C. November Revolution of 1917 (October on the old unreformed Russian calendar)
   1. A relatively easy takeover by the Bolsheviks of the national government in Petrograd (later Leningrad) in an armed insurrection--seizure of control also in most other urban centers, with the critical help of some soviets
   2. The greatest difficulty for the Bolsheviks not in gaining power but now in maintaining it--early reforms by Lenin:
      a. Conclusion of an armistice with Germany halting the war
      b. Extension of control over factories to the workers
      c. Rapid redistribution of land to the peasants
      d. Confiscation of church property & prohibition of religious instruction in schools
      e. Call for election to a new constituent assembly--disbanded in January, 1918 after Bolshevik opponents won the majority of seats
      f. Establishment of a secret police (Cheka) to counter opposition to the regime
   3. The most vital act for survival of the Bolshevik regime--negotiation of a humiliating peace treaty with Germany in March, 1918 at Brest-Litovsk:
      a. Loss by Russia of 60 million people, one-third of its European population, one-fourth of its European territory, one-third of its farmland, about half of its industry, & nine-tenths of its coal mines
      b. Belief by Lenin that many of those lost assets could be regained in the event of a German defeat in the war
      c. Conviction also that the Bolshevik example of peace might inspire a worldwide worker revolution
   4. The greatest threat to the new communist regime--Civil War (1917-21) between the Reds (Bolsheviks) and Whites (all opposition to them--Old Regime Tsarists, Kadets, Mensheviks, and SR's)
      a. A desperate & horrifying struggle with both sides committing terrible atrocities against a populace caught in the middle--10 million Russians dying of battle wounds, starvation, & disease
      b. Murder of the ex-tsar & his family at Ekaterinburg on July 16, 1918 by local Bolsheviks at the approach of Whites in the area near the Ural Mountains
      c. Reasons for White defeat & Red triumph--to be lectured on in class
D. Revolutionary aftermath in lecture material--economic policies of War Communism (1917-21) & the New Economic Policy or NEP (1921-27) and the 1st Five-Year Plan, the power struggle between Trotsky & Stalin, and the Purge Trials of the late-1930's

. Similarities in old Tsarist Russia and the new Communist Russia:
   A. A high degree of governmental centralization, meaning authoritarianism and dictatorship
   B. Suppression of civil liberties & human rights, with the use of secret police & censorship & terrorism
   C. Predominance of a small & privileged bureaucracy or elite in ruling the country
   D. An aggressive foreign policy with the emphasis on territorial expansion in all directions

E. Ambivalence toward Western culture & ideas--sometimes admiration & emulation, occasional hostility & repulsion

FASCISM

I. Background & Definition
   A. Similarity in Fascism & Communism--emergence of both of them as authoritarian or totalitarian systems of government & society that constitute 20th-century dictatorship
   B. Difference between the two in doctrinal development:
      1. Derivation of Communism from the ideology of one man--Karl Marx and the "orthodox" views of his early years
      2. Origination of Fascism in the doctrines of numerous thinkers & their writings of the late-19th & early-20th centuries that were especially critical of European life popular culture
         a. Fascism was ideologically not the product of a deliberately devised body of beliefs
         b. Instead its proponents improvised theories & policies as they went along usually to suit the requirements of the moment
         c. Major Fascist sources of inspiration were Social Darwinism and critics of democracy & liberalism
   C. Definition of Fascism--a right-wing, anti-democratic, & authoritarian regime established with the assistance of regular military elements and/or violent paramilitary groups for the socio-economic benefit of the "classes of order", meaning the upper & middle bourgeoisie and the old landed aristocracy
      1. Utilization by Fascists of a combination of tactics to attain political power:
         a. Some legal means such as elections & alliances with traditional conservative parties
         b. Heavy use of terrorism & thuggery by illegal, paramilitary groups such as Blackshirts & Brownshirts often organized by state officials who recognized fascists as anti-socialist & anti-communist
         c. Exploitation of an era of political, social, & economic crisis that they themselves helped to create through violence & fear
      2. Appeal by Fascist movements to those people in all sectors of society dissatisfied with life during the inter-war period--but especially to:
         a. Officers & veteran soldiers of World War I.--frustrated with civilian life or a rootless & jobless existence, national humiliation after the peace treaty, and widespread pacifist sentiments in response to prior horrors
         b. The lower middle class--threatened the most by economic disruptions, uncertainty, & depression and fearing a fall into working-class living conditions
         c. Wealthy industrialists & landowners--fearful of the growing political power of the working class and the threat during the 1920's & 1930's of communist revolution
   D. General causes for the rise of Fascism:
      1. Fear by the upper classes of a threatened electoral victory or revolution from left-wing political parties representing the lower classes:

  a. In fact, the greatest gains in political power in Western Europe during the years prior to the war were made by socialist parties, which were the largest single political party in Germany & France
  b. In the past, the bourgeoisie had generally supported liberalism & democracy--however, by the 1920's democracy seemed to be threatening middle-class money, property, & status--thus they now favored conservatism or even authoritarianism in many European countries
 2. Colossal demoralization & desperation following the:
  a. Disasters of the Great War
  b. Disappointments of the peace treaty
  c. Universal frustrations over wounded national pride
  d. Massive suffering after the world economic collapse of 1929-30

I. Characteristics of Fascism
 A. Nationalism--a fanatical patriotism as well as glorification of the national past & its future destiny of greatness--deliberate encouragement of ethnic identification rather than socio-economic class identification
 B. Racism--occasional stress on ethnic (erroneously called "racial") superiority with the designation of other nations or ethnics (like Jews) or nonconformists (such as Gypsies, homosexuals, & intellectuals) as objects of derision & persecution and as scapegoats on whom to blame problems
 C. Militarism--emphasis on military values such as order & discipline, hierarchy, absolute obedience to authority, glorification of violence & war, territorial conquest as the basis of national destiny, and policies of expansionism & armaments buildup
  1. Hitler declared: "Mankind has grown strong through eternal struggle, and will only perish through eternal peace."[2]
  2. Ignorant or unthinking people incapable of understanding, articulating, or coping with their problems & frustrations will often resort to violence as a means of expressing dissatisfaction with their world--aggression is a way of striking out against failure
  3. Also, the normal inclinations toward conformity & the herd-mentality would lead many ordinary people to join the larger groups & mass movements of the 1930's
  4. Moreover, some individuals derive pleasure from brutalizing, victimizing, dominating, & inflicting pain on others--what we sometimes call sadism
 D. Authoritarianism--the relationship between the government & the people in which the latter possess very few if any rights or freedoms, and the former reserves the power & "authority" to do whatever it wishes with its population of subjects:
  1. Thus the rule by a dictator or "leader" (Der Fuhrer, Il Duce) who embodies the popular will
  2. Complete contempt for individual civil liberties, democracy, liberalism, constitutions, & parliamentary institutions
  3. Prominence of the goal to manipulate & exploit the masses of people in spite of occasional rhetoric to the contrary--belief in the masses being unfit to rule--scorn & disdain for the abilities of commoners

        4. Importance of the theory that government should belong to the
           intellectually & physically superior few to rule for the good
           of all
        5. Constant employment of censorship of the press & literature &
           media, coercion, secret police activities, concentration
           camps, and elimination (often liquidation) of most or all
           opposition
   E. Totalitarianism--a form of 20th-century dictatorship demanding
      "total" control of public & private life by the central govern-
      ment, thus supremacy over everything in society:
        1. National domination by an autocracy, or government with unlim-
               ited powers--use of the word "paternalism" to imply that gov-
               ernment would care for the populace in a system where the
           people had no rights, only duties to the state
        2. Impossibility, in reality, of government to exert total con-
           trol--yet persistent efforts by fascists to regiment society
           through the following:
             a. Economic planning & regulation by the national government
                in a system known as "corporate" or state capitalism
             b. Total authority over the media (newspapers, radio, film)
                through state ownership or censorship
             c. Domination of education & academics, social organizat-
                ions, artistic endeavors, and sports
        3. Use of the term "Corporate State" for the method of control--
           organization of all of society & the economy into groups or
           bodies or "corps" through which the national government man-
           aged everything in theory
             a. Establishment in the economy of councils known as <u>syndic-
                ates</u> representing members of the same profession in bus-
                    inesses & industry & professions and including govern-
                ment officials for supervision
             b. Effort by Fascism with the "Corporate State" to break
                down class identification as forecast by Marx and to
                promote community interests over individual interests
        4. In the economy, replacement of laissez-faire or free enter-
           prise practices where they still existed with a governmental-
           ly planned & managed economy coordinated by the central state
           for maximum efficiency & upper-class profits
             a. Preservation of private property but application of gov-
                ernmental authority to protect that property & its pro-
                fits for the wealthy few
             b. Provision of nothing for workers--no right to strike &
                fixation of wages usually at quite a low level
        5. Frequent reference by Fascism to itself as "national social-
           ism" to distinguish its movement from Communism, which was
           called "popular socialism":
             a. In Communism, the people as a whole theoretically benefit
                in equal shares from such a regime, whereas...
             b. In Fascism, the regime frankly favors the "better" people
                & wealthy & business community over the masses & working
                class
             c. Fascism is <u>not</u> "socialistic" for the above reason and be-
                cause socialism implies government ownership of at least
                some means of production--Fascism involves only govern-
                ment regulation & planning and not outright ownership

                d. In Fascism, a foundation of capitalism & the profit motive & middle class dominance are retained--the most accurate description of Fascism economically is "state capitalism"
                e. Fascist leaders often emphasized the word "socialism" as populist demagoguery to attract gullible lower-class people to their movements while privately making deals upper-class individuals
        6. Recruitment by Fascism of most of its leadership from the opportunist, brutal, ignorant, & criminal elements of every society, thus contradicting its theory & rhetoric of personifying the superior segment of the nation
    F. Anti-communism--violent opposition to socialist & communist parties and labor organizations--hatred because of their internationalism, pacifism, & stress on equality
    G. Anti-intellectualism--contempt for knowledge & learning and those who possess it
        1. Rejection of rational thought & critical thinking--Hermann Goring once said: "When I hear anyone speak of culture, I reach for my revolver."[3]
        2. Stress on emotion & intuition & will over reason & logic & rational faculties--in other words, always unthinking action over thoughtful consideration
        3. Emphasis on ritual, loud noise, & mindless behavior--songs, slogans, chants, ridiculous salutes & marches, flashy uniforms, bands, parades, mass rallies, etc.
        4. Examples:
            a. "Believe! Obey! Fight!"[4]
            b. "Down with intelligence, and long live death!"[5]
            c. "He who has steel has bread."[6]
            d. "To die is to be happy; to be happy is to die."[7]
    H. Alliance with traditional religious institutions
        1. Negotiation of bargains & deals by all Fascist regimes with traditional religious organizations such as the Catholic, Orthodox, & Lutheran Churches
        2. Natural affinities & common goals in seeking hierarchy, authoritarianism, passive obedience & subservience of the popular masses, and the frequent use of antisemitism, scapegoating, & intolerance toward nonconformist minorities
III. Contradictions, Ambiguities, & Absurdities of Fascism
    A. Racism--basis of their belief in "racial superiority" and "racial purity" on pseudo-science & ridiculous notions, considering the extensive racial & ethnic mixture in Europe that had existed for thousands of years
    B. Totalitarianism--this remaining an unfulfilled goal, with fascists always obliged to share power & to compromise with traditional conservative forces such as the Catholic & Protestant churches, the military establishments, industrialists, land barons, & sometimes monarchy
    C. Anticommunism--true only within their countries--otherwise, fascist regimes had the most cordial relations with the Soviet Union during the inter-war years of all European nations
    D. Law, order, & morality--these subjects constantly preached yet routinely ignored by fascists--total disregard for judicial & legal procedures and moral conduct--rampant governmental corruption & inefficiency due to cronyism, incompetent ideologues, and bureau-

cratic in-fighting by an unscrupulous power-hungry party elite
   E. Militarism--much bombast by fascists yet unprepared for the ordeal of war as it would be experienced in World War II.
   F. Authoritarianism--claim by the "leader" to embody the "will of the people", yet there was always a condescending scorn & no real concern for the masses of people
   G. Ideology vs. reality--assertion by Fascism that it promoted better government & people & society, yet usually it was the rule of opportunistic, ruthless, & often sociopathic persons with no qualms about betraying allies & enemies alike and ready to alter ideology & strategy to fit the needs of the moment or to save themselves

INTERNATIONAL CRISES OF THE 1930'S

I. Introduction
   A. Occurrence of successive acts of aggression & treaty violations by the Fascist nations leading to World War II. in 1939
   B. Reasons why the democracies did not respond effectively during the 1930's to totalitarian aggression:
      1. Preoccupation by the Allies (democracies) with numerous domestic social & economic problems caused by the Great Depression
      2. Attitudes of defeatism & demoralization in the face of rising power & successes of Germany & Japan
      3. Movements of pacifism in the democracies--thus anti-war sentiments in remembrance of the horrors & senselessness of the World War I.
      4. Retreat of America into isolation, thus doing nothing to stop Fascist expansionism
      5. Fears of Communist Russia as potentially an even greater threat to bourgeois capitalism than Fascism
      6. Weakness & incapacity of the League of Nations to punish Fascist militarism
      7. Divisions among the Allies over what policies to pursue, especially considering the apparent unfairness of the Treaty of Versailles
II. The Series of Crises Leading to War
   A. Japanese Invasion of Manchuria in 1931
      1. Existence of Manchuria (a vast province in northeastern China possessing tremendous resources) as still under the sovereignty of a weak Chinese Republic yet very vulnerable
      2. Belief by Japanese leaders in the need for Manchuria in order that Japan survive as a great power--launch of an undeclared war in September, 1931 and completion of the conquest by 1933
      3. Failure of the League in this first major test--condemnation of Japan but with no effective punitive measures--Japanese withdrawal from the League in 1933
      4. Invasion of other areas of China in succeeding years with Japanese armies committing horrifying atrocities against the civilian population in a prelude to the grim future
   B. German Rearmament: 1933-35
      1. Withdrawal from the League by Germany in 1933
      2. Denunciation of the disarmament clauses of the Versailles Treaty in March, 1935--announcement of the existence of an air force & the application of conscription to the armies
      3. Committal of these acts as the first open violations of Ver-

sailles by Germany--condemnation but no action by the League as well as Allied division over the proper response
C. Italian Conquest of Ethiopia in 1935-36
   1. A colonial war by Mussolini against this northeastern African nation mainly to gain national prestige & to avenge the humiliating Italian defeat there in 1896
   2. Conquest in several months--use of poison gas & aerial bombardment against natives armed with spears & shields
   3. Response by the League--a vote of censure & economic sanctions against Italy in November, 1935--yet the list of commodities denied to Italy in trade prohibitions did not include oil, which was the only thing urgently required by Italy for a continuation of the war--thus ridiculous ineffectiveness
   4. No action taken by the democracies--official end of the sanctions by the League in July, 1936--withdrawal from the League by Mussolini in December, 1937
D. German Occupation of the Rhineland in 1936
   1. Remilitarization of the region in March--a matter of perfect timing with the democracies embroiled in the Ethiopian Crisis
   2. Protest by the League of this violation of Versailles, but no firm action taken--conclusion today that France in 1936 could have probably defeated Germany easily--thus recognition of this move by Hitler as a bold risk that succeeded
   3. Impact of Versailles unfairness--persuasion by many people everywhere that Germany had a right to occupy militarily its own territory
   4. Loss in 1936 by the Allies of their last chance during this crisis to destroy Hitler's regime without a major war--consequence of a tremendous increase of Hitler's popularity in Germany
E. Spanish Civil War: 1936-39
   1. Establishment of the Spanish Republic in 1931 yet inheritance of colossal weaknesses of poverty & illiteracy & socio-economic divisions while facing strongly entrenched conservative groups: the Catholic Church, army, large landowners, & rich industrialists & businessmen
   2. Support of the Republic from disunited rural & urban democrats and especially from labor unions--thus socialist programs & anti-clericalism antagonizing conservatives
   3. The fundamental difficulty--inauguration in the early 1930's of liberal reforms in a backward nation lacking a strong middle class to support them, and also lacking a stable & peaceful environment in which to develop
   4. Disappearance of the political center & polarization of Spain into two extremes:
      a. A Communist-supported Left, known as the Loyalists of the Republic
      b. A Fascist-led Right, known as the Insurgents & Falangists under the authority of General Francisco Franco
   5. Commencement of the Civil War in 1936 as conservatives united militarily to overthrow the Republic
   6. International reaction--agreement by France & Britain (fearing the influence of Communists in the Republic) on a policy of neutrality & non-intervention, but dispatch by Germany & Italy of weapons & troops to the Falangists, and shipment by Russia of some assistance to the Loyalists

      7. Emergence of this brutal & savage Civil War as a preview and a testing ground for the tactics & weaponry of World War II.
      8. Tragic results--victory of the Falangists by March, 1939 in a final campaign of mass executions & terror against Loyalists
F. The Rome-Berlin Axis: October, 1936--negotiation of a formal alliance between Italy & Germany
G. The Anti-Comintern Pact: 1936-37--agreements among Japan, Germany, & Italy to oppose Communism, thus a three-way alliance against Russia with the creation of the Rome-Berlin-Tokyo Axis
H. Seizure of Austria in 1938
      1. Existence of Austria as a small & weak nation with an unbalanced economy & numerous social problems--wish by most Austrians to maintain national independence in spite of being ethnically German
      2. Desire by Hitler & German nationalists for <u>Anschluss</u>, or "amalgamation" or unity of Austria with Germany in an expression of national expansion & self-determination
      3. German manipulation of the Austrian Nazi Party to instigate turmoil & chaos--paralysis of the Austrian government--encounter by this German invasion of almost no resistance in March--proclamation of unity of the two states on March 13
      4. Response of no action by the democracies--conviction by many that this move only affected the Germans & not other nationalities, despite German terrorism on Austrian opponents
      5. Significant gains for Hitler in terms of money, population, resources, industry, & geographical penetration into southeastern Europe that surrounded Czechoslovakia on three sides
I. The Czech Crisis in 1938
      1. Survival of Czechoslovakia as the only true democracy in Eastern Europe and as an economically strong & fairly stable nation of 15 million people
      2. Yet containment of numerous minorities including 3 million Germans residing along the western borders in a region known as the Sudetenland
      3. Encouragement by Hitler of the Sudeten German Party (a puppet Nazi group) to demand autonomy & then annexation to Germany--Czech resistance and preparations for war
      4. Appearance of war at that time as an inevitability--international tensions mounting to fever pitch--delivery by Hitler of hysterically belligerent speeches with the announcement of war imminence to the German generals in November, 1937--mobilization of the British fleet & French army
      5. Belief then & today by military experts that Germany would suffer quick defeat in a war against Czechoslovakia (with a good army & extensive border fortifications), France, Britain, and Russia
      6. Adoption instead of a continuation by Britain & France of the policy of "appeasement", or conciliating & buying off the aggressor with concessions of territories & nations at the expense of principle & reason in hopes of satiating the enemy
      7. Request by British P.M. Neville Chamberlain of personal conferences with Hitler to defuse the crisis & avoid war--support from French premier Daladier--response by Hitler with increasingly extravagant claims

       8. Final meeting at Munich with Hitler, Mussolini, Chamberlain, & Daladier but without representation from Russia & Czechoslovakia
J. Munich Conference: September 29, 1938
    1. A dramatic climax of shame & humiliation for Britain & France in their sacrifice of Czechoslovakia to avoid a risky major war--surrender of the Sudetenland & Czech border forts to Germany without the consultation of Czechoslovakia and leaving the latter betrayed, defenseless, & helpless
    2. Yet euphoric celebrations in the West & overwhelming praise for Chamberlain's attainment of an honorable "Peace in our time."[8]
    3. Consequent loss of prestige by the Western democracies in Eastern Europe that never again completely revived until the death of Communism in 1989
K. Occupation of all of Czechoslovakia by Germany: March, 1939
    1. Final extinction of the Czech state, as Nazi forces behaved with characteristic bestiality
    2. Abrupt end also of the Allied policy of appeasement in a British & French pledge & commitment of assistance to Poland if attacked by Germany
    3. Incorrect assumption by Hitler that appeasement still prevailed & that war on Poland would not provoke a general conflict
L. Invasion & Conquest of Albania by Italy: April, 1939
    1. Jealousy on the part of Mussolini for the spectacular successes of Hitler
    2. Preoccupation by the democracies with Poland, thus no action taken to assist Albania
M. German-Russian Pact: August 23, 1939
    1. Desire by Hitler & Germany to prevent a simultaneous two-front conflict like World War I.--distrust of the democracies by Stalin after Munich--Western fears of what actually occurred later, meaning Soviet occupation of Central & Eastern Europe
    2. Negotiation of the Soviet-Nazi Nonaggression Pact committing both sides to neutrality in case of war against other nations
    3. Recognition of this "diplomatic revolution" between two traditional enemies as a shocking blow to the West & as a guarantee that the democracies could do nothing to prevent the dismemberment of Poland
N. German Invasion of Poland: September 1, 1939
    1. Marking the official beginning of World War II.
    2. Declaration of war on Germany by France & Britain, September 3
    3. Requirement of less than one month for Germany to overwhelm Poland

Chapter 14　　　　　　　　WORLD WAR II. & AFTER

I. World War II. (1939--45)
   A. Introduction
      1. Victory by the Allies in the most devastating conflict in history saved the Western World & democracy from destruction by fascist dictatorship & totalitarianism
      2. This triumph paved the way for a spectacular post-war economic & cultural regeneration
   B. Generalizations about the 2nd World War:
      1. A more global war than ever before, being fought in the Pacific & Asia as well as in Europe--thus the most extensive & far-reaching war in history
      2. A threefold field of action for the first time: air, land, & sea (as well as under the sea)--in fact, the most crucial & significant hostilities being waged in the air by fighter planes & bombers that most often determined outcomes elsewhere
      3. A war of movement rather than position, with no trench warfare as in World War I.--armies now fully mobile with huge forces rapidly ranging over hundreds of miles in a few days or weeks
         a. German development & initial use of <u>blitzkrieg</u> ("lightning-war")--stress on speed & quickness & mobility, coordination of attacks by airplanes & tanks, and use of motorized or mechanized vehicles for transporting troops & supplies
         b. Rapid adoption of these tactical & strategic methods by other major nations
      4. The most scientific & technological conflict in character so far in the human experience--great importance of new devices such as radar, sonar, rocket bombs, & atomic bombs in victory or defeat
      5. A truly "total" war, in the sense of destroying a roughly equal number of civilians & noncombatants as well as soldiers in battle--also featuring the destruction of much property in addition to war material--thus no one & nothing actually safe from the ravages of war
      6. Existence simultaneously of both a conflict between nations and a gigantic civil war within nations involving domestic collaborators with fascist occupation against resistance fighters employing guerrilla tactics & sabotage & assassination
   C. Primary participants & alliances:
      1. The Axis Powers of Germany, Italy, Hungary, & Japan
      2. Grand Alliance (or the "Allies") of Britain, France, the United States, Russia, China, as well as numerous smaller nations
   D. The <u>two</u> phases of the war:
      1. Axis powers triumphant nearly everywhere: 1939--42
      2. Allied rally & drive to full victory: 1942--45. Thus the most crucial year & turning point in the war was 1942
   E. Reasons for Allied triumph & Axis defeat:
      1. Russian manpower & human resources--two-thirds of all German war casualties occurring on the Eastern Front against the Soviet Union
      2. American industrial might plus managerial & organizational skills--one of the vital keys to Allied victory being the outproduction of the Axis--we were the "great arsenal of democ-

racy"[1], in the words of President Franklin Delano Roosevelt
3. British inspiration through dedicated resistance & iron will against heavy odds early in the war--also provision of an emotional & psychological edge by the vigorous energy & brilliant oratory of Prime Minister Winston Churchill, who offered his nation nothing less than "blood, toil, tears, & sweat"[2]
4. Unrealistic German goals of world conquest & unlimited expansion, resulting in overextension of their empire beyond the means of control--also German totalitarian methods of repression, racism, brutality, & genocide eventually alienating most conquered peoples into resistance
5. Recklessness & ignorance of Hitler--always emotionally unstable & at times hysterical as well as highly superstitious & poorly educated--increasingly losing touch with reality during the war & suffering from a serious disease of the nervous system--the leadership of Japan & Italy equally incompetent

F. Results of World War II:
1. An end of the international supremacy & predominance of Western (Britain & France) and Central (Germany) Europe--Germany crushed permanently as a military power
2. Emergence of the United States & Russia as the two strongest powers in the world--defeat & partition of Germany creating a power vacuum in Europe & making Russia the mightiest nation on the Continent until 1989
3. Development of the atomic bomb bringing into existence a weapon initially capable of destroying civilization on the planet and later capable of destroying all of humanity
4. Enormous cost of the war, with only estimates possible:
   a. At least 50 million soldiers killed & an equal number of civilians killed from bombings, mass extermination & deportation policies, postwar famines, and epidemics of disease
   b. The psychological & emotional shock & trauma incalculable yet overwhelming & appalling--the battle damage staggers the imagination--huge areas of Russia & Germany totally devastated and many cities entirely levelled
   c. Estimate of the damage & cost of fighting the war--$1,400 billion at 1940's rates of exchange
5. Colossal magnitude of inhuman atrocities:
   a. Impressment of millions of people by the Germans for slave labor camps & industries--hostages & civilians rounded up & shot in reprisal for the resistance of others
   b. German use of mass extermination centers with gas chambers & crematory ovens for the systematic liquidation of over seven million "inferior" peoples by the supposedly racially superior "master race" (Herrenvolk in German)
   c. Introduction by the Germans of a new infamous word to describe their horrors: genocide--the destruction of an entire ethnic group, attempted in their extermination of more than six million Jews, known as the Holocaust

G. Theaters & phases of the 2nd World War:
1. Poland: September, 1939
   a. Official commencement of war with the German invasion of Poland--conquest in less than a month despite heroic Polish efforts--this campaign witnessing the 1st use of blitzkrieg tactics--Russian occupation of the eastern

region of Poland in a partition agreement with Germany
   b. Seizure by Russia shortly thereafter of the Baltic states of Lithuania, Latvia, & Estonia--no direct assistance for these nations forthcoming from their Western allies due to the long distances & hopeless futility
   c. Immediate emergence in Poland of a highly effective Resistance movement among the civilian population--it was <u>the</u> most effective Resistance movement anywhere during the war, in spite of greater fame for the French one
   d. Declaration of war in the West by Britain & France, yet no attack by them on a vulnerable Germany--this strange situation called the <u>Sitzkrieg</u> ("Phony War") & lasting until May, 1940--a reflection of their attitude of hesitancy & defensiveness behind French fortifications along the German border known as the Maginot Line

2. Denmark & Norway: April, 1940
   a. Occupation of Denmark easily on April 9 and Norway within the next two weeks
   b. Particular German desire for Norway because of its strategic airports & seaports from which later to attack Britain--also of value to them were timber & iron ore
3. Low Countries: May, 1940
   a. Blitzkrieg on May 10 to outflank the Maginot Line--murderous bombing of Rotterdam killing 30,000 civilians--the Netherlands or Holland capitulating in four days, Belgium surrendering two weeks later
   b. Horrifying atrocities committed by the Nazis--many Jews transported to death camps in Germany
4. France: May-June, 1940
   a. Shocking defeat of France in little more than one month--the reasons why:
      (1) Possession by the Germans of 3 to 1 superiority in air power, usually the most critical factor of all
      (2) Low morale & defeatism in the French forces, partly due to colossal losses in World War I.
      (3) A one-front war for Germany unlike the 1st WW--neutrality of Russia in the east this time
      (4) Qualitative difference in more modern weaponry for the Germans, in spite of relative quantitative equality of troops & tanks & artillery
      (5) Better German strategy of aggressive attack while the British & French trying merely to survive defensively--yet French soldiers fighting at least as well as Germans--almost all modern wars are won by technology more than bravery
   b. German division of France territorially into two parts:
      (1) Direct German occupation of northern & western areas of France along the oceans
      (2) Vichy France--establishment of a puppet fascist regime in southern & eastern areas outwardly under French leaders yet really subordinate to Germany
   c. Flight of several tens of thousands of French soldiers to Britain to continue the struggle under a brilliant & inspiring leader, Charles de Gaulle--this group known as the Free French

5. Britain: August to November, 1940
    a. The Battle of Britain (also called the "Blitz") now fought exclusively in the air between opposing air forces (Luftwaffe vs. Royal Air Force) as Hitler prepared for an invasion of the Isles
    b. Possession by Germany at that time of insufficient means to conquer Britain, as we understand the situation in retrospect--yet the Germans having a much larger air force at the outset of the fighting
    c. Persistence of bombings & dog-fights for four months--London targeted for [57] consecutive nights in a German effort to terrorize the British into submission
    d. Gradual shift in momentum to Britain because of three factors: development of a radar warning-system, better aircraft, & superior fighter pilots
    e. Evocation by the efforts & heroism of RAF pilots of one of Churchill's greatest comments: "Never in the field of human conflict was so much owed by so many to so few."[3]
    f. Another critical factor--German failure to concentrate on bombing industries & air fields rather than population centers--eventual loss of interest in Britain by Hitler as preparations advanced for campaigns elsewhere
6. North Africa: 1941-43
    a. German tank divisions with Italian troops overrunning North Africa toward British Egypt--yet failure to take it due to inadequate support
    b. Later rout of Axis forces there by an Allied combination of American, French, & British armies
7. The Balkans: April to June, 1941
    a. Easy destruction by the Germans of Yugoslavia & Greece and occupation of Rumania & Bulgaria
    b. Yet a fateful consequence in these operations for the Germans of delaying their invasion of Russia for several weeks & hastening winter conditions
8. Russia: June 22, 1941--44
    a. Application by the Germans of racist theories & policies especially toward the Russians, the latter being regarded by the former as mindless & uncivilized & brutish animals
    b. Pursuit in Russia more than anywhere else of German desires for expansionism (<u>Lebensraum</u>, or "living space") for future German colonization
    c. Russian advantages in the war & reasons for victory:
        (1) Geographical enormity & limitless space of land-- great distances from Germany led to overextension of supply lines & eventual ineffectiveness
        (2) A much larger population for manpower: 170 million Russians to 70 million Germans
        (3) Familiarity with the extreme weather conditions of summer heat & winter cold
        (4) Superior strategy of initial retreat & use of the "scorched earth policy" (destruction of everything during their retreat, leaving no food or water or shelter for the advancing Germans)
        (5) Intensification by the invasion of nationalistic aspirations in defense of the Russian fatherland

            d. Turning point in the Battle of Stalingrad (November, 1942--February, 1943)--the biggest & most significant battle of the war--seizure of the offensive by the Russians in the fighting thereafter
    9. United States:
        a. American entrance in the war after the Japanese surprise attack on our Pacific Fleet in Hawaii at Pearl Harbor on December 7, 1941
        b. Decision to concentrate initially on waging war in Europe against Hitler before focusing on victory in the Pacific against Japan
    10. Battle of the Atlantic: 1941--43
        a. German use of submarines to destroy Allied shipping, to threaten Britain's survival, & to prevent American involvement in the fighting--tremendous German successes throughout much of 1942
        b. American victory in 1943 with the employment of radar & sonar detection devices, speedy escort vessels for the ship convoys, and a multitude of aircraft to scour the the sea routes
    11. D-Day: June 6, 1944--massive Allied amphibious invasion of Normandy, France from England demonstrating spectacular American capabilities in large-scale organizational & managerial skills
    12. Lecture material on the end of war in Europe (VE-Day: May 7, 1945) and the war in the Pacific (VJ-Day: September 2, 1945) as well as the dropping of atomic bombs and the wartime conferences shaping the post-war world

II. International Affairs After 1945
    A. Introduction
        1. Unique results of World War II. in the emergence of Communist Russia & previously isolationist America as the two most powerful nations in the world, for the first time in history
        2. Both nations lacking experience in the realm of big-power international politics & thus committing enormous blunders in world affairs as a consequence
        3. All of the traditional powers (Britain, France, Germany) now generally on the sidelines without any major influence in the world
        4. Maneuvering by the U.S. & Russia even before the finish of the 2nd World War for potential advantages in post-war rivalries & hostilities by making deals with Nazi Germans for information about the future enemy
        5. This leading to the "Cold War": 1945--89
    B. Characteristics of the Cold War:
        1. Absence of open war & total peace--Americans & Russians never coming to blows directly, yet constant tensions & crises creating an atmosphere of potential belligerence at any time
        2. Constant threats against each other & maneuvers for advantage in anticipation of future war
        3. Existence of rival military alliance systems on both sides:
            a. American formation of NATO (North Atlantic Treaty Organization) for the European theater, & SEATO (Southeast Asia Treaty Organization) for the Far East

            b. Russian formation of the Warsaw Pact of East European
               puppet-communist-regime nations, and the Sino-Soviet
               Pact with China after the latter became communist in 1948
      4. Development of heavy armaments in a race for superiority
      5. Use of propaganda to portray a struggle between virtue & evil,
         which never existed in reality:
            a. Proclamation by the U.S. in particular of a showdown be-
               tween democracy & totalitarianism, freedom vs. tyranny
            b. Accuracy of these terms in describing Russia, yet American
               support also of a policy of propping up & defending &
               arming countless fascist regimes that routinely committed
               horrifying atrocities & human-rights abuses against their
               own people
            c. Justification of this unprincipled policy by sinister Am-
               erican politicians & leaders with the admonition that
               democratic governments in Third World nations were often
               too unstable & thus vulnerable to communist revolutions
            d. Commitment by both big powers of much money to aid their
               supporters in other nations--extension by the Truman
               (President Harry: 1945-53) Doctrine of military & econom-
               ic assistance to all nations threatened by communist ag-
               gression, & continuation of this policy by American gov-
               ernments for decades
            e. The Marshall Plan (named for Secretary of State George)--
               provision of American money to rebuild Western Europe's
               shattered economies--while seemingly a humanitarian gest-
               ure, its main purpose was quickly to revive societies &
               restore bourgeois capitalism in order to prevent demo-
               cratic socialists or communists from winning elections
               immediately after the war

C. Features of American foreign policy:
   1. A sharp reaction against the appeasement policies of the
      1930's & earlier American isolationism
         a. Rise of the view that making concessions & surrendering
            territories to dictators had only encouraged their
            aggression
         b. American swing now toward the opposite extreme of
            frequent unwillingness to make any compromises at all
   2. Policy of containment--a judgment that enemy territorial
      expansion must be prevented or "contained" by armed
      resistance, which encouraged a rigid corollary:
   3. The domino theory--a belief that the loss of a single
      country would lead to the fall of successive nations which
      might ultimately result in demise for the entire "free
      world" to communist aggression--thus the regard toward any
      failure to defend territories as intolerable weakness
   4. Idea of monolithic communism--an incorrect notion that all
      communist nations constituted one gigantic political force
      working against democracy, thus ignoring the fact that
      modern nationalism (the most powerful ideology in the
      modern world) motivated selfish & distinct behavior in even
      communist states
   5. Diplomatic inflexibility--the belief in & practice of the
      above views resulting in many uncompromising &
      confrontational positions--what Secretary of State John

Foster Dulles in fact called his policy of "brinkmanship", the consequence being a:
D. Series of international crises:
1. The Berlin Blockade in 1949
   a. Russian closure of all land & water routes from West Germany to West Berlin, the latter being completely surrounded by territories of Communist East Germany
   b. American response in a massive airlift of supplies to relieve the blockaded city--nothing done by Russia to impede this operation, & later all restrictions lifted
2. Korean War: 1950--53
   a. Creation by post-war treaties of a communist North Korea & a fascist South Korea, each aggressively wishing to absorb the other
   b. Invasion of the South by the North--intervention on the side of the South by the U.S.A. & the U.N. forces-- then intervention on the side of the North by Communist China
   c. Heavy losses on all sides & protracted negotiations-- the result in a treaty roughly establishing a status quo antebellum that still remains today
   d. American frustrations in Korea anticipating disaster in Vietnam--the hopelessness & futility of a land war in Asia
3. Construction of the Berlin Wall: 1961--built by the Russians to prevent East Germans from fleeing to freedom in West Berlin--protests but no action by America--eventually the wall became a perfect symbol of & monument to the failure of the entire communist system
4. Cuban Missile Crisis: 1962
   a. Existence of these events as the closest point the world ever came to nuclear war--Russian leader Krushchev seeking to test & challenge an inexperienced new president John Kennedy with the introduction of offensive weapons into Cuba
   b. American response--a naval blockade of Cuba & demands fo the removal of missiles, yet with a concession of the pledge to respect the territorial integrity of Cuba in the future (meaning no more American invasions)
   c. Thus the attainment of a compromise
   d. Response by both sides to the tremendous tensions during the crisis in a real sense of urgency (for a while) to reduce the perils of atomic war--the results:
      (1) The beginnings of negotiations to ban nuclear testing, with treaties ensuing
      (2) Establishment of the "Hot Line" between Washington & Moscow in October, 1963 to avert future wars with direct communication
      (3) Commencement of wheat sales to Russia
5. Vietnam War: 1964--75
   a. American intervention in South Vietnam to prevent the collapse of a fascist regime to communist North Vietnam
   b. Demonstration by this conflict of the limitations & unworkability of the containment-domino theory policies
      (1) Conservatives had warned for years that if Vietnam fell, then following it would be Thailand, Burma,

                    Malaysia, Singapore, Indonesia, the Philippines,
                    Japan, Hawaii, San Francisco, (even St. Mark's
                    Lighthouse?)
            (2) In fact, none fell nor were they even threatened
                after our departure from Vietnam

II. Western Europe Since 1945
    A. Achievement of a remarkable & brilliant recovery from the devastation & horrors of World War II. by featuring the establishment of relatively stable democratic governments, spectacular economic revival & expansion, and cultural regeneration
    B. The creation of the Common Market in 1957 as particularly significant in this revival--reference to it often as the EEC (European Economic Community), or more today as simply the EC (European Community):
        1. Its initial priority to integrate & unify Western Europe economically by the abolition or lowering or fair adjustment of tariff barriers among its participants for the benefit of all
        2. More & more economic cooperation & coordination eventually bringing greater political, social, & cultural unity and interdependence--thus effectively eliminating future dangers of war between the major European nations
        3. The original members in 1957 known as "the Six": France, West Germany, Italy, the Netherlands, Belgium, & Luxembourg--later members in 1973 including Denmark, Britain, & Ireland--joining in 1981 was Greece and in 1985 were Spain & Portugal, to comprise a total of twelve nations
        4. In 1994 Austria, Finland, & Sweden voted for membership--in the future most or all of Europe will integrate with the EC
        5. Existence of the EC today as the most important & powerful free trade area in the world, including over 300 million people
        6. A key condition for membership application to the EC--prior establishment & functioning operation of a democratic form of government--thus simultaneous promotion of economic prosperity <u>and</u> political democracy
    C. Impressive achievements of the major nations:
        1. Germany (reunification of West & East in 1989 following the fall of communism)--the most powerful industrial complex in Europe renowned internationally for the high quality of its technological products as well as for its very efficient & orderly society
        2. France:
            a. Also superb in science, technology, & organization--possession of probably the finest public transportation system in the world with its excellent Paris subway (Metro) & TGV trains routinely attaining 200 mph
            b. Typical leadership in styles & fashions for clothing, cuisine, & art (after all, our words "culture", "civilization", "finesse", & "chic" are French)
        3. Holland (the Netherlands)--a very energetic, tolerant, well-educated, & resourceful people (the Dutch)--major prominence in international trade, with Rotterdam being the port city with the greatest volume of trade per year in the world
        4. Scandinavia (Norway, Sweden, Denmark, Finland)--attainment of the most significant social, economic, & political advances in the world for women, featuring the most extensive social ser-

vices in health & education & public welfare of any societies anywhere (they are several decades ahead of us in these areas)
   5. Switzerland--famous banking & financial center in Europe maintaining the most stable & valuable currency in the world--also celebrated for its institutions & practices of direct local democracy
   6. Italy--a chaotic & inefficient society riddled with political corruption & incompetence, yet populated with an extremely imaginative & creative people, and boasting the world's most popular food (pizza) & greatest music (Puccini & Verdi operas, in your professor's prejudiced opinion)
   7. Ireland--arguably the most friendly, gregarious, humor-loving, & literate (in terms of books read annually) people in all of Europe, who also produce the world's finest brand of beer (Guinness) and best whiskey (again, in your author's judgment)
D. Great Britain--the exception to most European nations in its steady decline from wealth & power & greatness--the major problems and reasons for decline of post-war Britain:
   1. Rapid loss & surrender of its empire after World War II:
      a. Prior rule by Britain for four centuries of more land & people than any nation in history, yet disintegration occurring with amazing speed
      b. Achievement of independence between 1947 & 1980 for some [49] colonial territories from Asia to the Americas, with the British sometimes leaving voluntarily, usually being pressured, occasionally being thrown out by armed rebellion & popular resistance, and often expelled by a combination of all three methods
      c. This collapse of the British Empire regarded as "the most enormous transfer of power in history"
      d. Yet a very poor adjustment or adaptation by Britain & the British economically & psychologically to these losses of markets, raw materials, & overseas investment areas as well as the diminution of global influence
   2. Decline of industry--failure to modernize & diversify manufacturing as well as to anticipate future economic trends & developments, the results being high rates of unemployment, social misery, & a drain on the welfare system
   3. An antiquated & fairly rigid class structure with generally passive lower-class acceptance of upper-class dominance--perpetuation of much cronyism & favoritism & unwarranted privileges & advantages for the "old boy net(work)"
   4. Persistence of the traditional ideal of aspiring to become a leisured country gentleman--this being a reflection of the continuous admiration for the old aristocratic lifestyle of idleness & inactivity & non-productivity--thus the investment of much money in rural estates rather than in business
   5. A basically backward rather than forward-looking mentality---this being a consequence of their love of tradition & the past and a discouragement from confronting the serious problems & challenges of the present & future--examples:
      a. Wistful yet ridiculous references by many British to the glories & greatness of the "empire" (existing only in the imagination) and patriotic utterances "for queen & country" (should one be ready to die for the residents of Buckingham Palace?)

  b. Veneration of, emulation of, & profound interest in the royal family as occupying much of the time & energies of the nation--existence of the royal family as the perfect symbol of decadence, obsolescence, sloth, & stupidity and as a detriment to a democratic society
  c. Preservation of many attitudes & practices from the past (such as titles & silly status symbols) having no relevance to a very changed modern world

V. Differences in Western Europe and America
 A. Manifestation by both Western European nations and the United States simultaneously of:
  1. Some "democratic" characteristics of fairness, equal opportunity, shared sacrifices, & commitment of society to all of its members, and....
  2. Certain "aristocratic" characteristics of elitist privilege & status, accumulation by a few people of enormous wealth & power, and occasional reward of talent & effort
 B. Yet possession by most Western European nations of some critical practices & institutions making them more "democratic" than American society:
  1. Nationalized public transportation systems providing usually swift, efficient, & moderately-priced service within & between nations for the lower class in addition to the middle & upper classes
  2. Socialized health services available to & affordable by all--most European families are not economically devastated by major or protracted illness, as are most American families
  3. Tax structures making it more difficult for the rich to avoid significant contributions--imposition in Europe especially of high inheritance taxes on accumulated fortunes
   a. In America the wealthy always finding ways to avoid paying their share of taxes
   b. The Americans who usually must contribute the largest percentage of their incomes are the roughly 35% of the lower middle class, the group least capable of paying taxes other than the poor
  4. Often free or very cheap university education for the qualified of all classes--in America, money & family influence still determining who attends universities more than the factors of intellectual capability & motivation
 C. Description of Russian society & Eastern Europe under communism for over forty years (1945--89) as essentially an "aristocracy of bureaucrats" who were mainly privileged & undeserving members of Communist Parties or their flunky friends
 D. Description of American society (in terms of its class structure) as an "aristocracy of investors & businessmen" whose privileged status & advantages in accumulating money are safeguarded by a multitude of government policies & laws
 E. Containment by American society, however, of probably more "class or social mobility" (opportunities for improvement) than any other in the world due to the unity & diversity of such a huge economy, our possession of bountiful natural resources, and inexcessive population numbers (although these advantages might be dissipating today)

V. Post-Colonialism in Africa
   A. Achievement earlier by the New Imperialism (1870--1920) of certain definite results:
      1. Domination or control of the entire world by the white (Caucasian) race, but...
      2. Appearance of the beginnings of native rejection of white supremacy & domination--emergence of an embryonic sense of nationalism among natives demanding eventual self-determination & political independence
         a. Evidence of this restlessness initially & appropriately in the colonies of Britain & France, the two most exemplary democracies in the world
         b. Occurrence of a learning process by the natives of absorbing from their overlords the ideas of representative government, rule by law, and "liberty, equality, fraternity" that contradicted British & French policies & practices
   B. Development during the Inter-war Era (between the two World Wars: 1919--39) of mounting problems, tensions, & hostilities between the natives & their European rulers, occasionally evoking promises of eventual independence or dominion status
   C. Then, after 1945, came the liberation of former colonies in Africa, Asia, & the Middle East--this emancipation being the most spectacular development in international affairs since 1945 yet prior to the collapse of communism in 1989-91
   D. Use today of the term "Third World" to describe underdeveloped & poor nations mainly in Africa & Asia, but also parts of Latin America & the Middle East.
   E. Remainder of many problems originating in the colonial experience among the African nations achieving independence during the 1950's and 1960's
   F. Post-colonial problems in Africa originating with European rule:
      1. Inconsistency & inharmony of ethnic & national boundaries:
         a. Drawing of territorial borders & boundaries earlier in the 19th century in London, Paris, & Berlin and basis on geographical factors rather than on ethnic or tribal considerations
         b. Results--division of some tribal groups living together in one region into two or three separate nations, where they were relegated to minority status in each one
         c. Thus the provocation by European governments of domestic as well as international conflicts among different African tribes & states after independence
      2. Economic dependency & weakness:
         a. Allowance by the exploitative nature of imperialism for no economic diversification in Africa or elsewhere
         b. Little or no native industry permitted to develop (importation of manufactured products from Europe), little or no investment capital accumulated by natives, and colonial raw materials mandated for export to Europe in payment for imported European manufactures
         c. Thus existence of African nations after independence as one-crop or one-mineral economies (mainly for export) having no industrial base & no investment money to develop it--persistence of economic dependency on the outside world

            d. Frequent talk by Africans of the arrival of "political in-
               dependence, but not economic independence"--it is often
               true today that more influence is exerted on African
               economies in New York, Paris, & London than in African
               capital cities
      3. Exacerbation of class & cultural differences among Africans:
            a. Partial success earlier by European governments in "assim-
               ilating" an African upper-class elite & minority with
               European culture & language & institutions
            b. Assimilation--the act or process of absorbing a new & dif-
               ferent culture, language, & institution--in other words,
               the "Europeanization" of some Africans
            c. Yet the vast majority of native Africans overwhelmingly
               not being assimilated, thus intensifying social & cultur-
               al differences as well as conflicts among the Africans
               themselves
            d. Furthermore, a tiny number of whites often remaining after
               independence who retained much wealth & sometimes much
               land (earlier expropriated from the natives)--thus per-
               petuating a seriously inequitable distribution of wealth
      4. Political inexperience--deliberate neglect by Europeans during
         colonialism to develop representative institutions potentially
         providing natives some experience in self-government--thus
         independence understandably brought errors & pain
      5. Educational deficiencies:
            a. Establishment of colonial schools by the Europeans to edu-
               cate & assimilate only a small minority of Africans and
               to provide elementary preparation for bureaucratic work-
               ers but not for people with decision-making or managerial
               skills
            b. Possession of college degrees by only a very few native
               Africans at the time of independence--then a lack of suf-
               ficient for schools by the new governments--a near non-
               existence of trained teachers in the independent states
            c. The consequence: a tragic predominance of ignorance
      6. military ascendancy:
            a. Foundation by the Europeans of the army as the most organ-
               ized & racially integrated & bureaucratized institution
               during colonial times
            b. Unfortunately, more native Africans gaining experience in
               armies than in any other institution
   c. Emergence of the military in most countries after independence as the
      most powerful institution in society--today over 50% of all African
      nations are ruled by military dictatorships
      7. An example of the contrasting fates of European nations & their
         former colonies:
            a. Ironically, small & impoverished Portugal became the first
               European nation to exploit the people & resources of Af-
               rica in the modern world during the late-15th century...
            b. And, it was the last nation to leave its colonies in 1973-
               -74 following a revolution in 1973 against a fascist re-
               gime in Portugal
            c. Its colonies of Angola & Mozambique granted independence
               by the new provisional government after being systematic-
               ally pillaged & misruled for centuries

       d. Evolution of Portugal thereafter into a fairly stable democracy that joined the Common Market & achieved modest yet impressive advances economically & socially in the last two decades
       e. Meanwhile, its former colonies wracked by civil wars, military governments, economic regression, & ongoing nightmares

G. Post-colonial African problems originating with African traditions:
  1. Inter-tribal warfare--endurance of hostilities between different clans & ethnic groups for thousands of years & pre-dating European or even Arabic penetration, the latter beginning in the 600's A.D. with Islam
     a. Regard for excessive tribalism by most scholars as the greatest "curse of Africa"
     b. Usually, European slave traders not capturing potential slaves directly but merely purchasing them from Africans as prisoners-of-war who resulted from tribal warfare
     c. Pursuit of somewhat similar practices earlier by the Arabs
  2. Slavery--a condition of involuntary servitude in which the victim is owned or at least dominated by an overlord
     a. Again, origination of this problem many millennia ago and at least traceable to the beginnings of humanity & to the earliest civilization of Egypt
     b. Slavery & the slave trade later receiving an enormous impetus throughout the northern half of Africa from the rise & spread of Islam by 600 A.D.
     c. Residence by the Prophet Mohammed in a slave-raiding & slave-owning & polygynous society where the custom was for men of a defeated group to be executed and for women & children to be taken as slaves by the victors
     d. Thus the addition by Islamic & Arabic slavery of the concept of male sexual domination of women to the traditional condition of forced labor
     e. Recently, since European decolonization after WW II, the institution of slavery in Moslem regions returning to become a major & mounting problem
     f. Abolition of slavery (like the idea of democracy) is a European importation into Africa
     g. Ironically, some black American radicals have correctly yet naively rejected the religion of Christianity as a "slave religion" only to embrace the even more slave-oriented & authoritarian & unthinking religion of Islam
  3. Military & aristocratic predominance--practices by the vast majority of African tribes for millennia of glorifying & rewarding a warrior caste (as in Europe)--thus colonial rule perpetuating an old tradition rather than creating a new one
  4. Economic & cultural backwardness--prior to European penetration, sub-Saharan Africa (the roughly southern half of the continent below a narrow belt of savannas grasslands along the lower fringes of the Sahara Desert) was lacking in:
     a. Alphabets & forms of writing
     b. Use of the wheel for transportation
     c. Sails for ships, or animal-drawn plows
     d. Science, higher mathematics, & advanced technology

                    e. Centralized & bureaucratically-organized nations

I. Modern Japan & the West
   A. Introduction
      1. Today, in 1994, Japan has the 2nd most powerful national economy in the world--it could be number one in a decade--there are important things about Japan that we should know
      2. Japan is the most Westernized of all Asiatic nations, although it has retained many of its native Japanese characteristics--thus Japan is both like & unlike ourselves in critical ways
      3. Always geography & climatic conditions strongly shape the experiences & characteristics of a people--this is especially true of Japan
   B. Impact of geography
      1. Existence as a mountainous island-group east of China--over 3,000 islands included in the Japanese archipelago, but only four relatively large ones
         a. The eastern sides warmed by the Japan Current & receiving abundant rain--these areas being the location for most centers of Japanese life
         b. Development by the Japanese of a sensitive appreciation for scenic natural beauty and of a profound love of their native land
         c. The rugged & mountainous terrain became the most important factor in determining weak national government & political decentralization for much of the pre-modern era
      2. Existence of few natural resources, many barren regions, and a shortage of good farm land--yet with the normal habitation of a relatively large population occupying a small area
         a. For example, today approximately 120 million Japanese inhabit a living space & area smaller than the state of Connecticut--thus collective effort & togetherness became necessities for survival early in their history
         b. These circumstances leading to the development of certain celebrated characteristics: a strong sense of community, emphasis on conformity & identification with the group, desire for social consensus at any price, and willingness to sacrifice for the common good of all society
         c. Thus geographic conditions bringing cohesiveness to its population as well as social consciousness
         d. In America abundant resources & land encouraging individualism & self-reliance--in Japan the opposite circumstances stimulating conformity, social commitment, self-discipline, and respect for authority
         e. Challenge-&-response theory of history--the belief that awesome problems & difficulties stimulate in some peoples (such as the ancient Greeks) qualities enabling them to achieve great success:
            (1) Creativity, imagination, competitiveness, & appreciation of knowledge as a tool for practical purposes
            (2) Development of these qualities by the Japanese--thus this historical theory being very relevant to them
         f. Geographic encouragement also of the long-term tendency toward a commercial economy emphasizing trade with the outside world, with the importation of food & raw materials and the exportation of manufactures

3. Subjection to frequent natural catastrophes such as earthquakes, typhoons, & tidal waves--contribution of these phenomena to the Japanese collective paranoia, sense of impending disaster, and overwhelming need to plan for future survival
4. Relative isolation--separation of Japan from mainland Asia by 115 miles, thus close enough to benefit from the great Chinese civilization but distant enough to be capable of selecting or rejecting as desired--the long distance of Japan from the major centers of older Asian continental cultures resulting in:
    a. Crucial short periods of close cultural borrowing (mainly from China), but usually based on Japanese initiative
        (1) Japanese civilization becoming a blend of native Japanese and alien Chinese elements
        (2) Chinese refusal to recognize Japan as an equal--Chinese introduction of a condescending term for the nation as "Jih-pen" (Where the Sun Rises)--Japanese pronunciation of the same word as "Nippon"
    b. Long periods of relatively isolated & separate development
        (1) The most famous being the "Centuries of Isolation" (1641--1853) that followed a century of significant contact & commerce with several European nations
        (2) During the era from the 17th to the 19th century, only the Dutch of the Netherlands among the non-Oriental nations allowed to trade on a very limited & restricted basis at the port of Nagasaki
        (3) Occurrence of occasional violent reactions to the outside world, outsiders, & those Japanese influenced by outsiders--a typical xenophobic response to foreign things as alien & dangerous to & corrupting of native purity
        (4) Japan never invaded & conquered by a foreign power until 1945--thus its culture remaining notably homogeneous
    c. A very high degree of ethnic purity or population homogeneity--the Japanese were a people of mixed origins who developed thereafter with few additions of blood & genes--consequently, they are one of the ethnically purest nationalities or peoples in the world
C. Explanations in contemporary times for Japanese business success & economic power throughout the world:
    1. Superior traits of the common people--deferential obedience to higher authority, personal energy & drive, professional pride & dedication, natural inclinations toward cooperation & collaboration, identification with the group & community, individual willingness to sacrifice for the common good of all, impressive self-discipline
    2. Contrasting views by management toward labor:
        a. American laborers usually regarded as tools or instruments to be exploited by employers for huge personal profits & investment gains--thus resulting in an adversarial relationship between management & labor and reflecting upper-class greed & selfishness
        b. Even the best American businesses plagued by chronic problems with worker alienation, absenteeism, drug abuse, and alcoholism

c. Japanese laborers usually more contented and treated more fairly & humanely by management, with greater job security & health benefits & considerate bosses who consult with workers more frequently & who accept lower salaries than their American counterparts
3. Different attitudes toward the future:
   a. Tendency for Japanese workers to save more money and their companies to reinvest greater profits in long-term projects as well as in research & development
   b. These tendencies in sharp contrast to the American obsession with short-term spending & profits
   c. Derivation of these attitudes from the Japanese sense of community & common purpose & willingness to sacrifice for future benefits
4. The nature of their people, society, & priorities:
   a. Possession by Japan of a better educated population, lower crime rates, a more equitable distribution of wealth, and more admirable traits of respect & courtesy toward others
   b. These factors contrasting dramatically with American lawlessness & disorder, racial turmoil, & class antagonisms
5. Impressive flexibility & adaptability & pragmatism of the Japanese people--adept at improving on processes & products introduced earlier by other nations
6. Economic ideology & policy:
   a. Worship by Americans of "free enterprise" theories and the minimal role of national government in organizing & coordinating & planning a modern economy
   b. More collaboration in Japan of all three economic sectors (government, business, & labor) to promote common goals & objectives for the betterment of the entire country under the initiative of the national government
   c. The key word in explaining success or failure: teamwork-- the Japanese work together better in nearly every way at almost every level than the people of any other major nation economically
7. Military spending:
   a. Expenditure by Japan since 1945 of less than 2% annually on defense & less than any other great power--there is no popular support for the aggressive expansionism that climaxed in the catastrophe of World War II.
   b. Expenditure by the U.S. since 1945 of over 15% of its annual GNP on the military, with much of that money devoured by waste, fraud, & abuse or poured into unproductive projects contributing eventually to lower standards of living, massive national debts, economic strangulation, and decline in competitiveness for certain consumer products & markets
8. Opposite opinions toward learning:
   a. Manifestation in Japan of a profound reverence for knowledge & for people who possess it, especially teachers-- Japanese realization that "knowledge is power" & that education is essential for survival
   b. Prevalence in America of a strong undercurrent of anti-intellectualism (a contempt for learning & educated people) glorifying ignorance & mediocrity as admirable democratic virtues of the "common man"

9. Summary--this is not to portray Japan as perfect or worthy of complete emulation; the Japanese have problems & weaknesses of their own--yet they are better prepared than nearly every other nation in the world for survival & strength in the 21st century

VII. The Collapse of Communism in the 1980's (elaboration in lecture material
  A. Reasons for the failure of Communism in Russia:
     1. Economic inefficiency--over-regulation & centralization often lacking the capability to respond to local needs while frequently ignoring "market forces" of supply & demand and denying rewards to those who labored energetically or thought creatively
     2. Massive military spending--gradual strangulation of the economy due to heavy expenditures on armaments lacking the positive financial spin-off effects of spending on consumer products
     3. Very low standards of living in comparison to the West:
        a. Steady improvements in living standards for nearly three decades after WW II. but stagnation & then decline by the late-1970's because of the reasons being discussed here
        b. Achievement by the Soviet system, nevertheless, of much higher standards of living than Tsarist capitalism
     4. Ideological betrayal in the perpetuation of aristocratic privilege--extension of higher status & favoritism to party officials & athletes & artists conforming to Soviet standards
     5. Popular resignation, cynicism, & alienation--a significant majority of Russians gave up all hope of a better future and reacted in disgust by refusing to work hard or even work at all
     6. Role of the modern media--focus of increasing exposure & publicity by foreign television & journalism on Soviet backwardness in contrast to Western progress--rising availability of this information to the Russian people
  B. Unfolding of events:
     1. Recognition by Soviet dictator Leonid Brezhnev (1964-82) of the mounting disintegration of the Russian economy & society as well as its increasing inability to stifle dissent & rebellion in the East European satellite states
        a. Emergence in Poland of the labor union Solidarnosz organized in 1980 by Lech Walesa--rapid growth & immense strength--uniqueness in attracting urban industrial workers and rural farmers in a nation-wide, anti-government association supported by a very popular Catholic Church--failure by the Polish government to suppress the union
        b. Refusal by Brezhnev to countenance reform, yet awareness that his handpicked successor would do so
     2. Mikhail Gorbachev (March, 1985--November, 1991)
        a. Personality--ambitious, determined, intelligent, energetic, knowledgeable, successful in the Soviet system yet definitely possessing maverick & independent tendencies
        b. Background--a religious mother, a nonconformist uncle imprisoned for a few years, an independent thinker with a reputation for innovation & reform & achievement

3. Embarkation on a revolutionary crash program of reform policies:
     a. <u>Glasnost</u> (openness)--injection of democratic changes such as freedom of the press, speech, assembly, travel, & religion
     b. <u>Perestroika</u> (restructuring)--infusion of capitalistic practices & policies into the communist economy to encourage more productivity, individual incentives, & growth
     c. Extension of more self-rule to the satellite or colonial states of the Soviet empire
4. Results of his reforms--much chaos & disorder & rebellion on the domestic & international scene with rapidly declining popularity & support for Gorbachev--when he finally left power, less than 20% of the Russian people favored or approved of him:
     a. Alienation of the Communist Party (his original power base) for introducing reforms & dismantling the dictatorship & eliminating their privileges, yet also...
     b. Alienation of the popular masses for not reforming faster & for unleashing the economic anarchy & decline
5. Enormity of his significance & impact--he was the first Russian ruler in all of history to prepare the nation for democracy

III. An Issue of Centrality in the Modern World
  A. How to resist against tyranny and to defend moral principles when confronted with superior military force? Employment of several different means by people living in the past two centuries:
     1. Principle of popular armed insurrection--a mass uprising as most famously demonstrated in 1789 France during Bastille Day and the July Revolution spreading all over the country--yet this example in history has been very rare
     2. Guerrilla warfare--unconventional & irregular hit-&-run methods of fighting against superior forces by inferior groups suffering from a condition of weakness--1st demonstration of great effectiveness in Spain against Napoleonic armies--later in the Boer War (1899-1902), especially in World War II., & in Vietnam among many other places
     3. Terrorism--random & unexpected destruction of property or murder of opponents representing the established order by alienated groups or individuals--this strategy has accomplished little change in the world beyond the harassment & partial intimidation of a government or population
     4. Civil disobedience or passive resistance--a nonviolent refusal to cooperate with established authority by utilizing means such as strikes & boycotts & ostracism (or "shunning") of those dealing with the designated enemy
        a. First expression of these ideas by American (New England) author & eccentric Henry David Thoreau in his celebrated essay, <u>Resistance to Civil Government</u> in 1849
        b. Employment by the Irish in their long struggle to achieve national independence from British colonial rule:
           (1) 1st use of the term "boycott" in a refusal to work for or cooperate with Charles Boycott (an agent for an absentee landlord) in 1880 during the Land War of 1879-82), in which Irish leader C.S. Parnell called

                    for non-cooperation & shunning
            (2) The Anglo-Irish War (1919-22), featuring passive re-
                sistance by the Irish majority combined with guer-
                illa warfare by the Irish Republican Army, or IRA
            (3) Emergence of Irish independence as a powerful incen-
                tive to nationalist movements against colonial rule
                (especially British) all over the world
        c. Application of satyagraha ("soul force") by Mohandas Gandhi
           (1869-1948) in India effectively against British rule
        d. Utilization of bus & store boycotts by Martin Luther King
           in the Civil Rights Movement of the 1960's
        e. Deliberate use of these tactics in Poland by Lech Walesa &
           Solidarnosz to resist governmental oppression & to shut
           down the economy--unintentional employment in Russia by
           the disaffected masses against the hopelessness of Soviet
           life
    B. Overall assessment--the greatest effectiveness in the struggle
       against powerful forces of oppression has resulted from non-violent
       rather than violent resistance--the final words of advice are the
       last utterance of American labor militant Joe Hill in 1915: "Don't
       mourn for me--organize!"[4]

X. Quotations
    A. Doc Barry has decided to leave his dedicated students with some pro-
       found, pessimistic, & optimistic words of wisdom from sages down
       through the ages
    B. Don't ask if there will be questions from this material on the final
       exam--the answer is an emphatic YES!
    C. Quotations:
        1. H.G. Wells (1866--1946), British novelist & historian: "Human
           history becomes more and more a race between education and
           catastrophe."[5] Which side are you on?
        2. Oscar Wilde (1854--1900), Irish playwright & critic: "There is
           no sin except stupidity." & "The truth is rarely pure, and
           never simple."[6]
        3. Voltaire (1694--1778), brilliant French intellectual & cultural
           contributor in every regard: "I disapprove of what you say,
           but I will defend to the death your right to say it." &
           "Superstition sets the whole world in flames; philosophy
           quenches them."[7]
        4. Heinrich Heine (1797--1856), German poet & philosopher: "When-
           ever books are burned men also, in the end, are burned."[8]
        5. Mark Twain (1835--1910), American novelist & raconteur, on the
           propensity of pathetic yet manipulative people to quote facts
           & figures: "There are three kinds of lies: lies, damned lies,
           and statistics."[9] Wonder what Sam Clemons would say about
           our contemporary politicians & businessmen?
        6. Bertrand Russell, 20th century British philosopher-mathematic-
           ian: "Most people would rather die than think (rationally)--
           and in fact do so."[10]
        7. Johann Wolfgang von Goethe (1749--1832), awesome German play-
           wright & commentator, on the role of nonconformists who criti-
           cize society in order to improve it: "The world only goes for-
           ward because of those who oppose it."[11]
        8. Lillian Hellman (1905--88), American writer: "I cannot and will
           not cut my conscience to fit this year's fashions."[12] Could

she find a place on this campus?
9. On the essence of modern politics and the central explanation for the election of most of our politicians, a quote from Robert Bolt's A Man For All Seasons, in which King Henry VIII. (1509--47) addresses Sir Thomas More: "There are those like (the Duke of) Norfolk who follow me because I wear the crown, and there are those like Master (Thomas) Cromwell who follow me because they're jackals with sharp teeth and I am their lion, and there is a mass (of people) that follows me---because it follows anything that moves..."[13]
10. Winston Churchill (1874--1965), British statesman & historian: "...democracy is the worst form of government, except for all those other forms that have been tried from time to time."[14]
11. George Bernard Shaw (1856--1950), Anglo-Irish playwright: "Liberty means responsibility. That is why most men dread it." & "The greatest of evils and the worst of crimes is poverty."[15]
12. William Faulkner (1897--1962), American novelist, upon accepting the Nobel Prize For Literature after writing some of the most powerful yet depressing works ever on the general themes of the degeneracy of white Southern rednecks: "I believe that man will not merely endure, he will prevail."[16]
13. Thomas Jefferson (1743--1826), American president & Renaissance man: "I am mortified to be told that...the sale of a book can become a subject of inquiry...as an offense against religion...Is this then our freedom of religion?"[17]
14. Joseph de Maistre (1753--1821), French philosopher & commentator: "Every nation has the government it deserves."[18] What does this tell us about ourselves?
15. Alexander Solzhenitsyn (1918--), Russian novelist in his 1970 Nobel Lecture: "The salvation of mankind lies only in making everything the concern of all."[19]
16. Jonathan Swift (1667--1745), Anglo-Irish novelist and critic of Man's inhumanity to his fellow Man, his Epitaph inscribed on the wall above his gravestone in St. Patrick's Cathedral in Dublin: Death is "Where fierce indignation can no longer tear his heart."[20]
17. Leo Tolstoy (1828--1910), Russian novelist: "It is amazing how complete is the delusion that beauty is goodness."[21]
18. George Santayana (1863--1952), Spanish historian & commentator: "Progress, far from consisting in change, depends on retentativeness...Those who cannot remember the past are condemned to fulfill it."[22]
19. Doc Barry (dates unknown), after excruciating defeat in the Indiana high school basketball tournaments many moons ago: "It's time to throw in the towel, sponge, and water bucket."

ENDNOTES

Chapters 1 & 2

1. Isaiah Berlin, <u>The Crooked Timber of Humanity</u> (New York: Random House, 1992) vii. Another translation from the original German by R.G. Collingwood is provided: "Out of the cross-grained timber of human nature nothing quite straight can be made."
2. <u>The Oxford Dictionary of Quotations</u>, 3rd ed. (New York: Oxford University Press, 1980) 414.
3. <u>Oxford Dictionary of Quotations</u>, 568.
4. J. Christopher Herold, ed., <u>The Mind of Napoleon</u> (New York: Columbia University Press, 1961) 105.
5. Herbert J. Muller, <u>The Uses of the Past</u> (New York: Oxford University Press, 1957) 60.
6. Muller, <u>Uses of the Past</u>, 60.
7. Richard Leakey and Roger Lewin, <u>Origins Reconsidered: In Search of What Makes Us Human</u> (New York: Doubleday, 1994) 512.
8. Tom B. Jones, <u>From the Tigris to the Tiber: An Introduction to Ancient History</u> (Homewood, Illinois: The Dorsey Press, 1969) 36.
9. Herodotus, <u>The Persian Wars</u>, trans. George Rawlinson (New York: Random House, 1942) 633. The original translation of Mr. Rawlinson has been modified by this author into a more contemporary rendition.

Chapter 3

1. Muller, <u>Uses of the Past</u>, 101.
2. Muller, <u>Uses of the Past</u>, 123.
3. Muller, <u>Uses of the Past</u>, 122n.
4. Orlando Patterson, <u>Freedom in the Making of Western Culture</u> (New York: Harper-Collins, 1991) 42.
5. Wallace K. Ferguson and Geoffrey Bruun, <u>A Survey of European Civilization</u>, 4th ed. (Boston: Houghton Mifflin Company, 1969) 39.
6. H.D.F. Kitto, <u>The Greeks</u> (London: Penguin Books, 1962) 228-229.
7. Edith Hamilton, <u>The Greek Way</u> (New York: W. W. Norton & Company, 1964) 42.

Chapter 4

1. Herbert J. Muller, <u>Freedom in the Ancient World</u> (New York: Harper & Row, 1961) 249-250.
2. Muller, <u>Freedom in the Ancient World</u>, 257.
3. Muller, <u>Uses of the Past</u>, 226.
4. Ferguson & Bruun, <u>A Survey of European Civilization</u>, 62-64.

Chapter 5

1. Ferguson & Brunn, <u>European Civilization</u>, 124.

Chapter 6

1. Muller, <u>Uses of the Past</u>, 170.
2. Muller, <u>Uses of the Past</u>, 173.
3. Muller, <u>Uses of the Past</u>, 174.
4. <u>The Holy Bible</u>, Revised Standard Version (Cleveland: The World Publishing Company, 1962), Old Testament, 2 [Genesis 2:17].

. The Holy Bible, OT, 3 [Genesis 3:16].
. The Holy Bible, New Testament, 160 [I. Corinthians 7:29].
. The Holy Bible, NT, 152 [Romans 13:2].
. The Holy Bible, NT, 181 [Ephesians 2:8].
. Elaine Pagels, Adam, Eve, and the Serpent (New York: Random House, 1988) 109. Ms. Pagels provides the direct quote from St. Augustine's De Civitate Dei.
0. Pagels, 111-113. Again St. Augustine is quoted from De Civitate Dei.
1. George H. Sabine, A History of Political Theory, 3rd ed. (New York: Holt, Rinehart and Winston, 1961) 368.

hapter 7

. Crane Brinton, John B. Christopher, Robert Wolff, A History of Civiliz-
  1967) 465.
. Oxford Dictionary of Quotations, 140.
. Ferguson & Bruun, A Survey of European Civilization, 371.
. William Shakespeare, The Complete Works of William Shakespeare (London: Abbey Library, 1977) 825. More precisely, this quotation in from Macbeth: Act I, Scene iv, Lines 7-8.
. Ferguson & Bruun, A Survey of European Civilization, 479.

hapter 8

. Ferguson & Bruun, A Survey of European Civilization, 567.
. Oxford Dictionary of Quotations, 107. This quote was apparently first stated by Edward Bulwer-Lytton in 1838 in his poem Richelieu.
. Ferguson & Bruun, A Survey of European Civilization, 571.
. Ferguson & Bruun, A Survey of European Civilization, 571.
. Brinton, Christopher, Wolff, A History of Civilization, II., 54.

hapter 9

. Ferguson & Bruun, A Survey of European Civilization, 571.
. Jonathon Green, ed., The Book of Political Quotes (New York: McGraw-Hill, 1982) 12.

hapter 10

. Robert C. Tucker, ed., The Marx-Engels Reader, 2nd ed. (New York: W.W. Norton & Company, 1978) 145. Tucker includes Marx's "Theses on Feuerbach, No. XI".
. "A Contribution to the Critique of Political Economy", Marx-Engels Reader, 4.
. "Manifesto of the Communist Party", Marx-Engels Reader, 473.
. "Critique of the Gotha Program", Marx-Engels Reader, 538.
. "Address of the Central Committee to the Communist League", Marx-Engels Reader, 505.
. "Conspectus on Bakunin: After the Revolution", Marx-Engels Reader, 546. The editor translates Marx's German text into English as "...the so-called people's will disappears..."
. "Critique of the Gotha Program", Marx-Engels Reader, 531.

Chapter 11

1. Gordon Wright, France in Modern Times (Chicago: Rand McNally, 1970) vi.
2. Wright, France in Modern Times, vi.
3. Paul A. Gagnon, France Since 1789 (New York: Harper & Row, 1972) 88.

Chapter 12

1. Donald D. Horward, "Lectures on Napoleonic Europe" (unpublished lectures at Florida State University) 1969.
2. Fritz Fischer, World Power or Decline (New York: W.W. Norton & Company, 1974) xvi-xviii.
3. Paul Halpern, "Lectures on the Causes & Background of World War I." (unpublished lectures at Florida State University) 1970.
4. Oxford Dictionary of Quotations, 42.
5. Oxford Dictionary of Quotations, 152.

Chapter 13

1. Oxford Dictionary of Quotations, 152.
2. Monte Finkelstein, "Lectures on European Fascism" (unpublished lectures at Florida State University) 1984.
3. Roland N. Stromberg, European Intellectual History since 1789, 2nd ed. (Englewood Cliffs, N.J.: Prentice-Hall, 1975) 252.
4. Herman Finer, Mussolini's Italy, 2nd ed. (New York: Grosset & Dunlap, 1965.
5. Monte Finkelstein, "Lectures on European Fascism" (unpublished lectures at Florida State University) 1984.
6. Finkelstein, "Lectures on European Fascism", 1984.
7. Finkelstein, "Lectures on European Fascism", 1984.
8. Oxford Dictionary of Quotations, 139.

Chapter 14

1. Odford Dictionary of Quotations, 407.
2. Oxford Dictionary of Quotations, 149.
3. Oxford Dictionary of Quotations, 150.
4. Book of Political Quotations, 105.
5. Oxford Dictionary of Quotations, 568.
6. Oxford Dictionary of Quotations, 572.
7. Oxford Dictionary of Quotations, 561.
8. Oxford Dictionary of Quotations, 244.
9. Oxford Dictionary of Quotations, 187. This statement is also attributed to British Prime Minister (1874-80) Benjamin Disraeli.
10. Muller, Uses of the Past, 60.
11. Horward, "Lectures on Napoleonic Europe".
12. Oxford Dictionary of Quotations, 244.
13. Robert Bolt, A Man For All Seasons (New York: Random House, 1962) 31-32.
14. Book of Political Quotations, 16.
15. Oxford Dictionary of Quotations, 497.
16. Abraham Lass, ed., A Students's Guide to 50 American Novels (New York: Washington Square Press, 1966) 216.
17. "Jefferson as quoted in a letter of M. Dufief in 1814", Louisville Courier-Journal, Forum, A10.
18. Oxford Dictionary of Quotations, 327.

9. <u>Oxford Dictionary of Quotations</u>, 531.
0. <u>Oxford Dictionary of Quotations</u>, 528. The most inspirational source of this citation is the site itself.
1. <u>Oxford Dictionary of Quotations</u>, 551.
2. <u>Oxford Dictionary of Quotations</u>, 414.

REFERENCES

Berlin, Isaiah. <u>The Crooked Timber of Humanity</u>. New York: Random House, 1992.

Bolt, Robert. <u>A Man For All Seasons</u>. New York: Random House, 1962.

Brinton, Crane. Christopher, John B. Wolff, Robert L. <u>A History of Civilization</u>. 2 vols. 3rd ed. Englewood Cliffs, New Jersey: Prentice-Hall, 1967.

Finer, Herman. <u>Mussolini's Italy</u>. (2nd ed.) New York: Grosset & Dunlap, 1965.

Finkelstein, Monte. "Unpublished lectures on European Fascism", at Florida State University, 1984.

Fischer, Fritz. <u>World Power or Decline</u>. New York: W.W. Norton & Company, 1974.

Gagnon, Paul A. <u>France Since 1789</u>. New York: Harper & Row, 1972.

Green, Jonathon (Comp.). <u>The Book of Political Quotes</u>. New York: McGraw-Hill, 1982.

Halpern, Paul. "Unpublished lectures on the Causes & Background of World War I.", at Florida State University, 1970.

Hamilton, Edith. The <u>Greek Way</u>. New York: W.W. Norton & Company, 1964.

Herodotus. <u>The Persian Wars</u> (George Rawlinson, Trans.). New York: Random House, 1942.

Herold, J. Christopher (Ed.). <u>The Mind of Napoleon</u>. New York: Columbia University Press, 1961.

Horward, Donald D. "Unpublished lectures on Napoleonic Europe", at Florida State University, 1969.

Jones, Tom B. <u>From the Tigris to the Tiber: An Introduction to Ancient History</u>. Homewood, Illinois: The Dorsey Press, 1969.

Kitto, H.D.K. <u>The Greeks</u>. London: Penguin Books, 1962.

Lass, Abraham (Ed.). <u>A Student's Guide to 50 American Novels</u>. New York: Washington Square Press, 1966.

Leakey, Richard and Lewin, Roger. <u>Origins Reconsidered: In Search of What Makes Us Human</u>. New York: Doubleday, 1994.

<u>Louisville Courier-Journal</u>.

Muller, Herbert J. <u>Freedom in the Ancient World</u>. New York: Harper & Row, 1962.

Muller, Herbert J. <u>The Uses of the Past</u>. New York: Oxford University Press, 1947.

Pagels, Elaine. <u>Adam, Eve, and the Serpent</u>. New York: Random House, 1988.

Patterson, Orlando. <u>Freedom in the Making of Western Culture</u>. New York: Harper-Collins, 1991.

Sabine, George H. <u>A History of Political Thought</u> (3rd ed.). New York: Holt, Rinehart and Winston, 1961.

Shakespeare, William. <u>The Complete Works of William Shakespeare</u>. London: Abbey Library, 1977.

Stromberg, Roland N. <u>European Intellectual History since 1789</u> (2nd ed.). Englewood Cliffs, N.J.: Prentice-Hall, 1975.

<u>The Holy Bible</u> (Revised Standard Version). Cleveland: The World Publishing Company, 1962.

<u>The Oxford Dictionary of Quotations</u> (3rd ed.). New York: Oxford University Press, 1980.

Tucker, Robert C. <u>The Marx-Engels Reader</u>. (2nd ed.). New York: W.W. Norton & Company, 1978.

Chapter 1   SUBJECT MATTER FOR ESSAY EXAMS

Prehistory and the Study of History

1. A definition of "History" and explanation for its great significance & uniqueness in comparison to other subjects.

2. In understanding the human experience, we emphasize the knowledge provided by Marx, Freud, Darwin, & Einstein. What does that tell us about the subject of History?

3. The attainment of absolute certainty or knowledgeable probability in the study of History and the reason why that is so.

4. The main reason for studying History.

5. The primary purpose for Americans to study European History.

6. The difference between Prehistory and History. The meaning of the "Neolithic Revolution" and its progress beyond the Paleolithic Age. The contrast between a "culture" and a "civilization" as well as the three features of the latter.

7. Where geographically did Western Civilization begin and where were the Europeans at the time?

8. Definitions of "race" and "ethnic group" and a knowledge of the European linguistic branches & dialects.

9. The fundamental definition of "religion" as well as the explanations why religion has always exercised such tremendous power over human beings. Also, the source for humanity's belief in "immortality".

10. The conclusions about Mankind drawn from a study of Prehistory.

11. The origins for male domination of females and warfare, and the factors & developments contributing to the formation of rigid class structures with the advent of civilizations.

12. The class system--freemen, slaves, peasants, & aristocracy. The existence of a "class struggle" in the Ancient World.

Chapter 2 SUBJECT MATTER FOR ESSAY EXAMS

Ancient Middle East

1. The achievements and contributions to civilization of the Egyptians, the various peoples of Mesopotamia, and the diverse peoples of the Fertile Crescent.

2. The geographical differences between Egypt and Mesopotamia as well as the consequences of those differences.

3. The importance of river valleys, flood waters, irrigation systems, and agriculture to these early civilizations.

4. Egyptian religion and the career of Akhenaton. The enormous impact on the Western World of Zoroastrianism: dualism, messianism, & apocalyse.

5. The Hebrews--reasons for their uniqueness & peculiarity, the Torah, Moses' political objective for the Ten Commandments, the Jewish Revolt against Rome, the Diaspora, Masada, monolatry, how Judaism was refined into pure monotheism.

6. Map identification of places and peoples.

Chapter 3   SUBJECT MATTER FOR ESSAY EXAMS

                            Greece--Hellas

1. Reasons why the Greeks were so brilliant, creative, & remarkable. An understanding of their ethnic composition, their attitude toward change & travel & others' ideas, and their typical characteristics.

2. Geographical circumstances of Greece and how they influenced Greek history.

3. Definitions of the different forms of government and how the average city-state evolved.

4. Beliefs & practices of the two different types of religion.

5. Comparison & contrast between Athens and Sparta.

6. Democratic institutions in Athens--names & functions of the Ekklesia, Boule, Strategoi, Heliaea, Areopagus as well as the term ostracism.

7. Differences between ancient Greek democracy and modern Western democracy.

8. Explanations why the Greeks won the Persian Wars, what caused the Peloponnesian Wars, and what the results were.

9. Major developments during the "Golden Age of Athens".

10. Achievements and contributions of the Hellenic Greeks: humanism, classical standards of culture, the open society, rational thought, beginnings of modern science, banking & commercial capitalism, origination of drama & comedy & history & athletic games.

11. Negative qualities & weaknesses of the Greeks.

12. Importance of the conquests by Alexander the Great.

13. Identification of terms such as Sophists, hoplite, Ionians, hubris, Thermopylae, Salamis, anthropomorphism, Iliad, Orphism, Delphi.

Chapter 4   SUBJECT MATTER FOR ESSAY EXAMS
                           Rome: Republic & Empire

1. The famous Roman values and character-traits contributing to greatness.

2. Government of the Republic: definition of a "republic", the powers and responsibilities of positions such as consuls & tribunes, of institutions such as the Centuriate & Plebian Assemblies, and especially of the Senate. The impact of the political analysis by Polybius.

3. The reasons why Rome developed a warlike spirit & desires for expansion and the reasons why Rome was so successful at war. Why were the later organizational changes in the armies by Marius so fateful?

4. The causes for the fall of the Republic as a form of government.

5. An explanation of what made Julius Caesar so brilliant & successful.

6. Measures adopted by Augustus & other early emperors to consolidate their absolute power and to transform the city-state into a world-state and empire.

7. The great achievements and contributions to Western Civilization by the Romans.

8. The causes for the decline & fall of the Roman Empire: social, economic political, military, and other. An analysis of how slavery contributed perpetually to Rome's difficulties.

9. The reasons for the triumph of Christianity over the pagan religions of the Empire, especially its status as a small, minority group.

10. Terms of identification: Aenaeas, S.P.Q.R., Punic Wars, Octavian, Etruscans, Spartacus, Nobiles, Optimates & Populares, Saul of Tarsus, syncretism, authoritarianism.

Chapter 5   SUBJECT MATTER FOR ESSAY EXAMS

The Middle Ages

1. How the Middle Ages gets its name.

2. The capabilities or legacies of Roman civilization lost during the Middle Ages. The meaning of the "idea of the one world of Rome".

3. An explanation of what the Byzantine Empire was, its strengths & reasons for long survival as well as its weaknesses. Its significance & influence on history of the Western World.

4. The doctrine and practices of Islam as well as the personality & fascinating career of Mohammed. The cultural achievements of the Moslem World during the Medieval Era. The difference between the sects of Sunnis and Shi'ites.

5. The Frankish Kingdom: who the Franks were and the accomplishments associated with each of their famous kings. The reasons why the kingdom disintegrated so quickly in the 9th century.

6. The Vikings or Norsemen: who they were, where they were from, and what contributions they made to European Civilization.

7. The results of the Norman Conquest of England in 1066.

8. The main features of the feudal system. How manorialism was distinguished from feudalism.

9. An explanation of why the Middle Ages was known as the "Age of Faith" and what the main political power struggle was during the Medieval Era.

10. The improvements in Western Europe during the "Economic & Social Revolution" of the High Middle Ages.

11. A general description of the Crusades as well as their results and importance to Europe.

12. Terms of identification: Caesaropapism, chivalry, Drang nach Osten, Mecca & Medina, Estates-General, bourgeoisie, commutation, autarky, Iconoclastic Controversy, Treaty of Verdun.

Chapter 6   SUBJECT MATTER FOR ESSAY EXAMS
                          Renaissance--Reformation

1. An explanation of the general significance of the Late Middle Ages--
   Renaissance Era as one of profound change and transition.

2. The meaning of the word "Renaissance". The achievements of the Italian
   Renaissance generally in painting, literature, philosophy, music, and
   science. The reasons why the Renaissance achieved its highest and
   fullest development in Italy & not elsewhere, and the reasons for its
   decline and destruction there by the mid-16th century. An explanation
   of humanism and the importance of secularization.

3. Some things of importance economically, socially, politically, or cul-
   turally about the major Italian States of the period such as Milan,
   Florence, Venice, Naples, the Papal States, Genoa, & Savoy-Piedmont.
   The modern politics of Machiavelli.

4. How the Northern Renaissance differed from the Italian Renaissance.

5. The teachings & legacies of both St. Paul and St. Augustine such as the
   Curse of Original Sin & predestination. The reason why there are so
   many varieties of Christianity.

6. Causes of the Reformation: events such as the Babylonian Captivity &
   Great Schism & Conciliar Movement, the meaning of such terms as "just
   price" & reasonable wage & usury, words such as indulgences & simony &
   dispensation, the significance of the "rise of national consciousness"
   and the radical reforms of John Wycliff.

7. Martin Luther: his conclusion on how to achieve salvation, his "reforms
   or departures from Catholicism, and the reasons for the success of his
   revolt.

8. Calvinism: its significance & uniqueness & appeal to the bourgeoisie.
   Anglicanism: its beginnings in England & the Elizabethan Compromise.
   Anabaptism: its importance for the future of religion in the Western
   World. Unitarianism: its main feature.

Chapter 7   SUBJECT MATTER FOR ESSAY EXAMS

                  Early Modern Europe--Age of Absolutism

1. Characteristics of the modern "nation-state".

2. The Hapsburg Empire of Charles V. in the 1st half of the 16th century: how it was accumulated, what its primary territories were, what its disadvantages were, and what the general consequences were of his many wars.

3. The Age of Philip II. of Spain: (1556-98)--his four goals or policies, the causes of the Dutch Revolt against Spanish rule & the reasons for its eventual success, the general consequences of his involvement in the French Wars of Religion, and the results of his invasion of England with the Spanish Armada in 1588.

4. The French Wars of Religion: identification of the two sides, how the Valois Dynasty contributed to the problems, the role of Henri de Bourbon (Henry IV.), and the significance of the Edict of Nantes.

5. England under Elizabeth I. (1558-1603): her talents & personality, the achievements of her reign, the reason for the necessity of a final conquest of Ireland, her rivalry with her cousin Mary Stuart, Queen of Scotland as well as the causes of the latter's demise.

6. The reasons for the rapid decline of Spain in the 17th century from greatness to a 2nd-rank power.

7. The economic policies of mercantilism: its primary goal as well as its specific practices & principles.

8. The causes and results of the Thirty Years' War (1618-48) in Germany.

9. The English Revolution (1640-60): an explanation of the relationship between Crown & Parliament at the outset, the two central problems of England in this century, the opponents & winner in the Civil War (1642-46), the role of Cromwell & the army in this conflict, assumption of control of the Long Parliament by the radicals and the fate of King Charles I., a description of the Republic or Puritan Commonwealth during the Rump Parliament and why this period (1649-53) was known as the Reign of Terror & Virtue, what the Protectorate was, the general beliefs of groups such as the Levellers & Diggers, and the positive accomplishments of the Revolution.

10. The Age of Louis XIV. (1643--1715) of France: the meaning of the theory of "the divine right of kings", an explanation of his greatness as well as weaknesses, the main reason for the later decline of the economy, the significance of the Palace of Versailles and the king's role in the promotion of French culture, the motivation for the king's religious intolerance, and finally some of the Revolutionary roots & origins in his reign.

11. Peter the Great (1689--1725) of Russia: the condition & status of Russia at the beginning of his reign, the significance of his Westernization Policy, some of his reforms, his policy toward the Orthodox Church, the importance of his new capital city, the outcome of the Great Northern War, and the results of his reign.

Chapter 8 SUBJECT MATTER FOR ESSAY EXAMS

The Old Regime of 18th Century Europe

1. A description of what the Old Regime was, its characteristics, and the class structure of this society.

2. The two forces undermining and destabilizing its institutions.

3. The results of the commercial revolution, the trends in agriculture, & the features of the factory system.

4. The factors in European History preparing Europe for the Industrial Revolution and the reasons for the early head-start of England in it.

5. The Enlightenment: what was it generally & what did it try to achieve, the key words of the Enlightenment, the reform program in the realms of economics, justice, & education, the ideas of Deism & how it differed from traditional Christianity as well as a definition of anticlericalism.

6. The political thought of the Enlightenment: Locke's arguments in Two Treatises on Government and his meaning of "popular sovereignty" as well as how it was not truly democratic. Voltaire's views & why they were typical of the day. The opinions of Montesquieu and their impact on the American Constitution. The beliefs of Rousseau in their anticipation of democracy in the "general will", revolution, socialism, nationalism, and cultural romaniticism.

Chapter 9   SUBJECT MATTER FOR ESSAY EXAMS

French Revolution & Napoleon

1. Causes and background of the Revolution--conditions in France during the years leading up to 1789.

2. Reason for the Revolution being the greatest & most significant in all of history.

3. Differences between the French and American Revolutions.

4. How the Estates-General converted itself into the National Assembly.

5. The four July Revolutions, especially Bastille Day and the Great Fear.

6. The importance of the Women's March to Versailles, the role in the Revolution played by the Paris Commune, the significance of the September Massacres, and the Battle of Valmy.

7. Reforms of the National Assembly.

8. The provisions & importance of the Civil Constitution of the Clergy.

9. Reasons why the Jacobin Club & Party achieved control of the national government.

10. Reign of Terror--reasons why, measures applied to the war & civil war & economy & society & culture, the power struggle, role of Robespierre & the Republic of Virtue.

11. Babeuf as the first communist.

12. Thermidorean Reaction--what generally happened.

13. Napoleon--his reforms & achievements, the reasons for his downfall.

14. Meaning of "liberalism" and "nationalism", the political spectrum of Left Wing and Right Wing.

15. Terms such as cahiers, sans-culottes, levee en masse, maximum, assignats, emigres.

16. Congress of Vienna--its general purpose, principles, how it was successful and a failure.

Chapter 10 SUBJECT MATTER FOR ESSAY EXAMS

Industrial Revolution

1. Results & consequences of the Industrial Revolution--whether things increase or decrease, improve or worsen--a list of things will be provided for such things as living standards, gap between rich & poor, etc.

2. Identification & explanation of the "opiates of the masses".

3. A description of classical economics and the main ideas of thinkers such as Malthus, Bentham, & J.S. Mill. The general beliefs of Utopian Socialism and its proponent Saint-Simon.

4. Marx and Marxism--his educational background, the significance to him of the year 1848, the study of political economy, the terms "eclecticism" & determinism.

5. The dialectical interpretation of history by Hegel and how Marx changed it and what his final prediction was for the thesis, antithesis, & synthesis.

6. Marx's three "laws of history" and his labor theory of surplus value.

7. An explanation of what Marx believed would eventually happen to the state after the establishment of communism.

8. A description of some of the fallacies & weaknesses of Marxist ideology as well as his failed predictions.

9. Marx's accurate observations of the world.

10. The positive impact of Marx--<u>positivism</u> and the idea of alienation.

11. A couple of differences originally between unionism and socialism.

Chapter 11   SUBJECT MATTER FOR ESSAY EXAMS

                          19th Century Europe

- An explanation of the quote: "The history of the 19th century can be understood as the expansion & spread throughout the world of English institutions and French ideas."

- The means by which both Britain & France were developing representative & democratic governments, but in different ways.

- France: the four political traditions & programs emerging from the original French Revolution of 1789, some accomplishments of Napoleon III. & the main reason why he gambled on wars late in his reign, what the Paris Commune was & what socio-economic group supported it, what was at issue & what the outcome was of the Crisis of Seize Mai, and some characteristics of politics during the 3rd Republic.

- Dreyfus Affair (1894-99): the forces of democracy (Left) vs. those of authoritarianism (Right), the fate of Alfred Dreyfus himself, the role of Clemenceau & Emile Zola in the scandal, the consequences regarding the army officer corps & the Catholic Church & the cause of Royalism & the Socialists in France. How Zionism emerged from the Affair and what it meant.

- Italian Unification: the man & the Italian state most responsible for the movement, the foreign nation assisting the movement, and the foreign country being purged from its domination of Italy, the problems & weaknesses of Risorgimento prior to 1859.

- Unification of Germany: the role of Bismarck & Prussia, how Bismarck obtained the money for army buildup, the methods he employed to achieve his objectives, meaning of the term Herrenvolk and whom the Germans blamed their past problems.

- Austria: what its mid-century difficulties were, the German & Hungarian & Slavic nationalities situation, the significance & shortcomings of the Ausgleich of 1867.

- The general condition of Russia during the 19th century.

- Great Britain--its sources of power & wealth, the people gaining voting rights by the major Reform Bills of 1832, 1867, 1884, & 1918, the accomplishment of the Parliament Act of 1911, the characteristics of Victorian Morality.

Chapter 12   SUBJECT MATTER FOR ESSAY EXAMS

The New Imperialism through World War I.

1. A definition of "imperialism", and the differences between the Old Imperialism and the New Imperialism. The new nations participating in the pursuit of colonies as well as how the New Imperialism affected areas such as Africa, China, the Middle East, and South America.

2. The reasons explaining European superiority over the non-European areas of the world, or why small European nations were able to conquer & dominate vast numbers of people & territories outside of Europe.

3. British Empire--the two types of colonies & some examples, the meaning of "indirect rule" as well as dominion status.

4. The countries of Africa that preserved their independence from European nations and which European state was defeated in battle by native Africans--the reasons for the rapid rise to greatness of Japan.

5. The results of the New Imperialism.

6. Darwin & Darwinism--a definition of "evolution" and explanation of certain expressions such as "survival of the fittest". The contemporary view of "punctuated equilibrium" by Stephen Jay Gould. The phenomenon of Social Darwinism and the ideas strengthened by it.

7. Sigmund Freud--what ideas & practices he originated and what was meant by the "seduction theory" & "infantile fantasies theory"; the concept of the unconscious and how it contributed to mankind being fundamentally irrational, barbarous, & troubled; why his theories were unacceptable to Victorian society and later fashionable by the 1920's.

8. The causes of World War I.--the general & underlying & long-term causes and the most immediate cause of the war--the role played negatively by nationalism, the German emperor, & the German high command in its view of "world power or decline".

9. World War I.--the advantages & disadvantages of the Allies & the Central Powers, what major nations were on opposite sides, the reason why the Schlieffen Plan failed, the term "war of attrition", German violation of Belgian neutrality, a description of the war on the Western Front as well as the weapons employed extensively for the first time, the Gallipoli Campaign, and the role in the Middle East of T.E. Lawrence.

Chapter 13　　　　　　SUBJECT MATTER FOR ESSAY EXAMS

The Inter-War Era: 1919--39

1. The Treaty of Versailles: the basis on which the German government requested the Armistice on November 11, 1918; the four monarchies overturned by the war; the impediments to the making of a moderate & permanent peace; the provisions applied to Germany; the nations emerging from the disintegration of Austria-Hungary; the common term for Yugoslavia; and expressions such as "Balkanization of Europe", Diktat, "war-guilt" clause, & mandate system; the meaning of "Lost Generation".

2. The four leaders of the Peace Conference and the roles they played--President Wilson and his 14 Points--reasons for the failure of the Treaty--why the U.S. rejected the Treaty & the disastrous consequences thereof.

3. The Russian Revolution--general condition of the economy & society during the 25 years before war & revolution; whether or not Russia was progressing or regressing during that time; the opposition political parties and their programs for reform & change; who took power & who was overthrown during the 1917 Revolutions in March & November; the two unpopular policies pursued by the provisional government installed in March and the main leader of the Duma; a definition of "soviet"; the capabilities that enabled Lenin & Trotsky & the Bolsheviks to come to power; the first actions of the Bolshevik regime after seizing power; the educational & socio-economic background of the Bolshevik Party members; the reasons why the Reds defeated the Whites in the Civil War; the policies of War Communism and the NEP as well as how Stalin achieved rapid urbanization & industrialization; the meaning of nationalizattion and collectivization; and how Stalin outmaneuvered Trotsky to become dictator of Russia.

4. Fascism--the ideological or doctrinal development of it and how it differed from Communism; the socio-economic class benefitting most from a Fascist regime; the types of people victimized as scapegoats in Fascist societies; the difference between totalitarianism and authoritarianism; the meaning of the term anti-intellectualism and how it contributed to the success of a Fascist regime; an explanation of how a Fascist economy of "national socialism" is not truly socialistic and what its nature really is; the workings of the "Corporate State".

5. Adolf Hitler--the major influences of his troubled youth; the source of his ideas, especially antisemitism; a summary of his talents making him a good leader and his flaws making him a poor leader; the factors that bring him to power as dictator of Germany; the methods he employed to create a prosperous economy.

6. International Crises of the 1930's--reasons why the democracies did not respond effectively to totalitarian aggression; how the League of Nations responded to this series of crises generally; why economic sanctions against Italy during the Ethiopian Crisis failed; what Hitler did to exploit the Ethiopian Crisis; who supported & opposed the Spanish Republic and how the great powers reacted to the Spanish Civil War, and which side won; the <u>Anschluss</u> with Austria and the Allied policy of appeasement and the reasons why Hitler justified his aggression toward

such countries as Czechoslovakia with its Sudetenland; the shameful events at the Munich Conference; and the implications of the "diplomatic revolution" between Nazi Germany & Soviet Russia; the beginnings of World War II. with the invasion of Poland.

Chapter 14   SUBJECT MATTER FOR ESSAY EXAMS

                              World War II. & After

1. The reasons for Allied triumph & Axis defeat in World War II.

2. The literal meaning of <u>blitzkrieg</u> and some features of this modern type of warfare, explanations for the rapid defeat of France in 1940, the meaning of "total war", the fields of action during the fighting as well as how & where the Battle of Britain & the Battle of the Atlantic were fought, the significance of Stalingrad, the importance of guerrilla warfare & Resistance movements.

3. The four most important leaders of the war for the Allies. The reasons Truman gave for dropping the atomic bombs on Japan as well as the true reasons for the events.

4. International Affairs during the Cold War: the controversy over Yalta, an explanation of the containment policy, domino theory, monolithic communism, and the reaction to appeasement. The results of the Korean War, the Cuban Missile Crisis, and the Vietnam War on American foreign policy.

5. Europe Since 1945: the significance of the Common Market or EEC, the original six members, the key condition for joining, some impressive things about the major West European nations during the post-war era, reasons for the decline from greatness of Britain, and some of the ways that Europe is more "democratic" than America.

6. Explanations how & why geographical & other natural conditions influenced the history & character of Japan, a mention of the most famous traits & characteristics of the Japanese, and the reasons for Japanese business success & increasing economic domination.

7. Post-Colonialism in Africa: a definition of "assimilation"; contemporary African problems originating with European rule in the areas of ethnic & national boundaries, economic weakness, class differences, political inexperience, educational deficiencies, and military preponderance; present African problems originating with African traditions.

8. Reasons for the failure & collapse of Communism in Russia & Eastern Europe as well as the powerful role played by Mikhail Gorbachev in dismantling the Soviet system with his policies of <u>glasnost</u> & <u>perestroika</u> & extension of self-rule to the satellite states, plus the consequences of his revolutionary changes.

9. An understanding of the several ways to resist against tyranny and to defend moral principles when confronted with superior military force. The tremendous effectiveness of passive resistance & civil disobedience & non-violent refusal to cooperate with established authority by strikes & boycotts & ostracism. The impact of H.D. Thoreau & the Irish & Gandhi & M.L. King & Lech Walesa & Russians under Communism.

10. An explanation of a few famous quotations by celebrated individuals.